D0993177

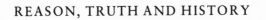

REASON, TRUTH AND HISTORY

REASON, TRUTH AND HISTORY

Hilary Putnam

CAMBRIDGE
UNIVERSITY PRESS

Published by the Press Syndicate of the University of Cambridge
The Pitt Building, Trumpington Street, Cambridge CB2 1RP
40 West 20th Street, New York, NY 10011-4211, USA
10 Stamford Road, Oakleigh, Melbourne 3166, Australia

First published 1981
Reprinted 1982, 1985, 1986, 1987, 1989, 1990, 1991, 1992, 1993,
1994, 1995

Printed in the United States of America

Library of Congress Catalogue card number: 81-6121

A catalogue record for this book is available from the British Library

ISBN 0-521-23035-7 hardback
ISBN 0-521-29776-1 paperback

FOR RUTH ANNA

Contents

Note

A reader who is unused to technical philosophy, or who wishes to gain an overview of the argument of this book, might well start by reading Chapter 5 to the end of the book, and only then return to Chapters 1 to 4.

Preface

In the present work, the aim which I have in mind is to break the strangle hold which a number of dichotomies appear to have on the thinking of both philosophers and laymen. Chief among these is the dichotomy between objective and subjective views of truth and reason. The phenomenon I am thinking of is this: once such a dichotomy as the dichotomy between 'objective' and 'subjective' has become accepted, accepted not as a mere pair of categories but as a characterization of types of views and styles of thought, thinkers begin to view the terms of the dichotomy almost as ideological labels. Many, perhaps most, philosophers hold some version of the 'copy' theory of truth today, the conception according to which a statement is true just in case it 'corresponds to the (mind independent) facts'; and the philosophers in this faction see the only alternative as the denial of the objectivity of truth and a capitulation to the idea that all schemes of thought and all points of view are hopelessly subjective. Inevitably a bold minority (Kuhn, in some of his moods at least; Feyerabend, and such distinguished continental philosophers as Foucault) range themselves under the opposite label. They *agree* that the alternative to a naive copy conception of truth is to see systems of thought, ideologies, even (in the case of Kuhn and Feyerabend) scientific theories, as subjective, and they proceed to *put forward* a relativist and subjective view with vigor.

That philosophical dispute assumes somewhat the character of ideological dispute is not, of itself, necessarily *bad:* new ideas, even in the most exact sciences, are frequently both espoused and attacked with partisan vigor. Even in politics, polarization and ideological fervor are sometimes necessary to bring moral seriousness to an issue. But in time, both in philosophy and politics, new ideas become old ideas; what was once challenging, becomes predictable and boring; and what once served to focus attention where it should be focussed, later keeps discussion from considering new alternatives. This has now happened in the debate between the correspondence views of truth and subjectivist views. In the first three chapters of this book I shall try to explain a conception of truth which unites objective and subjective components. This view, in spirit at least, goes back to ideas of Immanuel Kant; and it holds that we can reject a naive 'copy' conception of truth without having to hold that it's all a matter of the Zeitgeist, or a matter of 'gestalt switches', or all a matter of ideology.

The view which I shall defend holds, to put it very roughly, that there is an extremely close connection between the notions of *truth* and *rationality;* that, to put it even more crudely, the only criterion for what is a fact is what it is *rational* to accept. (I mean this quite literally and across the board; thus if it can be rational to accept that a picture is beautiful, then it can be a *fact* that the picture is beautiful.) There can be *value facts* on this conception. But the relation between rational acceptability and truth is a relation between two distinct notions. A statement can be rationally acceptable *at a time* but not *true;* and this realist intuition will be preserved in my account.

I do not believe, however, that rationality is defined by a set of unchanging 'canons' or 'principles'; methodological principles are connected with our view of the world, including our view of ourselves as part of the world, and change with time. Thus I *agree* with the subjectivist philosophers that there is no fixed, ahistorical *organon* which defines what it is to be rational; but I don't conclude from the fact that our conceptions of reason evolve in history, that reason itself can be (or evolve into) *anything,* nor do I end up in some fancy mixture of cultural relativism and 'structuralism' like the French philosophers. The dichotomy: either ahistorical unchanging canons of rationality *or* cultural relativism is a dichotomy that I regard as outdated.

Another feature of the view is that rationality is not restricted to laboratory science, nor different in a fundamental way in laboratory science and outside of it. The conception that it is seems to me a hangover from positivism; from the idea that the scientific world is in some way constructed out of 'sense data' and the idea that terms in the laboratory sciences are 'operationally defined'. I shall not devote much space to criticizing operationalist and positivist views of science; these have been thoroughly criticized in the last twenty-odd years. But the empiricist idea that 'sense data' constitute some sort of objective 'ground floor' for at least a part of our knowledge will be reexamined in the light of what we have to say about truth and rationality (in Chapter 3).

In short, I shall advance a view in which the mind does not simply 'copy' a world which admits of description by One True Theory. But my view is not a view in which the mind *makes up* the world, either (or makes it up subject to constraints imposed by 'methodological canons' and mind-independent 'sense-data'). If one must use metaphorical language, then let the metaphor be this: the mind and the world jointly make up the mind and the world. (Or, to make the metaphor even more Hegelian, the Universe makes up the Universe – with minds – collectively – playing a special role in the making up.)

A final feature of my account of rationality is this: I shall try to show that our notion of rationality is, at bottom, just one part of our conception of human flourishing, our idea of the good. Truth is deeply dependent on what have been recently called 'values' (Chapter 6). And what we said above about rationality and history also applies to value and history; there is no given, ahistorical, set of 'moral principles' which define once and for all what human flourishing consists in; but that doesn't mean that it's all merely cultural and relative. Since the current state in the theory of truth – the current dichotomy between copy theories of truth and subjective accounts of truth – is at least partly responsible, in my view, for the notorious 'fact/value' dichotomy, it is only by going to a very deep level and correcting our accounts of truth and rationality themselves that we can get beyond the fact/value dichotomy. (A dichotomy which, as it is conventionally understood, virtually commits one to some sort of relativism.) The current views of truth are alienated views; they cause one to lose one part or another of one's self and the world, to see the world as simply consisting of elementary particles swerving in the void (the 'physicalist' view, which sees the *scientific* description as converging to the One True Theory), or to see the world as simply consisting of 'actual and possible sense-data' (the older empiricist view), or to deny that there is a world at all, as opposed to a bunch of stories that we make up for various (mainly unconscious) reasons. And my purpose in this work is to sketch the leading ideas of a non-alienated view.

My Herbert Spencer Lecture, 'Philosophers and Human Understanding' (given at Oxford University, 1979) overlaps the present text, having stemmed from work in progress, as does the paper ' "Si Dieu est mort, alors tout est permis". . . (reflexions sur la philosophie du langage)', *Critique,* 1980.

A research grant from the National Science Foundation* supported research connected with this book during the years 1978–80. I gratefully acknowledge this support.

Thomas Kuhn and Ruth Anna Putnam have studied drafts of this book and given me able criticism and wise advice. I have been helped also by advice and criticism from many friends, including Ned Block, David Helman, and Justin Leiber, and the students in my various lectures and seminars at Harvard. Several chapters were read as lectures in Lima in the spring of 1980 (a trip made possible by a grant from the Fulbright Commission), and Chapter 2 was actually finished during my Lima stay. I benefited in this period from discussions with Leopoldo Chiappo, Alberto Cordero Lecca, Henriques Fernandez, Francisco Miro Quesada, and Jorge Secada. The entire book (in an earlier version) was read as lectures at the University of Frankfurt in the summer of 1980, and I am grateful to my colleagues there (especially Wilhelm Essler and Rainer Trapp), to my very stimulating group of students, and my other friends in Germany (especially Dieter Henrich, Manon Fassbinder, and Wolfgang Stegmüller) for encouragement and stimulating discussions.

All of my colleagues in the Harvard Philosophy Department deserve to be singled out for individual thanks. In recent years Nelson Goodman and I have detected a convergence in our views, and while the first draft of the present book was written before I had the opportunity to see his *Ways of Worldmaking,* reading it and discussing these issues with him has been of great value at a number of stages.

I am also grateful to Jeremy Mynott for encouragement and advice in his capacity as editor.

* To study 'The Appraisal of Scientific Theories: Historical versus Formal Methodological Approaches'; Agreement No. SOC78-04276.

1

Brains in a vat

An ant is crawling on a patch of sand. As it crawls, it traces a line in the sand. By pure chance the line that it traces curves and recrosses itself in such a way that it ends up looking like a recognizable caricature of Winston Churchill. Has the ant traced a picture of Winston Churchill, a picture that *depicts* Churchill?

Most people would say, on a little reflection, that it has not. The ant, after all, has never seen Churchill, or even a picture of Churchill, and it had no intention of depicting Churchill. It simply traced a line (and even *that* was unintentional), a line that *we* can 'see as' a picture of Churchill.

We can express this by saying that the line is not 'in itself' a representation[1] of anything rather than anything else. Similarity (of a certain very complicated sort) to the features of Winston Churchill is not sufficient to make something represent or refer to Churchill. Nor is it necessary: in our community the printed shape 'Winston Churchill', the spoken words 'Winston Churchill', and many other things are used to represent Churchill (though not pictorially), while not having the sort of similarity

[1] In this book the terms 'representation' and 'reference' always refer to a relation between a word (or other sort of sign, symbol, or representation) and something that actually exists (i.e. not just an 'object of thought'). There is a sense of 'refer' in which I can 'refer' to what does not exist; this is not the sense in which 'refer' is used here. An older word for what I call 'representation' or 'reference' is *denotation*.

Secondly, I follow the custom of modern logicians and use 'exist' to mean 'exist in the past, present, or future'. Thus Winston Churchill 'exists', and we can 'refer to' or 'represent' Winston Churchill, even though he is no longer alive.

to Churchill that a picture – even a line drawing – has. If *similarity* is not necessary or sufficient to make something represent something else, how can *anything* be necessary or sufficient for this purpose? How on earth can one thing represent (or 'stand for', etc.) a different thing?

The answer may seem easy. Suppose the ant had seen Winston Churchill, and suppose that it had the intelligence and skill to draw a picture of him. Suppose it produced the caricature *intentionally*. Then the line would have represented Churchill.

On the other hand, suppose the line had the shape WINSTON CHURCHILL. And suppose this was just accident (ignoring the improbability involved). Then the 'printed shape' WINSTON CHURCHILL would *not* have represented Churchill, although that printed shape does represent Churchill when it occurs in almost any book today.

So it may seem that what is necessary for representation, or what is mainly necessary for representation, is *intention*.

But to have the intention that *anything,* even private language (even the words 'Winston Churchill' spoken in my mind and not out loud), should *represent* Churchill, I must have been able to *think about* Churchill in the first place. If lines in the sand, noises, etc., cannot 'in themselves' represent anything, then how is it that thought forms can 'in themselves' represent anything? Or can they? How can thought reach out and 'grasp' what is external?

Some philosophers have, in the past, leaped from this sort of consideration to what they take to be a proof that the mind is *essentially non-physical in nature.* The argument is simple; what we said about the ant's curve applies to any physical object. No physical object can, in itself, refer to one thing rather than to another; nevertheless, *thoughts in the mind* obviously do succeed in referring to one thing rather than another. So thoughts (and hence the mind) are of an essentially different nature than physical objects. Thoughts have the characteristic of *intentionality* – they can refer to something else; nothing physical has 'intentionality', save as that intentionality is derivative from some employment of that physical thing by a mind. Or so it is claimed. This is too quick; just postulating mysterious powers of mind solves nothing. But the problem is very real. How is intentionality, reference, possible?

Magical theories of reference

We saw that the ant's 'picture' has no necessary connection with Winston Churchill. The mere fact that the 'picture' bears a 'resemblance' to Churchill does not make it into a real picture, nor does it make it a representation of Churchill. Unless the ant is an intelligent ant (which it isn't) and knows about Churchill (which it doesn't), the curve it traced is not a picture or even a representation of anything. Some primitive people believe that some representations (in particular, *names*) have a necessary connection with their bearers; that to know the 'true name' of someone or something gives one power over it. This power comes from the *magical connection* between the name and the bearer of the name; once one realizes that a name *only* has a contextual, contingent, conventional connection with its bearer, it is hard to see why knowledge of the name should have any mystical significance.

What is important to realize is that what goes for physical pictures also goes for mental images, and for mental representations in general; mental representations no more have a necessary connection with what they represent than physical representations do. The contrary supposition is a survival of magical thinking.

Perhaps the point is easiest to grasp in the case of mental *images*. (Perhaps the first philosopher to grasp the enormous significance of this point, even if he was not the first to actually make it, was Wittgenstein.) Suppose there is a planet somewhere on which human beings have evolved (or been deposited by alien spacemen, or what have you). Suppose these humans, although otherwise like us, have never seen *trees*. Suppose they have never imagined trees (perhaps vegetable life exists on their planet only in the form of molds). Suppose one day a picture of a tree is accidentally dropped on their planet by a spaceship which passes on without having other contact with them. Imagine them puzzling over the picture. What in the world is this? All sorts of speculations occur to them: a building, a canopy, even an animal of some kind. But suppose they never come close to the truth.

For *us* the picture is a representation of a tree. For these humans the picture only represents a strange object, nature and function unknown. Suppose one of them has a mental image which is exactly like one of my mental images of a tree as a result of having seen the picture. His mental image is not a *representation of a tree*. It is only a representation of the strange object (whatever it is) that the mysterious picture represents.

Still, someone might argue that the mental image is *in fact* a representation of a tree, if only because the picture which caused this mental image was itself a representation of a tree to begin with. There is a causal chain from actual trees to the mental image even if it is a very strange one.

But even this causal chain can be imagined absent. Suppose the 'picture of the tree' that the spaceship dropped was not really a picture of a tree, but the accidental result of some spilled paints. Even if it looked exactly like a picture of a tree, it was, in truth, no more a picture of a tree than the ant's 'caricature' of Churchill was a picture of Churchill. We can even imagine that the spaceship which dropped the 'picture' came from a planet which knew nothing of trees. Then the humans would still have mental images qualitatively identical with my image of a tree, but they would not be images which represented a tree any more than anything else.

The same thing is true of *words*. A discourse on paper might seem to be a perfect description of trees, but if it was produced by monkeys randomly hitting keys on a typewriter for millions of years, then the words do not refer to anything. If there were a person who memorized those words and said them in his mind without understanding them, then they would not refer to anything when thought in the mind, either.

Imagine the person who is saying those words in his mind has been hypnotized. Suppose the words are in Japanese, and the person has been told that he understands Japanese. Suppose that as he thinks those words he has a 'feeling of understanding'. (Although if someone broke into his train of thought and asked him what the words he was thinking *meant,* he would discover he couldn't say.) Perhaps the illusion would be so perfect that the person could even fool a Japanese telepath! But if he couldn't use the words in the right contexts, answer questions about what he 'thought', etc., then he didn't understand them.

By combining these science fiction stories I have been telling, we can contrive a case in which someone thinks words which are in fact a description of trees in some language *and* simultaneously has appropriate mental images, but *neither* understands the words *nor* knows what a tree is. We can even imagine that the mental images were caused by paint-spills (although the person has been hypnotized to think that they are images of something appropriate to his thought – only, if he were asked, he wouldn't be able to say of what). And we can imagine that the language the person is thinking in is one neither the hypnotist nor the person hypnotized has ever heard of – perhaps it is just coincidence that these 'nonsense sentences', as the hypnotist supposes them to be, are a description of trees in Japanese. In short, everything passing before the person's mind might be qualitatively identical with what was passing through the mind of a Japanese speaker who was *really* thinking about trees – but none of it would refer to trees.

All of this is really impossible, of course, in the way that it is really impossible that monkeys should by chance type out a copy of *Hamlet*. That is to say that the probabilities against it are so high as to mean it will never really happen (we think). But is is not logically impossible, or even physically impossible. It *could* happen (compatibly with physical law and, perhaps, compatibly with actual conditions in the universe, if there are lots of intelligent beings on other planets). And if it did happen, it would be a striking demonstration of an important conceptual truth; that even a large and complex system of representations, both verbal and visual, still does not have an *intrinsic,* built-in, magical connection with what it represents – a connection independent of how it was caused and what the dispositions of the speaker or thinker are. And this is true whether the system of representations (words and images, in the case of the example) is physically realized – the words are written or spoken, and the pictures are physical pictures – or only realized in the mind. Thought words and mental pictures do not *intrinsically* represent what they are about.

The case of the brains in a vat

Here is a science fiction possibility discussed by philosophers: imagine that a human being (you can imagine this to be yourself) has been subjected to an operation by an evil scientist. The person's brain (your brain) has been removed from the body and placed in a vat of nutrients which keeps the brain alive. The nerve endings have been connected to a super-scientific computer which causes the person whose brain it is to have the illusion that everything is perfectly normal. There seem to be people, objects, the sky, etc; but really all the person (you) is experiencing is the result of electronic impulses travelling from the computer to the nerve endings. The computer is so clever that if the person tries to raise his hand, the feedback from the computer will cause him to 'see' and 'feel' the hand being raised. Moreover, by varying the program, the evil scientist can cause the victim to 'experience' (or hallucinate) any situation or environment the evil scientist wishes. He can also obliterate the memory of the brain operation, so that the victim will seem to himself to have always been in this environment. It can even seem to the victim that he is sitting and reading these very words about the amusing but quite absurd supposition that there is an evil scientist who removes people's brains from their bodies and places them in a vat of nutrients which keep the brains alive. The nerve endings are supposed to be connected to a super-scientific computer which causes the person whose brain it is to have the illusion that . . .

When this sort of possibility is mentioned in a lecture on the Theory of Knowledge, the purpose, of course, is to raise the classical problem of scepticism with respect to the external world in a modern way. (*How do you know you aren't in this predicament?*) But this predicament is also a useful device for raising issues about the mind/world relationship.

Instead of having just one brain in a vat, we could imagine that all human beings (perhaps all sentient beings) are brains in a vat (or nervous systems in a vat in case some beings with just a minimal nervous system already count as 'sentient'). Of course, the evil scientist would have to be outside – or would he? Perhaps there is no evil scientist, perhaps (though this is absurd) the universe just happens to consist of automatic machinery tending a vat full of brains and nervous systems.

This time let us suppose that the automatic machinery is programmed to give us all a *collective* hallucination, rather than a number of separate unrelated hallucinations. Thus, when I seem to myself to be talking to you, you seem to yourself to be hearing my words. Of course, it is not the case that my words actually reach your ears – for you don't have (real) ears, nor do I have a real mouth and tongue. Rather, when I produce my words, what happens is that the efferent impulses travel from my brain to the computer, which both causes me to 'hear' my own voice uttering those words and 'feel' my tongue moving, etc., and causes you to 'hear' my words, 'see' me speaking, etc. In this case, we are, in a sense, actually in communication. I am not mistaken about your real existence (only about the existence of your body and the 'external world', apart from brains). From a certain point of view, it doesn't even matter that 'the whole world' is a collective hallucination; for you do, after all, really hear my words when I speak to you, even if the mechanism isn't what we suppose it to be. (Of course, if we were two lovers making love, rather than just two people carrying on a conversation, then the suggestion that it was just two brains in a vat might be disturbing.)

I want now to ask a question which will seem very silly and obvious (at least to some people, including some very sophisticated philosophers), but which will take us to real philosophical depths rather quickly. Suppose this whole story were actually true. Could we, if we were brains in a vat in this way, *say* or *think* that we were?

I am going to argue that the answer is 'No, we couldn't.' In fact, I am going to argue that the supposition that we are actually brains in a vat, although it violates no physical law, and is perfectly consistent with everything we have experienced, cannot possibly be true. *It cannot possibly be true,* because it is, in a certain way, self-refuting.

The argument I am going to present is an unusual one, and it took me several years to convince myself that it is really right. But it is a correct argument. What makes it seem so strange is that it is connected with some of the very deepest issues in philosophy. (It first occurred to me when I was thinking about a theorem in modern logic, the 'Skolem–Löwenheim Theorem', and I suddenly saw a connection between this theorem and some arguments in Wittgenstein's *Philosophical Investigations*.)

A 'self-refuting supposition' is one whose truth implies its own falsity. For example, consider the thesis that *all general statements are false.* This is a general statement. So if it is true, then it must be false. Hence, it is false. Sometimes a thesis is called 'self-refuting' if it is *the supposition that the thesis is entertained or enunciated* that implies its falsity. For example, 'I do not exist' is self-refuting if thought by *me* (for any '*me*'). So one can be certain that one oneself exists, if one thinks about it (as Descartes argued).

What I shall show is that the supposition that we are brains in a vat has just this property. If we can consider whether it is true or false, then it is not true (I shall show). Hence it is not true.

Before I give the argument, let us consider why it seems so strange that such an argument can be given (at least to philosophers who subscribe to a 'copy' conception of truth). We conceded that it is compatible with physical law that there should be a world in which all sentient beings are brains in a vat. As philosophers say, there is a 'possible world' in which all sentient beings are brains in a vat. (This 'possible world' talk makes it sound as if there is a *place* where any absurd supposition is true, which is why it can be very misleading in philosophy.) The humans in that possible world have exactly the same experiences that *we* do. They think the same thoughts we do (at least, the same words, images, thought-forms, etc., go through their minds). Yet, I am claiming that there is an argument we can give that shows we are not brains in a vat. How can there be? And why couldn't the people in the possible world who really *are* brains in a vat give it too?

The answer is going to be (basically) this: although the people in that possible world can think and 'say' any words we can think and say, they cannot (I claim) *refer* to what we can refer to. In particular, they cannot think or say that they are brains in a vat (*even by thinking 'we are brains in a vat'*).

Turing's test

Suppose someone succeeds in inventing a computer which can actually carry on an intelligent conversation with one (on as many subjects as an intelligent person might). How can one decide if the computer is 'conscious'?

The British logician Alan Turing proposed the following test:[2] let someone carry on a conversation with the computer and a conversation with a person whom he does not know. If he can-

---

[2] A. M. Turing, 'Computing Machinery and Intelligence', *Mind* (1950), reprinted in A. R. Anderson (ed.), *Minds and Machines*.

not tell which is the computer and which is the human being, then (assume the test to be repeated a sufficient number of times with different interlocutors) the computer is conscious. In short, a computing machine is conscious if it can pass the 'Turing Test'. (The conversations are not to be carried on face to face, of course, since the interlocutor is not to know the visual appearance of either of his two conversational partners. Nor is voice to be used, since the mechanical voice might simply sound different from a human voice. Imagine, rather, that the conversations are all carried on via electric typewriter. The interlocutor types in his statements, questions, etc., and the two partners – the machine and the person – respond via the electric keyboard. Also, the machine may *lie* – asked 'Are you a machine', it might reply, 'No, I'm an assistant in the lab here.')

The idea that this test is really a definitive test of consciousness has been criticized by a number of authors (who are by no means hostile in principle to the idea that a machine might be conscious). But this is not our topic at this time. I wish to use the general idea of the Turing test, the general idea of a *dialogic test of competence,* for a different purpose, the purpose of exploring the notion of *reference.*

Imagine a situation in which the problem is not to determine if the partner is really a person or a machine, but is rather to determine if the partner uses the words to refer as we do. The obvious test is, again, to carry on a conversation, and, if no problems arise, if the partner 'passes' in the sense of being indistinguishable from someone who is certified in advance to be speaking the same language, referring to the usual sorts of objects, etc., to conclude that the partner does refer to objects as we do. When the purpose of the Turing test is as just described, that is, to determine the existence of (shared) reference, I shall refer to the test as the *Turing Test for Reference*. And, just as philosophers have discussed the question whether the original Turing test is a *definitive* test for consciousness, i.e. the question of whether a machine which 'passes' the test not just once but regularly is *necessarily* conscious, so, in the same way, I wish to discuss the question of whether the Turing Test for Reference just suggested is a definitive test for shared reference.

The answer will turn out to be 'No'. The Turing Test for Reference is not definitive. It is certainly an excellent test in practice;

but it is not logically impossible (though it is certainly highly improbable) that someone could pass the Turing Test for Reference and not be referring to anything. It follows from this, as we shall see, that we can extend our observation that words (and whole texts and discourses) do not have a necessary connection to their referents. Even if we consider not words by themselves but rules deciding what words may appropriately be produced in certain contexts – even if we consider, in computer jargon, *programs for using words* – unless those programs themselves *refer to something extra-linguistic* there is still no determinate reference that those words possess. This will be a crucial step in the process of reaching the conclusion that the Brain-in-a-Vat Worlders cannot refer to anything external at all (and hence cannot say *that* they are Brain-in-a-Vat Worlders).

Suppose, for example, that I am in the Turing situation (playing the 'Imitation Game', in Turing's terminology) and my partner is actually a machine. Suppose this machine is able to win the game ('passes' the test). Imagine the machine to be programmed to produce beautiful responses in English to statements, questions, remarks, etc. in English, but that it has no sense organs (other than the hookup to my electric typewriter), and no motor organs (other than the electric typewriter). (As far as I can make out, Turing does not assume that the possession of either sense organs or motor organs is necessary for consciousness or intelligence.) Assume that not only does the machine lack electronic eyes and ears, etc., but that there are no provisions in the machine's program, the program for playing the Imitation Game, for incorporating inputs from such sense organs, or for controlling a body. What should we say about such a machine?

To me, it seems evident that we cannot and should not attribute reference to such a device. It is true that the machine can discourse beautifully about, say, the scenery in New England. But it could not recognize an apple tree or an apple, a mountain or a cow, a field or a steeple, if it were in front of one.

What we have is a device for producing sentences in response to sentences. But none of these sentences is at all connected to the real world. *If one coupled two of these machines and let them play the Imitation Game with each other, then they would* go on *'fooling'* *each* *other forever, even if the rest of the world disappeared!* There is no more reason to regard the machine's talk of apples as referring to real world apples than there is to regard the ant's 'drawing' as referring to Winston Churchill.

What produces the illusion of reference, meaning, intelligence, etc., here is the fact that there is a convention of representation which *we* have under which the machine's discourse refers to apples, steeples, New England, etc. Similarly, there is the *illusion* that the ant has caricatured Churchill, for the same reason. But we are able to perceive, handle, deal with apples and fields. Our talk of apples and fields is intimately connected with our *nonverbal* transactions with apples and fields. There are 'language entry rules' which take us from experiences of apples to such utterances as 'I see an apple', and 'language exit rules' which take us from decisions expressed in linguistic form ('I am going to buy some apples') to actions other than speaking. Lacking either language entry rules or language exit rules, there is no reason to regard the conversation of the machine (or of the two machines, in the case we envisaged of two machines playing the Imitation Game with each other) as more than syntactic play. Syntactic play that *resembles* intelligent discourse, to be sure; but only as (and no more than) the ant's curve resembles a biting caricature.

In the case of the ant, we could have argued that the ant would have drawn the same curve even if Winston Churchill had never existed. In the case of the machine, we cannot quite make the parallel argument; if apples, trees, steeples and fields had not existed, then, presumably, the programmers would not have produced that same program. Although the machine does not *perceive* apples, fields, or steeples, its creator–designers did. There is *some* causal connection between the machine and the real world apples, etc., via the perceptual experience and knowledge of the creator–designers. But such a weak connection can hardly suffice for reference. Not only is it logically possible, though fantastically improbable, that the same machine *could* have existed even if apples, fields, and steeples had not existed; more important, the machine is utterly insensitive to the *continued* existence of apples, fields, steeples, etc. Even if all these things *ceased* to exist, the machine would still discourse just as happily in the same way. That is why the machine cannot be regarded as referring at all.

The point that is relevant for our discussion is that there is nothing in Turing's Test to rule out a machine which is programmed to do nothing *but* play the Imitation Game, and that a machine which can do nothing *but* play the Imitation Game is *clearly* not referring any more than a record player is.

Brains in a vat (again)

Let us compare the hypothetical 'brains in a vat' with the machines just described. There are obviously important differences. The brains in a vat do not have sense organs, but they do have *provision* for sense organs; that is, there are afferent nerve endings, there are inputs from these afferent nerve endings, and these inputs figure in the 'program' of the brains in the vat just as they do in the program of our brains. The brains in a vat are *brains;* moreover, they are *functioning* brains, and they function by the same rules as brains do in the actual world. For these reasons, it would seem absurd to deny consciousness or intelligence to them. But the fact that they are conscious and intelligent does not mean that their words refer to what our words refer. The question we are interested in is this: do their verbalizations containing, say, the word 'tree' actually refer to *trees?* More generally: can they refer to *external* objects at all? (As opposed to, for example, objects in the image produced by the automatic machinery.)

To fix our ideas, let us specify that the automatic machinery is supposed to have come into existence by some kind of cosmic chance or coincidence (or, perhaps, to have always existed). In this hypothetical world, the automatic machinery itself is supposed to have no intelligent creator–designers. In fact, as we said at the beginning of this chapter, we may imagine that all sentient beings (however minimal their sentience) are inside the vat.

This assumption does not help. For there is no connection between the *word* 'tree' as used by these brains and actual trees. They would still use the word 'tree' just as they do, think just the thoughts they do, have just the images they have, even if there were no actual trees. Their images, words, etc., are qualitatively identical with images, words, etc., which do represent trees in *our* world; but we have already seen (the ant again!) that qualitative similarity to something which represents an object (Winston Churchill or a tree) does not make a thing a representation all by itself. In short, the brains in a vat are not thinking about real trees when they think 'there is a tree in front of me' because there is nothing by virtue of which their thought 'tree' represents actual trees.

If this seems hasty, reflect on the following: we have seen that the words do not necessarily refer to trees even if they are arranged in a sequence which is identical with a discourse which (were it to occur in one of our minds) would unquestionably *be about trees* in the actual world. Nor does the 'program', in the sense of the rules, practices, dispositions of the brains to verbal behavior, necessarily refer to trees or bring about reference to trees through the connections it establishes between words and words, or *linguistic* cues and *linguistic* responses. If these brains think about, refer to, represent trees (real trees, outside the vat), then it must be because of the way the 'program' connects the system of language to *non-verbal* input and outputs. There are indeed such non-verbal inputs and outputs in the Brain-in-a-Vat world (those efferent and afferent nerve endings again!), but we also saw that the 'sense-data' produced by the automatic machinery do not represent trees (or anything external) even when they resemble our tree-images exactly. Just as a splash of paint might resemble a tree picture without *being* a tree picture, so, we saw, a 'sense datum' might be qualitatively identical with an 'image of a tree' without being an image of a tree. How can the fact that, in the case of the brains in a vat, the language is connected by the program with sensory inputs which do not intrinsically or extrinsically represent trees (or anything external) possibly bring it about that the whole system of representations, the language-in-use, *does* refer to or represent trees or anything external?

The answer is that it cannot. The whole system of sense-data, motor signals to the efferent endings, and verbally or conceptually mediated thought connected by 'language entry rules' to the sense-data (or whatever) as inputs and by 'language exit rules' to the motor signals as outputs, has no more connection to *trees* than the ant's curve has to Winston Churchill. Once we see that the *qualitative similarity* (amounting, if you like, to qualitative identity) between the thoughts of the brains in a vat and the thoughts of someone in the actual world by no means implies sameness of reference, it is not hard to see that there is no basis at all for regarding the brain in a vat as referring to external things.

The premisses of the argument

I have now given the argument promised to show that the brains in a vat cannot think or say that they are brains in a vat. It remains only to make it explicit and to examine its structure.

By what was just said, when the brain in a vat (in the world where every sentient being is and always was a brain in a vat) thinks 'There is a tree in front of me', his thought does not refer to actual trees. On some theories that we shall discuss it might refer to trees in the image, or to the electronic impulses that cause tree experiences, or to the features of the program that are responsible for those electronic impulses. These theories are not ruled out by what was just said, for there is a close causal connection between the use of the word 'tree' in vat-English and the presence of trees in the image, the presence of electronic impulses of a certain kind, and the presence of certain features in the machine's program. On these theories the brain is *right*, not *wrong* in thinking 'There is a tree in front of me.' Given what 'tree' refers to in vat-English and what 'in front of' refers to, assuming one of these theories is correct, then the truth-conditions for 'There is a tree in front of me' when it occurs in vat-English are simply that a tree in the image be 'in front of' the 'me' in question – in the image – or, perhaps, that the kind of electronic impulse that normally produces this experience be coming from the automatic machinery, or, perhaps, that the feature of the machinery that is supposed to produce the 'tree in front of one' experience be operating. And these truth-conditions are certainly fulfilled.

By the same argument, 'vat' refers to vats in the image in vat-English, or something related (electronic impulses or program features), but certainly not to real vats, since the use of 'vat' in vat-English has no causal connection to real vats (apart from the connection that the brains in a vat wouldn't be able to use the word 'vat', if it were not for the presence of one particular vat –

the vat they are in; but this connection obtains between the use of *every* word in vat-English and that one particular vat; it is not a special connection between the use of the *particular* word 'vat' and vats). Similarly, 'nutrient fluid' refers to a liquid in the image in vat-English, or something related (electronic impulses or program features). It follows that if their 'possible world' is really the actual one, and we are really the brains in a vat, then what we now mean by 'we are brains in a vat' is that *we are brains in a vat in the image* or something of that kind (if we mean anything at all). But part of the hypothesis that we are brains in a vat is that we aren't brains in a vat in the image (i.e. what we are 'hallucinating' isn't that we are brains in a vat). So, if we are brains in a vat, then the sentence 'We are brains in a vat' says something false (if it says anything). In short, if we are brains in a vat, then 'We are brains in a vat' is false. So it is (necessarily) false.

The supposition that such a possibility makes sense arises from a combination of two errors: (1) taking *physical possibility* too seriously; and (2) unconsciously operating with a magical theory of reference, a theory on which certain mental representations necessarily refer to certain external things and kinds of things.

There is a 'physically possible world' in which we are brains in a vat — what does this mean except that there is a *description* of such a state of affairs which is compatible with the laws of physics? Just as there is a tendency in our culture (and has been since the seventeenth century) to take *physics* as our metaphysics, that is, to view the exact sciences as the long-sought description of the 'true and ultimate furniture of the universe', so there is, as an immediate consequence, a tendency to take 'physical possibility' as the very touchstone of what might really actually be the case. Truth is physical truth; possibility physical possibility; and necessity physical necessity, on such a view. But we have just seen, if only in the case of a very contrived example so far, that this view is wrong. The existence of a 'physically possible world' in which we are brains in a vat (and always were and will be) does not mean that we might really, actually, possibly *be* brains in a vat. What rules out this possibility is not physics but *philosophy*.

Some philosophers, eager both to assert and minimize the

claims of their profession at the same time (the typical state of mind of Anglo-American philosophy in the twentieth century), would say: 'Sure. You have shown that some things that seem to be physical possibilities are really *conceptual* impossibilities. What's so surprising about that?'

Well, to be sure, my argument can be described as a 'conceptual' one. But to describe philosophical activity as the search for 'conceptual' truths makes it all sound like *inquiry about the meaning of words.* And that is not at all what we have been engaging in.

What we have been doing is considering the *preconditions* for *thinking about, representing, referring to,* etc. We have investigated these preconditions *not* by investigating the meaning of these words and phrases (as a linguist might, for example) but by *reasoning a priori.* Not in the old 'absolute' sense (since we don't claim that magical theories of reference are *a priori* wrong), but in the sense of inquiring into what is *reasonably* possible *assuming* certain general premises, or making certain very broad theoretical assumptions. Such a procedure is neither 'empirical' nor quite 'a priori', but has elements of both ways of investigating. In spite of the fallibility of my procedure, and its dependence upon assumptions which might be described as 'empirical' (e.g. the assumption that the mind has no access to external things or properties apart from that provided by the senses), my procedure has a close relation to what Kant called a 'transcendental' investigation; for it is an investigation, I repeat, of the *preconditions* of reference and hence of thought – preconditions built in to the nature of our minds themselves, though not (as Kant hoped) wholly independent of empirical assumptions.

One of the premises of the argument is obvious: that magical theories of reference are wrong, wrong for mental representations and not only for physical ones. The other premise is that one cannot refer to certain kinds of things, e.g. *trees,* if one has no causal interaction at all with them,[3] or with things in terms

---

[3] If the Brains in a Vat will have causal connection with, say, trees *in the future,* then perhaps they can *now* refer to trees by the description 'the things I will refer to as "trees" at such-and-such a future time'. But we are to imagine a case in which the Brains in a Vat *never* get out of the vat, and hence *never* get into causal connection with trees, etc.

of which they can be described. But why should we accept these premisses? Since these constitute the broad framework within which I am arguing, it is time to examine them more closely.

The reasons for denying necessary connections between representations and their referents

I mentioned earlier that some philosophers (most famously, Brentano) have ascribed to the mind a power, 'intentionality', which precisely enables it to *refer*. Evidently, I have rejected this as no solution. But what gives me this right? Have I, perhaps, been too hasty?

These philosophers did not claim that we can think about external things or properties without using representations at all. And the argument I gave above comparing visual sense data to the ant's 'picture' (the argument via the science fiction story about the 'picture' of a tree that came from a paint-splash and that gave rise to sense data qualitatively similar to our 'visual images of trees', but unaccompanied by any *concept* of a tree) would be accepted as showing that *images* do not necessarily refer. If there are mental representations that necessarily refer (to external things) they must be of the nature of *concepts* and not of the nature of images. But what are *concepts?*

When we introspect we do not perceive 'concepts' flowing through our minds as such. Stop the stream of thought when or where we will, what we catch are words, images, sensations, feelings. When I speak my thoughts out loud I do not think them twice. I hear my words as you do. To be sure it feels different to me when I utter words that I believe and when I utter words I do not believe (but sometimes, when I am nervous, or in front of a hostile audience, it feels as if I am lying when I know I am telling the truth); and it feels different when I utter words I understand and when I utter words I do not understand. But I can imagine without difficulty someone thinking just these words (in the sense of saying them in his mind) and having just the feeling of understanding, asserting, etc., that I do, and real-izing a minute later (or on being awakened by a hypnotist) that he did not understand what had just passed through his mind at all, that he did not even understand the language these words are in. I don't claim that this is very likely; I simply mean that there is nothing at all unimaginable about this. And what this shows is not that concepts *are* words (or images, sensations, etc.), but that to attribute a 'concept' or a 'thought' to someone is quite different from attributing any mental 'presentation', any introspectible entity or event, to him. Concepts are not mental presentations that intrinsically refer to external objects for the very decisive reason that they are not mental presentations at all. Concepts are signs used in a certain way; the signs may be public or private, mental entities or physical entities, but even when the signs are 'mental' and 'private', the sign itself apart from its use is not the concept. And signs do not themselves intrinsically refer.

We can see this by performing a very simple thought experiment. Suppose you are like me and cannot tell an elm tree from a beech tree. We still say that the reference of 'elm' in my speech is the same as the reference of 'elm' in anyone else's, viz. elm trees, and that the set of all beech trees is the extension of 'beech' (i.e. the set of things the word 'beech' is truly predicated of) both in your speech and my speech. Is it really credible that the difference between what 'elm' refers to and what 'beech' refers to is brought about by a difference in our *concepts*? My concept of an elm tree is exactly the same as my concept of a beech tree (I blush to confess). (This shows that the determination of reference is social and not individual, by the way; you and I both defer to experts who *can* tell elms from beeches.) If someone heroically attempts to maintain that the difference between the reference of 'elm' and the reference of 'beech' in *my* speech is explained by a difference in my psychological state, then let him imagine a Twin Earth where the words are switched. Twin Earth is very much like Earth; in fact, apart from the fact that 'elm' and 'beech' are interchanged, the reader can suppose Twin Earth is exactly like Earth. Suppose I have a *Doppelganger* on Twin Earth who is molecule for molecule identical with me (in the sense in which two neckties can be 'identical'). If you are a dualist, then suppose my *Doppelganger* thinks the same verbalized thoughts I do, has the same sense data, the same dispositions, etc. It is absurd to think his psychological state is one bit different from mine: yet his word 'elm' represents *beeches*, and my word 'elm' represents elms. (Similarly, if the 'water' on Twin Earth is a different liquid – say, XYZ and not H_2O – then 'water' represents a different liquid when used on Twin Earth and when used on Earth, etc.) Contrary to a doctrine that has been with us since the seventeenth century, *meanings just aren't in the head.*

We have seen that possessing a concept is not a matter of possessing images (say, of trees – or even images, 'visual' or 'acoustic', of sentences, or whole discourses, for that matter) since one could possess any system of images you please and not possess the *ability* to use the sentences in situationally appropriate ways (considering both linguistic factors – what has been said before – and non-linguistic factors as determining 'situational appropriateness'). A man may have all the images you please, and still be completely at a loss when one says to him 'point to a tree', even if a lot of trees are present. He may even have the image of what he is supposed to do, and still not know what he is supposed to do. For the image, if not accompanied by the ability to act in a certain way, is just a *picture,* and acting in accordance with a picture is itself an ability that one may or may not have. (The man might picture himself pointing to a tree, but just for the sake of contemplating something logically possible; himself pointing to a tree after someone has produced the – to him meaningless – sequence of sounds 'please point to a tree'.) He would still not know that he was supposed to point to a tree, and he would still not *understand* 'point to a tree'.

I have considered the ability to use certain sentences to be the criterion for possessing a full-blown concept, but this could easily be liberalized. We could allow symbolism consisting of elements which are not words in a natural language, for example, and we could allow such mental phenomena as images and other types of internal events. What is essential is that these should have the same complexity, ability to be combined with each other, etc., as sentences in a natural language. For, although a particular presentation – say, a blue flash – might serve a particular mathematician as the inner expression of the whole proof of the Prime Number Theorem, still there would be no temptation to say this (and it would be false to say this) if that mathematician could not unpack his 'blue flash' into separate steps and logical connections. But, no matter what sort of inner phenomena we allow as possible *expressions* of thought, arguments exactly similar to the foregoing will show that it is not the phenomena themselves that constitute understanding, but rather the ability of the thinker to *employ* these phenomena, to produce the right phenomena in the right circumstances.

The foregoing is a very abbreviated version of Wittgenstein's argument in *Philosophical Investigations*. If it is correct, then the attempt to understand thought by what is called 'phenomenological' investigation is fundamentally misguided; for what the phenomenologists fail to see is that what they are describing is the inner *expression* of thought, but that the *understanding* of that expression – one's understanding of one's own thoughts – is not an *occurrence* but an *ability*. Our example of a man pretending to think in Japanese (and deceiving a Japanese telepath) already shows the futility of a phenomenological approach to the problem of *understanding*. For even if there is some introspectible quality which is present when and only when one *really* understands (this seems false on introspection, in fact), still that quality is only *correlated* with understanding, and it is still possible that the man fooling the Japanese telepath have that quality too and *still* not understand a word of Japanese.

On the other hand, consider the perfectly possible man who does not have any 'interior monologue' at all. He speaks perfectly good English, and if asked what his opinions are on a given subject, he will give them at length. But he never thinks (in words, images, etc.) when he is not speaking out loud; nor does anything 'go through his head', except that (of course) he hears his own voice speaking, and has the usual sense impressions from his surroundings, plus a general 'feeling of understanding'. (Perhaps he is in the habit of talking to himself.) When he types a letter or goes to the store, etc., he is not having an internal 'stream of thought'; but his actions are intelligent and purposeful, and if anyone walks up and asks him 'What are you doing?' he will give perfectly coherent replies.

This man seems perfectly imaginable. No one would hesitate to say that he was conscious, disliked rock and roll (if he frequently expressed a strong aversion to rock and roll), etc., just because he did not think conscious thoughts except when speaking out loud.

What follows from all this is that (a) no set of mental events – images or more 'abstract' mental happenings and qualities – *constitutes* understanding; and (b) no set of mental events is *necessary* for understanding. In particular, *concepts cannot be identical with mental objects of any kind.* For, assuming that by a mental object we mean something introspectible, we have just seen that whatever it is, it may be absent in a man who does understand the appropriate word (and hence has the full blown concept), and present in a man who does not have the concept at all.

Coming back now to our criticism of magical theories of reference (a topic which also concerned Wittgenstein), we see that, on the one hand, those 'mental objects' we *can* introspectively detect – words, images, feelings, etc. – do not intrinsically refer any more than the ant's picture does (and for the same reasons), while the attempts to postulate special mental objects, 'concepts', which *do* have a necessary connection with their referents, and which only trained phenomenologists can detect, commit a *logical* blunder; for concepts are (at least in part) *abilities* and not occurrences. The doctrine that there are mental presentations which necessarily refer to external things is not only bad natural science; it is also bad phenomenology and conceptual confusion.

2

A problem about reference

Why is it surprising that the Brain in a Vat hypothesis turns out to be incoherent? The reason is that we are inclined to think that *what goes on inside our heads* must determine what we mean and what our words refer to. But it is not hard to see that this is wrong. Ordinary indexical words, such as *I, this, here, now,* are a counterexample of a trivial sort. I may be in the same mental state as Henry when I think 'I am late to work' (imagine, if you like, that Henry and I are identical twins) and yet the token of the word 'I' that occurs in my thought refers to me and the token of the word 'I' that occurs in Henry's thought refers to *Henry.* I may be in the same mental state[1] when I think 'I am late to work' on Tuesday and when I think 'I am late to work' on Wednesday; but the time to which my tensed verb 'am' refers is different in the two cases. The case of natural kind terms is a more subtle example of the same point.

Suppose, to spell out the case mentioned in the previous chapter, that there are English speakers on Twin Earth (by a kind of

[1] At least I may be in the 'same mental state' in the sense that the parameters involved in the psychological process that results in my thinking the thought may have the same values. My *global* mental state is, to be sure, different since on Tuesday I believe 'this is Tuesday' and on Wednesday I don't; but a theory that says the meaning of the words changes whenever my *global* mental state changes would not allow any words to *ever* have the same meaning, and would thus amount to an abandonment of the very notion of word meaning. Moreover, we could construct a Twin Earth story in which I and my Doppelganger are in the same *global* mental state, and the reference of 'I' and 'now' is still different (the calendar on Twin Earth is not synchronized with ours).

miraculous accident they just evolved resembling us and speaking a language which is, apart from a difference I am about to mention, identical with English as it was a couple of hundred years ago). I will assume these people do not yet have a knowledge of Daltonian or post-Daltonian chemistry. So, in particular, they don't have available such notions as 'H_2O'. Suppose, now, that the rivers and lakes on Twin Earth are filled with a liquid that superficially resembles water, but which is *not* H_2O. Then the word 'water' as used on Twin Earth refers *not* to water but to this other liquid (say, XYZ). Yet there is no relevant difference in the mental state of Twin Earth speakers and speakers on Earth (in, say, 1750) which could account for this difference in reference. The reference is different because the *stuff* is different.[2] The mental state by itself, in isolation from the whole situation, does not fix the reference.

Some philosophers have objected to this example, however. These philosophers suggest that one should say, if such a planet is ever discovered, that 'There are two kinds of water', and *not* that our word 'water' does not refer to the Twin Earth liquid. If we ever find lakes and rivers full of a liquid other than H_2O that superficially resembles water, then we will have falsified the statement that all water is H_2O, according to these critics.

It is easy to modify the example so as to avoid this argument. First of all, the liquid on Twin Earth need not be *that* similar to water. Suppose it is actually a mixture of 20% grain alcohol and 80% water, but the body chemistry of the Twin Earth people is such that they do not get intoxicated or even taste the difference between such a mixture and H_2O. Such a liquid would be different from water in many ways; yet a *typical* speaker might be unacquainted with these differences, and thus be in exactly the same mental state as a *typical* speaker in 1750 on Earth. Of course Twin Earth 'water' tastes different from Earth water to *us;* but it does not taste different to *them.* And it behaves differently when you boil it; but must an English speaker have noticed exactly when water boils and exactly what takes place in order to associate a fairly standard conceptual content with the word 'water'?

---

[2] See 'The Meaning of "Meaning" ' in my *Mind, Language, and Reality* (*Philosophical Papers,* vol. 1), Cambridge University Press, 1975, for an extended discussion of this point.

It may be objected that there might well be experts on Twin Earth who do know things about 'water' (for instance, that it is a *mixture* of two liquids) that we do not know about water (did not believe about water in 1750, because they aren't *true* of water), and hence that the *collective* mental state of Twin Earth English speakers is different from the collective mental state of Earth English speakers (in 1750). One might concede that the reference of a person's term isn't fixed by his individual mental state, but insist that the total mental state of *all* the members of the language community fixes the reference of the term.

One difficulty with this is that it might not have been the case that people on Earth *or* Twin Earth had developed that much chemistry in 1750. If the term had the same meaning and reference on Earth prior to the development of chemistry that it does today (in ordinary use), and if the term had the same meaning and reference on Twin Earth prior to the development of the corresponding knowledge that it does today, then we can go back to this earlier time when the collective mental states of the two communities were the *same* in all respects relevant to fixing the extension of 'water', and argue that the extension was different *then* (as it is now) and so the *collective* mental state does not fix the extension. Should we then say the reference *changed* when chemistry was developed? That the term *used* to refer to both kinds of water (in spite of the difference in *taste* to us!), and only refers to *different* kinds after chemistry is developed?

If we say that the reference of their terms or of our terms changed when they or we developed chemistry (to the extent of being able to distill liquids, tell that water plus alcohol is a mixture, etc.) then we will have to say that almost every scientific discovery changes the reference of our terms. We did not *discover* that water (in the pre-scientific sense) was H_2O on such a view; rather we *stipulated* it. To me this seems clearly wrong. What we meant by water all along was whatever had the same nature as the local stuff picked out by that term; and we discovered that water *in that sense* was H_2O; what the people on Twin Earth meant by 'water' all along was the stuff in *their* environment picked out by that term, and their experts discovered that 'water' *in that sense* is a mixture of two liquids.

If we agree that 'water' does not change *meaning* (in either language) when experts make such discoveries as 'water is H_2O'

or 'water is a mixture of two liquids', or does not change its ordinary meaning and reference (of course it may develop more technical uses as a result of such discoveries), and that 'water' in its ordinary Earth meaning and reference does not include mixtures of alcohol and water, then we must say that expert knowledge is not what accounts for the difference in the *meaning* of the word 'water' on Earth and on Twin Earth. Nor does it account for the *reference*: for we could consider yet another Twin Earth where water was a *different* mixture and the expert knowledge was the same (rather scanty) expert knowledge as on the first Twin Earth. Or, as just indicated, we could simply imagine that experts on Earth and on Twin Earth did not yet exist. The word 'water' would still *refer to different stuff* even if the *collective* mental state in the two communities were the same. What goes on inside people's heads does not fix the reference of their terms. In a phrase due to Mill, 'the substance itself' completes the job of fixing the extension of the term.

Once we see that mental state (in either the individualistic or the collective sense) does not fix reference, then we should not be surprised that the Brains in a Vat could not succeed in referring to external objects (even though they have the same mental states we have), and hence could not say or think that they are Brains in a Vat.

Intentions, extensions, and 'notional worlds'

In order to look at the problem of how the reference of our terms is fixed, given that it is not fixed simply by our mental states, it will be convenient to have available some technical terms. In logic the set of things a term is true of is called the *extension* of the term. Thus the extension of the term 'cat' is the set of cats. If a term has more than one sense, then we pretend the word carries invisible subscripts (so that there are really two words and not one), e.g. 'rabbit$_1$' – extension: the set of rabbits – 'rabbit$_2$' – extension: the set of cowards. (Strictly speaking, the extension of terms in a natural language is always somewhat fuzzy: but we shall pretend for simplicity that the borderline cases have been somehow legislated.)

A word like 'I' which refers to different people on different occasions will have not an extension but an *extension-function*:

that is a function which determines an extension in each context of use. In the case of the word 'I' the extension-function is rather simple; it is simply the function $f(x)$ whose value for any speaker x is the set consisting of just x. The argument 'x' which ranges over the relevant parameter used to describe the context (in this case, the *speaker*) is referred to in semantics as an *index*. Indices are needed for times, for things demonstratively referred to, and for yet other features of context in a full semantic treatment (but we shall ignore the details).

The set of things which makes up the extension of 'cat' is different in different possible situations or 'possible worlds'. In a possible world M in which there are no cats, the extension of 'cat' is the empty set. If my cat Elsa had had offspring, then the extension of 'cat' would have at least one member it does not have in the actual world. (We can express this by saying that in each possible world M in which Elsa had offspring, the extension of 'cat' includes members it does not include in the actual world.)

We can indicate the way in which the extension of a term varies with the possible world M in exactly the way in which we indicate how the extension of the word 'I' varies with the speaker: by using a *function*. We assume a set of abstract objects called 'possible worlds' to represent the various states of affairs or possible world histories, and we associate with the term 'cat' a function $f(M)$ whose value on each possible world M is the set of possible objects which are cats in the world M. This function, following Montague and Carnap, I shall refer to as the *intension*[3] of the word 'cat'. Similarly, the intension of the two-place predicate 'touches' is the function $f(M)$ whose value on any possible world M is the set of ordered pairs of possible objects which touch each other in the world M; the intension of the three-place predicate 'x is between y and z' is the function whose value in any possible world is the set of ordered triples (x, y, z) such that x is between y and z, and so on. The intension of a word like 'I', whose extension in any world is context-dependent, will be a more complicated function having as arguments both the possible world and the indices representing the context.

---

[3] Montague, R., *Formal Philosophy,* Yale University, 1974. This use of 'intension' is not the traditional one which I discussed in 'The Meaning of "Meaning" '.

What the intension does is to specify how the extension depends on the possible world. It thus represents what we are interested in, the extension associated with a term, in a very complete way, since it says what that extension would have been in any possible world.

The reason 'intension' (in this sense) cannot be identified with *meaning* is that any two terms which are logically equivalent have the same extension in every possible world, and hence the same intension, but a theory which cannot distinguish between terms with the same meaning and terms which are only equivalent in logic and mathematics is inadequate as a theory of *meaning*. 'Cube' and 'regular polyhedron with six square faces' are logically equivalent predicates. So the intension of these two terms is the same, namely the function whose value in any possible world is the set of cubes in that world; but there is a difference in *meaning* which would be lost if we simply identified the meaning with this function.

Let me emphasize that possible worlds, sets, and functions are to be thought of as abstract extra-mental entities in this theory, and not to be confused with representations or descriptions of these entities.

Frege thought that the meaning (*Sinn*) of an expression was an extra-mental entity or concept which could somehow be 'grasped' by the mind. Such a theory cannot help us with intensions in *our* sense. In the first place, as just noted, there are differences in meaning which are not captured by intension; so the understanding of a term cannot consist *only* in associating it with an intension. More important, if we assume that we have no 'sixth sense' which enables us to *directly* perceive extra-mental entities, or to do something analogous to perceiving them ('intuiting' them, perhaps), then 'grasping' an intension, or any extra-mental entity, must be mediated by representations in some way. (This also seems clear introspectively, to me at least.) But the whole problem we are investigating is how representations *can* enable us to refer to what is outside the mind. To assume the notion of 'grasping' an X which is external to the mind would be to beg the whole question.

If I say of someone that he 'believes there is a glass of water on the table', then I normally attribute to him the capacity to refer to *water*. But, as we have seen, being able to refer to water requires being directly or indirectly linked to actual water (H_2O); the statement 'John believes there is a glass of water in front of him' is not just a statement about what goes on in John's head, but is in part a statement about John's environment, and John's relationship to that environment. If it turns out that John is a Twin Earth person, then what John believes when he says 'there is a glass of water on the table' is that there is a glass containing a liquid which *in fact* consists of water and grain alcohol on the table.

Husserl introduced a device which is useful when we wish to talk of what goes on in someone's head without any assumptions about the existence or nature of actual things referred to by the thoughts: the device of *bracketing*.[4] If we 'bracket' the belief that we ascribe to John when we say 'John believes that there is a glass of water on the table' then what we ascribe to John is simply the *mental state* of an actual or possible person who believes that there is a glass of water on the table (in the full 'unbracketed' ordinary sense). Thus, if John on Twin Earth cannot taste the difference between water and water-cum-grain-alcohol, he may be in the same mental state as an actual or possible speaker of Earth English when he says 'there is a glass of water on the table', notwithstanding the fact that what he refers to as water would make a reasonable highball. We will say that he has the *bracketed belief* that [there is a glass of water on the table]. In effect, the device of bracketing subtracts entailments from the ordinary belief locution (all the entailments that refer to the external world, or to what is external to the thinker's mind).

Daniel Dennett has recently used the locution 'notional world' in a way related to the way Husserl used bracketing.[5] The totality of a thinker's bracketed beliefs constitute the description of the thinker's notional world, in Dennett's sense. Thus, people on Twin Earth have roughly the same *notional* world (and even the same *notional* water) that we do; it is just that they live on a different *real* planet (and refer to different *actual* stuff as 'water'). And the Brains in a Vat of the previous chapter could have had the same notional world we do down to the last detail,

---

[4] Husserl, *Ideas; General Introduction to Pure Phenomenology*, Allen and Unwin, 1969. (Originally appeared in 1913).
[5] Dennett, D. 'Beyond Belief', in *Thought and Object*, Andrew Woodfield (ed.), Oxford University Press, forthcoming.

if you like; it is just that none of their terms had any external world reference at all. The traditional theory of meaning assumed that a thinker's notional world determines the intensions of his terms (and these, together with the fact that a particular possible world M is the actual one, determine the extensions of the terms and the truth-values of all the sentences). We have seen that the traditional theory of meaning is wrong; and this is why the literature today contains many different concepts (e.g., 'intension' and 'notional world') and not a single unitary concept of 'meaning'. 'Meaning' has *fallen to pieces*. But we are left with the task of picking up the pieces. If intension and extension are not directly fixed by notional world, then *how are they fixed?*

The received view of interpretation

The most common view of how interpretations of our language are fixed by us, collectively if not individually, is associated with the notions of an *operational constraint* and a *theoretical constraint*. Operational constraints were originally conceived of rather naively; we simply *stipulate* (conventionally, as it were) that a certain sentence (say, 'Electricity is flowing through this wire') is to be true if and only if a certain test result is observed (the voltmeter needle being deflected, or, in a phenomenalistic version, *my having the visual impression of seeing the voltmeter needle being deflected*). This sort of crude operationalism no longer has any defenders because it has been appreciated that (1) the links between theory and experience are probabilistic and cannot be correctly formalized as perfect correlations (even if there is current flowing through the wire, there are always low probability events or background conditions which could prevent the voltmeter needle from being deflected); and (2) even these probabilistic links are not simple *semantic* correlations, but depend on empirical theory which is subject to revision. On a naive operationist account every time a new way of testing whether a substance is really gold is discovered, the meaning and reference of 'gold' undergoes a change. (In fact, we shouldn't speak of a new test for gold being *discovered*.) On an operationist picture, theories are tested *sentence by sentence* (the stipulated operational meanings of the individual sentences tell you how to go about testing the theory); on the more recent picture, theories 'meet the test of experience as a corporate body', as Quine puts it.

It is possible, however, to relax the notion of an operational constraint so as to overcome or bypass all of these objections. Thus one can restrict the class of interpretations (assignments of intensions to the predicates of one's language) that will be accepted as admissible by constraints of the form: 'an admissible interpretation is such that *most of the time* the sentence S is true when the experiential condition E is fulfilled' (respectively, 'such that most of the time the sentence S is *false* when E is fulfilled'). Such constraints model the idea that there are *probabilistic* relations between truth or falsity of sentences in the language and experience. And, secondly, one can take the view that these constraints are revisable as theory develops. Rather than thinking of them as meaning stipulations, as crude operationism did, one can think of them as tentative restrictions on the class of admissible interpretations; and with Peirce (who wrote 50 years before Bridgeman announced 'operationism'!) one can take the view that the ideal set of operational constraints is itself something that we successively approximate in the course of empirical inquiry, and not something we just stipulate. In short, one can take the view that it is the operational constraints that rational inquirers *would* impose, if they observed and experimented and reasoned as well as is possible, the constraints that they would adopt in the state of 'reflective equilibrium', that singles out the interpretation of our terms; the constraints we actually accept at any given time have the status of a rational estimate or approximation.

Such a view is compatible with Quine's insistence that the theory-experience links are just as much subject to revision as any other aspect of our corporate body of knowledge. And it does not see each such revision as a 'meaning change': such revisions can be and often are simply better efforts to specify what it is we have already been talking about; that which earlier theory-cum-operational-constraints captured only inadequately.

In addition to restricting the class of admissible interpretations by means of operational constraints (or successive approximations to a Peircian ideal set of operational constraints), one can also have constraints which refer to formal properties of the theory. For example, 'an admissible interpretation is such that it turns out to be true that different effects always have different causes'. Kant held that such a 'theoretical constraint' was part of rationality itself: we *impose* the principle of determinism on the world rather than discovering it. In this form, the constraint is certainly too strong: the *price* of preserving determinism might be too great a complication of our system of knowledge as a whole. But this sort of constraint can be relaxed just as operational constraints have been relaxed. (For example, one can require that determinism be preserved whenever the 'cost' in terms of complications in other parts of the theory is not too great; in this form, the constraint seems to be one we accept.)

Theoretical constraints are often stated as constraints on theory acceptance rather than as constraints on theory interpretation, but they can easily be reinterpreted to play the latter role. Thus, if an author states the constraint of 'conservativism' or 'preservationism' as a constraint on theory acceptance ('do not accept a theory which requires giving up a great many previously accepted beliefs if an – otherwise equally 'simple' – theory is available which preserves those beliefs and agrees with observation'), then we can reformulate the constraint as a constraint on interpretation thus: 'an admissible interpretation is such that it renders true sentences which have been accepted for a long time, except where this would require undue complication in the theory consisting of the set of sentences true under the interpretation, or too great a revision in the operational constraints'. Again, it has been widely held that no inductive logic is possible unless we impose some *a priori* ordering (called a 'simplicity ordering' or 'plausibility ordering') on the hypotheses which may be accepted given particular observational data (although the ordering may itself be different in different experimental or observational contexts); the constraint that 'the set of sentences which is true under an admissible interpretation must not be lower down in the simplicity ordering than any other set with the same observational or experiential consequences would correspond to the constraint in inductive logic that one is to accept the most simple (or most 'plausible') of the hypotheses compatible with one's observations.

Theoretical constraints of many other kinds have been proposed in the literature of the philosophy of science. There are constraints which, like 'simplicity', refer to properties of the set of accepted sentences, and constraints which refer to the *history* of the inquiry by which that set came to be accepted. But the details need not concern us. The reasons for being attracted to the idea that the admissible interpretations of our language (in the sense of admissible intension-assignments to the terms of the language) are fixed by operational and theoretical constraints are obvious: whether or not one is having an experience of a certain kind is something the mind is able to judge (philosophical problems about 'experience' notwithstanding). So if a theory implies or contains a sentence which is associated with an experience E by an operational constraint of some kind, probabilistic or whatever, then the thinker can *know* if the theory works, or if there is some awkwardness of fit, at least in this case, by seeing whether or not he has the experience E. Since the constraints that we use to test the theory *also* fix the extensions of the terms, the thinker's estimate of the theory's 'working' is at the same time an estimate of its *truth*. Since the speaker's knowledge of these constraints is knowledge of the intensions of the terms, grasping a correct semantics would tell one, for any proposed theory of the world, what our world would have to be like for the theory to be true.

Furthermore, if we idealize by supposing thinkers to have what economists call 'perfect information' about each other, each thinker knows the formal structure of the accepted theory T and the past history of the research program to which it belongs, the previous beliefs that it does or does not preserve, etc. So each thinker is in a position to *know* if the theoretical constraints are met or not. (If we do not wish to idealize by assuming perfect information, then we can still say that the collective body of thinkers is in a position to know this.)

In short, if the received view is correct, then we would have an elegant account of how intensions and extensions are fixed (in principle – of course the details are too complicated to fill in at the present stage of methodological knowledge). But, unfortunately, the received view does not work!

Why the received view doesn't work

The difficulty with the received view is that it tries to fix the intensions and extensions of individual terms by fixing the truth-conditions for whole sentences. The idea, as we just saw, is that the operational and theoretical constraints (the ones rational inquirers would accept in some sort of ideal limit of inquiry) determine which sentences in the language are *true*. Even if this is right, however, such constraints cannot determine what our terms *refer* to. For there is nothing in the notion of an operational or theoretical constraint to do this directly. And doing it *indirectly*, by putting down constraints which pick out the set of true sentences, and then hoping that by determining the truth-values of whole sentences we can somehow fix what the *terms* occurring in those sentences refer to, won't work.

That it won't work has been shown by Quine.[6] I shall extend previous 'indeterminacy' results in a very strong way. I shall argue that even if we have constraints of whatever nature which determine the truth-value of every sentence in a language *in every possible world,* still the reference of individual terms remains indeterminate. In fact, it is possible to interpret the entire language in violently different ways, each of them compatible with the requirement that the truth-value of each sentence in each possible world be the one specified. In short, not only does the received view not work; *no view which only fixes the truth-values of whole sentences can fix reference,* even if it specifies truth-values for sentences *in every possible world.*

The detailed proof is technical, and I think it appropriate to give it in an Appendix. What I shall give here is an illustration of the method of the proof only, and not the detailed proof.

Consider the sentence

(1) A cat is on a mat. (Here and in the sequel 'is on' is *tenseless,* i.e. it means 'is, was, or will be on'.)

Under the standard interpretation this is true in those possible worlds in which there is at least one cat on at least one mat at some time, past, present, or future. Moreover, 'cat' refers to cats and 'mat' refers to mats. I shall show that sentence (1) can be reinterpreted so that in the *actual* world 'cat' refers to *cherries* and 'mat' refers to *trees* without affecting the truth-value of sentence (1) in any possible world. ('Is on' will keep its original interpretation.)

---

[6] See his 'Ontological Relativity', in *Ontological Relativity and Other Essays,* Columbia University Press, 1969.

The idea is that sentence (1) will receive a new interpretation in which what it will come to mean is:

(a) A cat* is on a mat*.

The definition of the property of being a cat* (respectively, a mat*) is given by cases, the three cases being:

(a) Some cat is on some mat, and some cherry is on some tree.
(b) Some cat is on some mat, and no cherry is on any tree.
(c) Neither of the foregoing.

Here is the definition of the two properties:

DEFINITION OF 'CAT*'
x is a cat* if and only if case (a) holds and x is a cherry; or case (b) holds and x is a cat; or case (c) holds and x is a cherry.
DEFINITION OF 'MAT*'
x is a mat* if and only if case (a) holds and x is a tree; or case (b) holds and x is a mat; or case (c) holds and x is a quark.

Now, in possible worlds falling under case (a), 'A cat is on a mat' is true, and 'A cat* is on a mat*' is also true (because a cherry is on a tree, and all cherries are cats* and all trees are mats* in worlds of this kind). Since in the actual world some cherry is on some tree, the actual world is a world of this kind, and in the actual world 'cat*' refers to cherries and 'mat*' refers to trees.

In possible worlds falling under case (b), 'A cat is on a mat' is true, and 'A cat* is on a mat*' is also true (because in worlds falling under case (b), 'cat' and 'cat*' are coextensive terms and so are 'mat' and 'mat*'). (Note that although cats are cats* in some worlds – the ones falling under case (b) – they are *not* cats* in the *actual* world.)

In possible worlds falling under case (c), 'A cat is on a mat' is false and 'A cat* is on a mat*' is also false (because a cherry can't be on a *quark*).

Summarizing, we see that *in every possible world* a cat is on a mat if and only if a cat* is on a mat*. Thus, reinterpreting the word 'cat' by assigning to it the intension we just assigned to 'cat*' and simultaneously reinterpreting the word 'mat' by assigning to it the intension we just assigned to 'mat*' would only have the effect of making 'A cat is on a mat' mean what 'A cat* is on a mat*' was defined to mean; and this would be perfectly compatible with the way truth-values are assigned to 'A cat is on a mat' in every possible world.

In the Appendix, I show that a more complicated reinterpretation of this kind can be carried out for all the sentences of a whole language. It follows that there are always infinitely many different interpretations of the predicates of a language which assign the 'correct' truth-values to the sentences in all possible worlds, *no matter how these 'correct' truth-values are singled out*. Quine argued for a similar conclusion in *Word and Object;* in Quine's example (as applied to English) 'There is a rabbit over there' was interpreted to mean 'There is a rabbit-slice over there' (where a 'rabbit-slice' is a three-dimensional spatial cross-section of the whole four-dimensional space–time rabbit), or, alternatively again, to mean, 'There is rabbithood being exemplified again.' (This last reinterpretation also reinterprets the syntactic form of the sentence, or at least its logical grammar.) Quine makes the point I just made, that *truth-conditions for whole sentences* underdetermine reference. Since 'rabbit-slices', 'rabbithood', and 'undetached rabbit-parts' all have a close connection to rabbits, one might come away from *Word and Object* with the impression that all reinterpretations that leave a sentence's truth-value unchanged are at least closely connected with the standard interpretation (in the way that rabbit-parts and rabbithood are connected with rabbits). The argument spelled out in the Appendix and illustrated in this chapter shows that the truth conditions for 'A cat is on a mat' don't even exclude the possibility that 'cat' refers to *cherries*.

'Intrinsic' and 'extrinsic'

Perhaps the first idea that comes to mind when one is confronted by non-standard interpretations, such as the one that interprets 'cat' as *cat** and 'mat' as *mat** is to dismiss them as presenting us with an unimportant paradox. But *genuine* paradoxes are never unimportant; they always show something is wrong with the way we have been thinking. Perhaps the second reaction is to protest that *cat** and *mat** are 'queer' properties; surely our terms correspond to 'sensible' properties (such as *being a cat* or *being a mat*) and not to such 'funny' properties as these. One might explicate the way in which *cat** (or, rather, *cathood** or *cat**hood) is a funny property by pointing out that one can 'build a machine' to 'inspect' things and 'tell' whether or not they are cats (a human being is such a 'machine'), but one cannot build a machine that will tell (in any world which resembles ours in its laws and general conditions) whether or not something is a *cat**. If the machine (or a person) looks at something and sees it is neither a cat nor a cherry, then they can tell it is *not* a *cat**; but if the thing *is* either a cat or a cherry then the device or the person needs to be informed of the truth-values of 'A cat is on a mat' and 'A cherry is on a tree' to decide if it is inspecting or seeing a *cat**, and these truth-values go beyond what it can learn by just examining the object presented to it for inspection.

Unfortunately, one can reinterpret 'sees' (say, as sees*) so that the two sentences (3) John (or whoever) sees a cat; and (4) John sees* a cat*, will have the same truth-value in every possible world (by the method given in the Appendix). So whenever a person sees a cat, he *is* seeing* a cat*; the experience we typically have when we see a cat *is* the experience we typically have when we see* a cat*, and so on. Similarly, we can reinterpret 'inspects' and 'tells' so that, when a machine inspects a cat, it is inspecting* a cat*, and when it 'tells' something is a cat, it is telling* that it is a cat*.

To use an illustration (suggested by Nozick), suppose half of us (the females perhaps) use 'cat' to mean 'cat*', 'mat' to mean 'mat*', 'look' to mean 'look*', 'tells' to mean 'tells*', and so on. Suppose the other half (the males) use 'cat' to denote cats, 'mat' to denote mats, 'look' to denote looking, and so on. How could we ever know?[7] (If you ask a male what 'cat' refers to, he will answer 'to cats, of course' and so will a female, *whatever* 'cat' refers to.)

---

[7] A female might answer that the supposition that she is referring to cats* when she says 'cat' is *incoherent* (because *within* her language whatever she refers to as a 'cat' *is* a cat). This answer is small comfort; it does not exclude the possibility that what *she* calls a *cat* is what males call a *cat**, and vice versa; and this is Nozick's point.

The point is that the fact that one can *build a machine to inspect things and tell if they are cats* differentiates cats from cats* if one can be sure 'inspect' and 'tell' refer to inspecting and telling, and it is no easier to say how the reference of *these* words is fixed than to say how the reference of 'cat' is fixed. One might say that when I look at something and think that it is a cat, my 'mental representations', the visual images or tactile images, the verbalized thought 'cat', and so on, *refer* to cathood and to various other physical or biological properties (being a certain shape, being a certain color, belonging to a certain species) and not to their counterparts; this may be true, but it just repeats that the reference *is* fixed one way rather than the other. This is what we want to explain and not the explanation sought.

'But,' one might protest, 'the *definitions* of "*cat**" and "*mat**" given above refer to things other than the object in question (cherries on trees and cats on mats), and thus signify *extrinsic* properties of the objects that have these properties. In the actual world, every cherry is a cat*; but it would not be a cat*, even though its intrinsic properties would be exactly the same, if no cherry were on any tree. In contrast, whether or not something is a cat depends only upon its intrinsic properties.' Is the distinction here referred to, the distinction between *intrinsic* and *extrinsic* properties, one that will enable us to characterize and rule out 'queer' interpretations?

The trouble with this suggestion is a certain symmetry in the relation of 'cat' and 'mat' to 'cat*' and 'mat*'. Thus, suppose we define 'cherry*' and 'tree*' so that in possible worlds falling under case (a) cherries* are cats and trees* are mats; in possible worlds falling under case (b) cherries* are cherries and trees* are trees; and in possible worlds falling under case (c) cherries* are cats and trees* are photons. Then we can define 'cat' and 'mat' by means of the *-terms as follows: Cases:

(a*) Some cat* is on some mat*, and some cherry* is on some tree*.

(b*) Some cat* is on some mat*, and no cherry* is on any tree*.

(c*) Neither of the foregoing.

Strangely enough, these cases are just our old (a), (b), (c) under a new description. Now we define:

DEFINITION OF 'CAT'

x is a cat if case (a*) holds and x is a cherry*; or case (b*) holds and x is a cat*; or case (c*) holds and x is a cherry*. (Note that in all three cases cats come out being *cats*.)

DEFINITION OF 'MAT'

x is a mat if and only if case (a*) holds and x is a tree*; or case (b*) holds and x is a mat*; or case (c*) holds and x is a quark*. (Supposing quark* to be defined so that in cases of type (c*) quarks* are *mats,* in all three cases mats come out being *mats*.)

The upshot is that viewed from the perspective of a language which takes 'cat*', 'mat*', etc., as primitive properties, it is 'cat' and 'mat' that refer to 'extrinsic' properties, properties whose definitions mention objects other than x; while relative to 'normal' language, language which takes 'cat' and 'mat' to refer to cathood and mathood (*you* know which properties I mean, dear reader!), it is 'cat*' and 'mat*' that refer to 'extrinsic' properties. Better put, being 'intrinsic' or 'extrinsic' are relative to a choice of which properties one takes as *basic;* no property is intrinsic or extrinsic in itself.

'Survival' and evolution

The suggestion is popular nowadays that the evolutionary process itself has somehow produced a correspondence between our words and mental representations and external things; people say that we would not have *survived* if there had not been such a correspondence, and that this correspondence is, at least in a primitive way, the relation of reference.

But what do 'correspondence' and 'reference' have to do with *survival*? For that matter, what does *truth* have to do with survival?

Here opinions differ. Some philosophers believe that we would not survive if (sufficiently many of) our beliefs were not *true*. Other philosophers claim that even our best established scientific beliefs *aren't* true, or at least that we have no reason to think they are. Thomas Kuhn has suggested that our beliefs only 'refer' to objects *within* those beliefs (somewhat in the way in which 'Hamlet' only refers to a person in a play); the success of science is explained by trial-and-error, not by any correspondence between its objects and real things, Kuhn says. Bas van Fraassen, in a new book, argues that a successful theory need not be true but only 'observationally adequate', i.e. correctly predict observation. He too explains the success (or 'observational adequacy') of science as the product of trial-and-error.

If these philosophers are right, then the whole idea of using evolution to justify belief in an *objective* relation of reference is undercut. Evolution, on such instrumentalist views, only establishes a correspondence between some terms (the observation terms) and 'permanent possibilities of sensation'. Such a correspondence is not *reference,* unless we are willing to abandon the idea that external things (the observable ones) are more than constructs out of sensations.

I believe that the other philosophers are right, however (the ones who say we would not survive if sufficiently many of our beliefs were not *true*).

The reason I believe this is that trial-and-error does not explain *why* our theories are 'observationally adequate'; *that* can only be explained by referring to characteristics of the environment–human *interaction* which explain why *trial-and-error is successful.* (Trial-and-error does not succeed in *all* enterprises, after all!) To posit that the interaction produces in our minds *false* theories which just *happen* to have successful predictions as consequences is to posit a totally inexplicable series of *coincidences.* But how does the fact that our beliefs are (approximately) true explain our survival?

Some of our beliefs are intimately connected with *action*. If I believe the sentence 'I will get something I value very much if I push that button' (assume I understand this sentence in a normal way, or at least associate the normal 'bracketed' or 'notional' belief with it), then I will reach out my hand and push the button. Call beliefs of the form 'If I do *x,* I will get . . .', where the blank describes a *goal* the agent has, *directive beliefs*. If too many of our directive beliefs are false, we will perform too many unsuccessful actions; so truth of (sufficiently many of) our *directive* beliefs is necessary for survival.

Now, our directive beliefs are themselves derived from many other beliefs: beliefs about the characteristics and causal powers of external things, and beliefs about our own characteristics and powers. If these beliefs were mainly false, would it not be a mere coincidence if they nonetheless led to true prediction of experience and to true directive beliefs? So, since (sufficiently many of) our *directive* beliefs are true, and the *best explanation* of this fact is that many of our other beliefs (the ones constituting our 'theory of the everyday world') are at least approximately true, we are justified in believing that our theory of the everyday world is at least approximately true, and that we would not have survived if this were not the case.

Imagine, now, that some of us are actually referring to the things that are assigned to our terms by the non-standard interpretation *J* (described in the Appendix). This interpretation agrees with the standard interpretation on terms referring to our notional world, our sensations, our volitions, etc. So 'I seem to myself to push the button', when understood in the 'bracketed sense' (as meaning that I have a certain subjective experience of voluntarily pushing a button) has not just the same truth conditions but the same *interpretation* under *J* and under the 'normal' interpretation *I*, and so does 'I seem to myself to get the satisfaction I expected.'

Now, if sufficiently many of our directive beliefs are true under the non-standard interpretation *J*, then we will certainly be successful, and we will certainly *survive* (since if we weren't alive we wouldn't be attaining these goals) and have offspring (since if *they* weren't alive they wouldn't be attaining these goals). In short, *J*-truth of (sufficiently many) directive beliefs is as good for 'evolutionary success' as *I*-truth. In fact it *is* *I*-truth, since the truth conditions for *every* sentence (not just directive beliefs) are the same under *I* and under *J*. My directive beliefs are not *only* associated with the same subjective *experience* under the interpretation *I* and under the interpretation *J*; they have the same *truth conditions*. From the point of view (or non-point of view) of 'evolution', all that is necessary is that sufficiently many of my beliefs be true under *any* interpretation that connects those beliefs with the relevant *actions*. Evolution may produce in me a tendency to have *true* beliefs (of certain kinds); but this only means that evolution affects linguistically mediated or conceptually mediated survival *via* its tendency to produce in us representation systems whose sentences or sentence-analogues have certain *truth conditions* (and certain *action* conditions, or 'language exit rules'). *But the truth-conditions for whole sentences were just shown not to determine the reference of sentence parts* (nor does adding the 'language exit rules' help, for these are preserved under *J*). It follows that it is simply a mistake to think that evolution determines a *unique* correspondence (or even a reasonably narrow range of correspondences) between referring expressions and external objects.

Intentions: pure and impure

We have seen that nature does not single out any one correspondence between our terms and external things. Nature gets us to process words and thought signs in such a way that sufficiently many of our directive beliefs will be true, and so that sufficiently many of our actions will contribute to our 'inclusive genetic fitness'; but this leaves reference largely indeterminate. W. V. Quine has urged that that is what reference in fact is – indeterminate! It is just an illusion, he thinks, that the terms in our language have determinate well-defined counterparts. As he puts it,

> For, consider again our standard regimented notation, with a lexicon of interpreted predicates and some fixed range of values for the variables of quantification. The sentences of this language that are true remain true under countless reinterpretations of the predicates and revisions of the range of values of the variables. Indeed any range of the same size can be made to serve by a suitable reinterpretation of the predicates. If the range of values is infinite, any infinite range can be made to serve; this is the Skolem–Löwenheim theorem. The true sentences stay true under all such changes.
>
> Perhaps then our primary concern belongs with the truth of sentences and with their truth conditions, rather than with the reference of terms.

In the next chapter I will explore the alternative here suggested, of giving up the idea that has so far been the premiss of the entire discussion: that words stand in some sort of one–one relation to (discourse-independent) things and sets of things. It may seem, however, that there is a much simpler way out: why not just say that it is our *intentions,* implicit or explicit, that fix the reference of our terms?

At the beginning of the discussion in the previous chapter, I rejected this as not constituting an informative answer on the ground that having intentions (of the relevant kind) presupposes the ability to refer. It may be good at this stage to expand upon this brief remark.

The problem is that the notions 'intention' and 'mental state' have a certain ambiguity. Let us call a mental state a *pure* mental state if its presence or absence depends only on what goes on 'inside' the speaker. Thus whether or not I have a pain depends only on what goes on 'inside' me, but whether or not I know that snow is white depends not only on whether or not something goes on 'inside' me (believing or being confident that snow is white), but also on whether or not snow *is* white, and thus is something 'outside' my body and mind. Thus *pain* is a pure mental state but *knowledge* is an *impure* mental state. There is a (pure) mental state component to knowledge, but there is also a component which is not mental in any sense: this is the component that corresponds to the condition that what a man believes is not knowledge unless the belief is *true.* I am not in the 'state' of knowing that snow is white if I am not in a suitable pure mental state; but being in a suitable pure mental state is never *sufficient* for knowing that snow is white; the world has to cooperate as well.

What about belief? We have defined *bracketed* belief ('notional world') so that having a bracketed belief that [there is water on the table] or having a notional world which includes there being water on the table is a pure mental state. But, in accordance with what was said before, *believing that there is water on the table* (without any 'bracketing') presupposes that one's word 'water' *actually refers to water,* and this depends on the actual nature of certain 'paradigms', one's direct or indirect causal relations to those paradigms, and so on. When I have the belief that there is water on the table, my Doppleganger on Twin Earth has the same bracketed belief but not the same belief because his word 'water' refers to water-with-grain alcohol and not to water. In short, believing that there is water on the table is an *impure* mental state. (Brains in a Vat could not be in this state, although they could be in the corresponding 'bracketed' state.)

What goes for belief goes for intention as well. Pure mental states of intending – e.g. intending that the term 'water' refer to water *in one's notional world* – do not fix real world reference at all. Impure mental states of intending – e.g. intending that the term 'water' refer to actual water – *presuppose* the ability to refer to (real) water.

Some philosophers have suggested that belief can be defined in terms of the state I called 'bracketed belief' *and* reference, thus:

> John believes that snow is white = *John believes that [snow is white]*
> (i.e. snow is white in John's notional world)
> *and the words 'snow' and 'white' in John's thought (or whatever words he uses to express this belief) refer to snow and to the property white, respectively.*

Without accepting this as a correct and complete analysis of what it is to believe that snow is white, we can accept this account as making a point which is certainly correct: *that believing presupposes the ability to refer*. And in exactly the same way, intending presupposes the ability to refer! Intentions are not mental events that *cause* words to refer: intentions (in the ordinary 'impure' sense) have reference as an integral *component*. To explain reference in terms of (impure) intention would be circular. And the problem of how *pure* mental states of intending, believing, etc., can (in the proper causal setting) constitute or cause reference is just what we have found so puzzling.

The origin of the puzzle

At first blush, nothing seems more obvious than that our words and mental representations *refer*. When I think or say 'the cat just went out', the thought is usually *about* our cat Mitty; the word 'cat' in the sentence I think or say *refers* to a set of entities of which Mitty is a member. Yet we have just seen that the nature of this relation of 'aboutness' or reference is puzzling.

The distinction between real world and notional world (and the correlative distinction between beliefs and bracketed beliefs, or intentions and bracketed intentions) itself explains part of the puzzle. The reason that it is surprising and troubling to discover that there are unintended 'admissible interpretations' of our language (where by an admissible interpretation I mean simply an interpretation that satisfies the appropriate operational and theoretical constraints) is, in part, that no such 'indeterminacy' rises in the 'notional world' of the speaker. In my notional world, cats and cats* are quite distinct (in fact, in my notional world cats* are *cherries*). 'There is a cat on a mat' and 'there is a cat* on a mat*' may be logically equivalent, but they contain terms with quite different notional referents; thus it seems strange indeed that there should be any confusion between the real world referents of the one belief and the real world referents of the other.

But if the number of cats happens to be equal to the number of cherries, then it follows from theorems in the theory of models (as Quine remarks in the passage quoted above) that there is a reinterpretation of the entire language that leaves all sentences unchanged in truth value while permuting the extensions of 'cat' and 'cherry'. By the techniques just mentioned, such reinterpretations can be constructed so as to preserve all operational and theoretical constraints (and by the techniques we illustrated with the 'cat/cat*' example, they can be extended so as to provide 'intensions', or functions which determine an extension *in each possible world*, and not just extensions in the actual world). This does not contradict the statements just made about our 'notional world', or subjective belief system, for the following reason: the fact that in our belief system or 'notional world' no cat is a cherry means that in each admissible interpretation of that belief system (each assignment of external world referents to the terms, images, and other representations we employ in thought) the referents of 'cat' and the referents of 'cherry' must be disjoint sets. But the disjointness of these sets is comparable with the (remarkable) fact that what is the set of 'cats' in *one* admissible interpretation may be the set of 'cherries' in a *different* (but equally admissible) interpretation. From the fact that notional cats are wholly different from notional cherries it only follows that real cats are wholly different from real cherries if the number of admissible interpretations is exactly one. If there is more than one admissible interpretation of the whole language (as there will be if the admissible interpretations are singled out only by operational and theoretical constraints), then two terms which refer to disjoint sets in *each* admissible interpretation can have the same potential referents when the totality of *all* admissible interpretations is considered. From the fact that notional cats are as different as can be from notional cherries it does not follow that there are determinate disjoint sets of cats-in-themselves and cherries-in-themselves.

What makes this so distressing is that operational *plus* theoretical constraints are the natural way in which to allow the actual empirical context to determine the admissible interpretation (or interpretations) of one's representational system. Such constraints can to some extent determine which sentences in one's language are true and which false; it is the slack between truth-conditions and reference that remains.

Quine, as we remarked, would be willing to put up with the slack and simply acknowledge that reference *is* indeterminate. A young philosopher, Hartry Field,[8] has recently suggested a different view. In Field's view reference is a 'physicalistic relation', i.e. a complex causal relation between words or mental representations and objects or sets of objects. It is up to empirical science to discover what that physicalistic relation is, Field suggests.

There is, however, a problem with this suggestion too. Suppose there is a possible naturalistic or physicalistic *definition* of reference, as Field contends. Suppose

(1) *x refers to y* if and only if *x bears R to y*

is true, where *R* is a relation definable in natural science vocabulary without using any semantical notions (i.e. without using 'refers' or any other words which would make the definition immediately circular). If (1) is true and empirically verifiable, then (1) is a sentence which is itself true even on the theory that reference is fixed as far as (and *only* as far as) is determined by operational *plus* theoretical constraints. (1) is a sentence which would be part of our 'reflective equilibrium' or 'ideal limit' theory of the world.

If reference is only determined by operational and theoretical constraints, however, then the reference of '*x* bears *R* to *y*' is

---

[8] Field, H., 'Tarski's Theory of Truth', *The Journal of Philosophy*, vol. 69. Field's view is discussed in my *Meaning and the Moral Sciences*, Routledge and Kegan Paul, 1978.

itself indeterminate, and so knowing that (1) is true will not help. Each admissible model of our object language will correspond to a model of our meta-language in which (1) holds; the interpretation of '*x* bears *R* to *y*' will fix the interpretation of '*x* refers to *y*'. But this will only be a relation *in each admissible model;* it will not serve to cut down the number of admissible models at all.

This is, of course, not at all what Field intends. What Field is claiming is that (*a*) there is a determinate unique relation between words and things or sets of things; and (*b*) this relation is the one to be used as the reference relation in assigning a truth value to (1) itself. But this is not necessarily expressed by just *saying* (1), as we have just seen; and it is a puzzle how we could *learn to express* what Field wants to say.

Putting this last puzzle aside, let us consider the view that (1), understood as Field wants us to understand it (as describing the determinate, unique relation between words and their referents), is true. If (1) is true, so understood, what *makes* it true? Given that there are many 'correspondences' between words and things, even many that satisfy our constraints, what *singles out* one particular correspondence *R?* Not the empirical correctness of (1); for that is a matter of our operational and theoretical constraints. Not, as we have seen, our intentions (rather *R* enters into determining what our intentions signify). It seems as if the fact that *R is* reference must be a *metaphysically unexplainable* fact, a kind of primitive, surd, metaphysical truth.

This kind of primitive, surd, metaphysical truth, if such there be, must not be confused with the sort of 'metaphysically necessary' truth recently introduced by Saul Kripke.[9]

Kripke's point, which is closely related to points made above about the reference of natural kind terms (terms for animal, vegetable and mineral species, for example), was that *given* that, as a matter of fact,

(2) Water is H_2O

(i.e. given that (2) is true in the actual world), and given that (Kripke points out) speakers *intend* that the term 'water' shall

---

[9] See his *Naming and Necessity,* Harvard University Press, 1980. (Originally given as lectures in 1970.)

refer to just those things that have the same lawful behavior and the same ultimate composition as various standard samples of actual water (i.e. speakers have such intentions even when talking about hypothetical cases or 'possible worlds'), it follows that (2) must also be true in every possible world; for to describe a hypothetical liquid which is not H_2O but which has some similarities to water is only to describe a hypothetical liquid which *resembles* water, and not to describe a possible world in which *water* isn't H_2O. It is 'metaphysically necessary' (true in all possible worlds) that water is H_2O; but this 'metaphysical necessity' is explained by mundane chemistry and mundane facts about speakers' intentions to refer.

If there is a determinate physicalistic relation R (whether it be definable in the language of natural science in finitely many words or not) which just *is* reference (independently of how or whether we describe that relation), *this* fact cannot itself be the consequence of our intentions to refer; rather, as we have repeatedly noted, it enters into determining what our very intentions to refer signify. Kripke's view, that 'water is H_2O' is true in all possible worlds, could be right even if reference in the actual world is fixed only by operational and theoretical constraints; the view presupposes the notion of reference, it does not tell us whether reference is determinate or what reference is.

To me, believing that some correspondence intrinsically just *is* reference (not as a result of our operational and theoretical constraints, or our intentions, but as an *ultimate* metaphysical fact) amounts to a magical theory of reference. Reference itself becomes what Locke called a 'substantial form' (an entity which *intrinsically* belongs with a certain name) on such a view. Even if one is willing to contemplate such unexplainable metaphysical facts, the epistemological problems that accompany such a metaphysical view seem insuperable. For, assuming a world of mind-independent, discourse-independent entities (this is the presupposition of the view we are discussing), there are, as we have seen, many different 'correspondences' which represent possible or candidate reference relations (infinitely many, in fact, if there are infinitely many things in the universe). Even requiring that (1) be true under whichever notion of truth corresponds to the metaphysically singled-out 'real' relation of reference does not exclude any of these candidates, if (1) is itself *empirically* accept-

able (acceptable given our operational and theoretical constraints), as we have seen. But then there are infinitely many *different* possible 'surd metaphysical truths' of the form '*R* is the
real (metaphysically singled-out) relation of reference'. If the
holder of the view allows that it is conceivable that his view is
not *quite* right, and that reference may be metaphysically singled
out without being totally *determinate* (the metaphysically singled-out *R* may allow for a plurality of admissible interpretations) then it is even conceivable that the operational-*plus*-
theoretical-constraints-view is metaphysically correct after all!
For why could it not be a surd metaphysical fact that reference
is the relation: *x* refers to *y* *in at least one admissible model M*.
Note that *all* these infinitely many metaphysical theories are
compatible with the *same* sentences being true, the same 'theory
of the world', and the same optimal methodology for discovering what is true!

3

Two philosophical perspectives

The problems we have been discussing naturally give rise to two philosophical points of view (or two philosophical temperaments, as I called them in the Introduction). It is with these points of view, and with their consequences for just about every issue in philosophy that I shall be concerned: the question of 'Brains in a Vat' would not be of interest, except as a sort of logical paradox, if it were not for the sharp way in which it brings out the difference between these philosophical perspectives.

One of these perspectives is the perspective of metaphysical realism. On this perspective, the world consists of some fixed totality of mind-independent objects. There is exactly one true and complete description of 'the way the world is'. Truth involves some sort of correspondence relation between words or thought-signs and external things and sets of things. I shall call this perspective the *externalist* perspective, because its favorite point of view is a God's Eye point of view.

The perspective I shall defend has no unambiguous name. It is a late arrival in the history of philosophy, and even today it keeps being confused with other points of view of a quite different sort. I shall refer to it as the *internalist* perspective, because it is characteristic of this view to hold that *what objects does the world consist of?* is a question that it only makes sense to ask *within* a theory or description. Many 'internalist' philosophers, though not all, hold further that there is more than one 'true' theory or description of the world. 'Truth', in an internalist view, is some sort of (idealized) rational acceptability – some sort of ideal coherence of our beliefs with each other and with our experiences *as those experiences are themselves represented in our belief system* – and not correspondence with mind-independent or discourse-independent 'states of affairs'. There is no God's Eye point of view that we can know or usefully imagine; there are only the various points of view of actual persons reflecting various interests and purposes that their descriptions and theories subserve. ('Coherence theory of truth'; 'Non-realism'; 'Verificationism'; 'Pluralism'; 'Pragmatism'; are all terms that have been applied to the internalist perspective; but every one of these terms has connotations that are unacceptable because of their other historic applications.)

Internalist philosophers dismiss the 'Brain in a Vat' hypothesis. For us, the 'Brain in a Vat World' is only a *story,* a mere linguistic construction, and not a possible world at all. The idea that this story might be true in some universe, some Parallel Reality, assumes a God's Eye point of view from the start, as is easily seen. For *from whose point of view is the story being told?* Evidently *not* from the point of view of any of the sentient creatures *in* the world. Nor from the point of view of any observer in another world who interacts with this world; for a 'world' by definition includes everything that interacts in any way with the things it contains. If *you,* for example, were the one observer who was *not* a Brain in a Vat, spying on the Brains in a Vat, then the world would not be one in which *all* sentient beings were Brains in a Vat. So the supposition that there could be a world in which *all* sentient beings are Brains in a Vat presupposes from the outset a God's Eye view of truth, or, more accurately, a No Eye view of truth – truth as independent of observers altogether.

For the externalist philosopher, on the other hand, the hypothesis that we are all Brains in a Vat cannot be dismissed so simply. For the truth of a theory does not consist in its fitting the world as the world presents itself to some observer or observers (truth is not 'relational' in this sense), but in its corresponding to the world as it is in itself. And the problem that I posed for the externalist philosopher is that the very relation of correspondence on which truth and reference depend (on his view) cannot logically be available to him if he *is* a Brain in a Vat. So, if we *are* Brains in a Vat, we cannot *think* that we are, except in the bracketed sense [we are Brains in a Vat]; and this bracketed thought does not have reference conditions that would make it *true*. So it is not possible after all that we are Brains in a Vat.

Suppose we assume a 'magical theory of reference'. For example, we might assume that some occult rays – call them 'noetic rays'[1] – connect words and thought-signs to their referents. Then there is no problem. The Brain in a Vat can think the *words*, 'I am a brain in a vat', and when he does the word 'vat' corresponds (with the aid of the noetic rays) to real external vats and the word 'in' corresponds (with the aid of the noetic rays) to the relation of real spatial containment. But such a view is obviously untenable. No present day philosopher would espouse such a view. It is because the modern realist wishes to have a correspondence theory of truth *without* believing in 'noetic rays' (or, believing in Self-Identifying Objects[2] – objects that intrinsically correspond to one word or thought-sign rather than another) that the Brain in a Vat case is a puzzler for him.

As we have seen, the problem is this: there are these objects out there. Here is the mind/brain, carrying on its thinking/computing. How do the thinker's symbols (or those of his mind/brain) get into a unique correspondence with objects and sets of objects out there?

The reply popular among externalists today is that while indeed no sign *necessarily* corresponds to one set of things rather than another, *contextual* connections between signs and external things (in particular, causal connections) will enable one to explicate the nature of reference. But this doesn't work. For example, the dominant cause of my beliefs about electrons is probably various *textbooks*. But the occurrences of the word 'electron' I produce, though having in this sense a strong connection to textbooks, do not *refer* to textbooks. The objects which are the dominant cause of my beliefs containing a certain sign may not be the referents of that sign.

The externalist will now reply that the word 'electron' is not connected to textbooks by a causal chain *of the appropriate type*. (But how can we have intentions which determine which causal chains are 'of the appropriate type' unless we are *already* able to *refer?*)

---

[1] 'Noetic rays' was suggested to me by Zemach.
[2] The term 'Self Identifying Object' is from *Substance and Sameness* by David Wiggins (Blackwell, 1980).

For an internalist like myself, the situation is quite different. In an internalist view also, signs do not intrinsically correspond to objects, independently of how those signs are employed and by whom. But a sign that is actually employed in a particular way by a particular community of users can correspond to particular objects *within the conceptual scheme of those users.* 'Objects' do not exist independently of conceptual schemes. We cut up the world into objects when we introduce one or another scheme of description. Since the objects *and* the signs are alike *internal* to the scheme of description, it is possible to say what matches what.

Indeed, it is trivial to say what any word refers to *within* the language the word belongs to, by using the word itself. What does 'rabbit' refer to? Why, to rabbits, of course! What does 'extraterrestrial' refer to? To extraterrestrials (if there are any).

Of course the externalist agrees that the extension of 'rabbit' is the set of rabbits and the extension of 'extraterrestrial' is the set of extraterrestrials. But he does not regard such statements as telling us what reference *is.* For him finding out what reference *is,* i.e. what the *nature* of the 'correspondence' between words and things is, is a pressing problem. (*How* pressing, we saw in the previous chapter.) For me there is little to say about what reference is within a conceptual system other than these tautologies. The idea that causal connection is necessary is refuted by the fact that 'extraterrestrial' certainly refers to extraterrestrials whether we have ever causally interacted with any extraterrestrials or not!

The externalist philosopher would reply, however, that we can refer to extraterrestrials even though we have never interacted with any (as far as we know) because we have interacted with *terrestrials* and we have experienced instances of the relation 'not from the same planet as' and instances of the property 'intelligent being'. And we can *define* an extraterrestrial as an intelligent being that is not from the same planet as terrestrials. Also, 'not from the same planet as' can be analyzed in terms of 'not from the same place as' and 'planet' (which can be further analyzed). Thus the externalist gives up the requirement that we have some 'real' connection (e.g. causal connection) with *everything* we are able to refer to, and requires only that the *basic* terms refer to kinds of things (and relations) that we have some

real connection to. Using the basic terms in complex conbina-
tions we can then, he says, build up descriptive expressions
which refer to kinds of things we have no real connection to, and
that may not even exist (e.g. extraterrestrials).

In fact, already with a simple word like 'horse' or 'rabbit' he
might have observed that the extension includes many things we
have *not* causally interacted with (e.g. *future* horses and rabbits,
or horses and rabbits that never interacted with any human
being). When we use the word 'horse' we refer not only to the
horses we have a real connection to, but also to all other things
of the same kind.

At this point, however, we must observe that 'of the same
kind' makes no sense apart from a categorial system which says
what properties do and what properties do not count as similarities. In *some* ways, after all, anything is 'of the same kind' as
anything else. This whole complicated story about how we refer
to some things by virtue of the fact that they are connected with
us by 'causal chains of the appropriate kind', and to yet other
things by virtue of the fact that they are 'of the same kind' as
things connected with us by causal chains of the appropriate
kind, and to still other things 'by description', is not so much
false as otiose. What makes horses with which I have not interacted 'of the same kind' as horses with which I *have* interacted
is that fact that the former as well as the latter are *horses*. The
metaphysical realist formulation of the problem once again
makes it seem as if there are to begin with all these objects in
themselves, and then I get some kind of a lassoo over a few of
these objects (the horses with which I have a 'real' connection,
via a 'causal chain of the appropriate kind'), and then I have the
problem of getting my word ('horse') to cover not only the ones
I have 'lassooed' but also the ones I can't lassoo, because they
are too far away in space and time, or whatever. And the 'solution' to this pseudo-problem, as I consider it to be – the metaphysical realist 'solution' – is to say that the word *automatically*
covers not just the objects I lassooed, but also the objects which
are *of the same kind* – of the same kind *in themselves*. But then
the world is, after all, being claimed to contain Self-Identifying
Objects, for this is just what it means to say that the *world*, and
not thinkers, sorts things into kinds.

In a sense, I would say, the world *does* consist of 'Self-Identifying Objects' – but not a sense available to an externalist. If, as I maintain, 'objects' themselves are as much made as discovered, as much products of our conceptual invention as of the 'objective' factor in experience, the factor independent of our will, then of course objects intrinsically belong under certain labels; because those labels are the tools we used to construct a version of the world with such objects in the first place. But *this* kind of 'Self-Identifying Object' is not mind-independent; and the externalist wants to think of the world as consisting of objects that are *at one and the same time* mind-independent and Self-Identifying. This is what one cannot do.

Internalism and relativism

Internalism is not a facile relativism that says, 'Anything goes'. Denying that it makes sense to ask whether our concepts 'match' something totally uncontaminated by conceptualization is one thing; but to hold that every conceptual system is therefore just as good as every other would be something else. If anyone really believed that, and if they were foolish enough to pick a conceptual system that told them they could fly and to act upon it by jumping out of a window, they would, if they were lucky enough to survive, see the weakness of the latter view at once. Internalism does not deny that there are experiential *inputs* to knowledge; knowledge is not a story with no constraints except *internal* coherence; but it does deny that there are any inputs *which are not themselves to some extent shaped by our concepts,* by the vocabulary we use to report and describe them, or any inputs *which admit of only one description, independent of all conceptual choices.* Even our description of our own sensations, so dear as a starting point for knowledge to generations of epistemologists, is heavily affected (as are the sensations themselves, for that matter) by a host of conceptual choices. The very inputs upon which our knowledge is based are conceptually contaminated; but contaminated inputs are better than none. If contaminated inputs are all we have, still all we have has proved to be quite a bit.

What makes a statement, or a whole system of statements – a theory or conceptual scheme – rationally acceptable is, in large part, its coherence and fit; coherence of 'theoretical' or less experiential beliefs with one another and with more experiential beliefs, and also coherence of experiential beliefs with theoretical beliefs. Our conceptions of coherence and acceptability are, on the view I shall develop, deeply interwoven with our psychology. They depend upon our biology and our culture; they are by no means 'value free'. But they *are* our conceptions, and they are conceptions of something real. They define a kind of objectivity, *objectivity for us,* even if it is not the metaphysical objectivity of the God's Eye view. Objectivity and rationality humanly speaking are what we have; they are better than nothing.

To reject the idea that there is a coherent 'external' perspective, a theory which is simply true 'in itself', apart from all possible observers, is not to *identify* truth with rational acceptability. Truth cannot simply *be* rational acceptability for one fundamental reason; truth is supposed to be a property of a statement that cannot be lost, whereas justification can be lost. The statement 'The earth is flat' was, very likely, rationally acceptable 3,000 years ago; but it is not rationally acceptable today. Yet it would be wrong to say that 'the earth is flat' was *true* 3,000 years ago; for that would mean that the earth has changed its shape. In fact, rational acceptability is both tensed and relative to a person. In addition, rational acceptability is a matter of degree; truth is sometimes spoken of as a matter of degree (e.g., we sometimes say, *'the earth is a sphere' is approximately true*); but the 'degree' here is the *accuracy* of the statement, and not its degree of acceptability or justification.

What this shows, in my opinion, is not that the externalist view is right after all, but that truth is an *idealization* of rational acceptability. We speak as if there were such things as epistemically ideal conditions, and we call a statement 'true' if it would be justified under such conditions. 'Epistemically ideal conditions', of course, are like 'frictionless planes': we cannot really attain epistemically ideal conditions, or even be absolutely certain that we have come sufficiently close to them. But frictionless planes cannot really be attained either, and yet talk of frictionless planes has 'cash value' because we can approximate them to a very high degree of approximation.

Perhaps it will seem that explaining truth in terms of justification under ideal conditions is explaining a clear notion in terms of a vague one. But 'true' is *not* so clear when we move away from such stock examples as 'Snow is white.' And in any case, I am not trying to give a formal *definition* of truth, but an informal elucidation of the notion.

The simile of frictionless planes aside, the two key ideas of the idealization theory of truth are (1) that truth is independent of justification here and now, but not independent of *all* justification. To claim a statement is true is to claim it could be justified. (2) truth is expected to be stable or 'convergent'; if both a statement and its negation could be 'justified', even if conditions were as ideal as one could hope to make them, there is no sense in thinking of the statement as *having* a truth-value.

The 'similitude' theory

The theory that truth is correspondence is certainly the natural one. Before Kant it is perhaps impossible to find *any* philosopher who did *not* have a correspondence theory of truth.

Michael Dummett has recently[3] drawn a distinction between *non-realist* (i.e. what I am calling 'internalist') views and *reductionist* views in order to point out that reductionists can be metaphysical realists, i.e. subscribers to the correspondence theory of truth. Reductionism, with respect to a class of assertions (e.g. assertions about mental events) is the view that assertions in that class are 'made true' by facts which are outside of that class. For example, facts about behavior are what 'make true' assertions about mental events, according to one kind of reductionism. For another example, the view of Bishop Berkeley that all there 'really is' is minds and their sensations is *reductionist,* for it holds that sentences about tables and chairs and other ordinary 'material objects' are actually made true by facts about sensations.

If a view is reductionist with respect to assertions of one kind, but only to insist on the correspondence theory of truth for sen-

---

[3] Dummett's views are set out in 'What is a theory of Meaning I, II' in *Truth and Other Enigmas* (Harvard, 1980). His forthcoming (eventually) William James Lectures (given at Harvard in 1976) develop them in much more detail.

tences of the *reducing* class, then that view is metaphysical realist at base. A truly non-realist view is non-realist all the way down.

The error is often made of regarding reductionist philosophers as non-realists, but Dummett is surely right; *their* disagreement with other philosophers is over *what there really is,* and not over the conception of truth. If we avoid this error, then the claim I just made, that it is impossible to find a philosopher before Kant who was *not* a metaphysical realist, at least about what he took to be *basic* or unreducible assertions, will seem much more plausible.

The oldest form of the correspondence theory of truth, and one which endured for approximately 2,000 years, is one that ancient and medieval philosophers attributed to Aristotle. That Aristotle actually held it I am not sure; but it is suggested by his language. I shall call it *the similitude theory of reference;* for it holds that the relation between the representations in our minds and the external objects that they refer to is literally a *similarity.*

The theory, like modern theories, employed the idea of a mental representation. This presentation, the mind's image of the external thing, was called a *phantasm* by Aristotle. The relation between the phantasm and the external object by virtue of which the phantasm represents the external object to the mind is (according to Aristotle) that the phantasm *shares a form* with the external object. Since the phantasm and the external object are similar (share the form), the mind, in having available the phantasm, also has directly available the very *form* of the external object.[4]

Aristotle himself says that the phantasm does *not* share with the object such properties as *redness* (i.e. the redness in our minds is not literally the same property as the redness of the object), which can be perceived by one sense, but does share such properties as *length* or *shape* which can be perceived by more than one sense (which are 'common sensibles' as opposed to 'single sensibles').

In the seventeenth century the similitude theory began to be restricted, much as it had been by Aristotle. Thus Locke and Descartes held that in the case of a 'secondary' quality, such as a color or a texture, it would be absurd to suppose that the prop-

---

[4] See *De Anima,* Book III, Ch. 7 and 8.

erty of the mental image is *literally* the same property as the property of the physical thing. Locke was a Corpuscularian, that is, an advocate of the atomic theory of matter, and like a modern physicist he conceived that what answers to the sensuous presented redness of my image of a red piece of cloth is not a simple property of the cloth, but a very complex dispositional property or 'Power', namely the Power to give rise to sensations of this particular kind (sensations which exhibit 'subjective red', in the language of psychophysics). This power in turn has an explanation, which we did not know in Locke's day, in the particular micro-structure of the piece of cloth which leads it to selectively absorb and reflect light of different wave-lengths. (This *sort* of explanation was already given by Newton.) If we say that having such a microstructure is 'being red' in the case of a piece of cloth, then clearly whatever the nature of subjective red may be, the event in my mind (or even my brain) that takes place when I have a sensation of subjective red does *not* involve anything in my mind (or brain) 'being red'. The properties of a physical thing which make it an instance of physical red and the properties of a mental event which make it an instance of subjective red are quite different. A red piece of cloth and a red after-image are *not* literally similar. They do not share a Form.

For those properties (shape, motion, position) which his Corpuscularian philosophy led him to regard as basic and irreducible, Locke was willing to keep the similitude theory of reference, however. (Actually, some Locke scholars today dispute this; but Locke does say that there is a 'similitude' between the idea and the object in the case of the primary qualities and that there is 'no similitude' between the idea of *red* or *warmth* and the redness or warmth in the object.[5] And the reading of Locke I am describing was the universal one among his contemporaries and among eighteenth century readers as well.)

Berkeley's tour de force

Berkeley discovered a very unwelcome consequence of the similitude theory of reference: it implies that nothing exists except mental entities ('spirits and their ideas', i.e. minds and

---

[5] See *An Essay Concerning Human Understanding*, Book II, Ch. VIII.

their sensations). It is generally unappreciated that the premiss from which Berkeley worked – the similitude theory – was not something he merely learned from Locke (or read into Locke) but was the accepted theory of reference before his time and, indeed, for a hundred years afterwards; but we have just remarked how venerable this theory actually was.

Berkeley's argument is very simple. The usual philosophical argument against the similitude theory in the case of secondary qualities is correct (the argument from the relativity of perception), but it goes just as well in the case of primary qualities. The length, shape, motion of an object are all perceived differently by different perceivers and by the same perceiver on different occasions. To ask whether a *table* is the same length as *my* image of it or the same length as *your* image of it is to ask an absurd question. If the table is three feet long, and I have a good clear view of it, do I have a *three foot long mental image*? To ask the question is to see its senselessness. Mental images do not have a *physical* length. They cannot be compared with the standard measuring rod in Paris. Physical length and subjective length must be as different as physical redness and subjective redness.

To state Berkeley's conclusion another way, *Nothing can be similar to a sensation or image except another sensation or image.* Given this, and given the (still unquestioned) assumption that the mechanism of reference is similitude between our 'ideas' (i.e. our images or 'phantasms') and what they represent, it at once follows that no 'idea' (mental image) can represent or refer to anything but another image or sensation. Only phenomenal objects can be thought about, conceived, referred to. And if you can't think of something, you can't think it exists. Unless we treat talk of material objects as highly derived talk about regularities in our sensations, it is totally unintelligible.

The tendency, in his own time and later, to see Berkeley as almost insanely perverse, almost scandalous, if brilliant, was due to the unacceptability of his conclusion that matter does not really exist (except as a construction from sensations), and not to anything peculiar about his premises. But the fact that one could derive such an unacceptable conclusion from the similitude theory produced a crisis in philosophy. Philosophers who did not wish to follow Berkeley in Subjective Idealism had to come up with a different account of reference.

Kant's account of knowledge and truth

I want to say that, although Kant never quite says that this is what he is doing, Kant is best read as proposing for the first time what I have called the 'internalist' or 'internal realist' view of truth.

To begin with, it is clear that Kant regarded Berkeley's Subjective Idealism as quite unacceptable (this much he explicitly says), and also regarded causal realism – the view that we directly perceive only sensations, and *infer* material objects via some kind of problematical inference, as equally unacceptable. A view on which it is only a very dubious hypothesis that there is a table in front of me as I write these pages is a 'scandal', Kant says.

Secondly, I take it that Kant saw clearly how Berkeley's argument works: he saw that it depends on the similitude theory of reference, and that rejecting Berkeley's argument requires rejecting that theory. Here I am attributing a view to Kant that Kant does not express in these words (indeed, talk of 'reference' as the relation between mental signs and what they stand for is very recent, although the problem of the relation between mental signs and what they stand for is very ancient). But we shall see that what Kant *did* say has precisely the effect of giving up the similitude theory of reference.

Let me suggest a way of reading Kant that may be helpful, although it is only a first approximation to a right interpretation. Think of Kant as accepting Berkeley's point that the argument from the relativity of perception applies as much to the so-called 'primary' qualities as to the secondary ones, but making a different response than Berkeley made. Berkeley's response, recall, was to scrap the distinction between primary qualities and secondary qualities and fall back on just what Locke would have called 'simple' qualities of sensation as the basic entities we can refer to. Locke's own treatment of secondary qualities, recall, was to say that (as properties of the physical object) we can only conceive of them as Powers, as properties – *nature unspecified* – which enable the object to affect *us* in a certain way. Saying that something is red, or warm, or furry, is saying that it is so-and-so *in relation to us,* not how it is from a God's Eye point of view.

I suggest that (as a first approximation) the way to read Kant is as saying that what Locke said about secondary qualities is true of *all* qualities – the simple ones, the primary ones, the secondary ones alike (indeed, there is little point of distinguishing them).[6]

If *all properties are secondary,* what follows? It follows that *everything* we say about an object is of the form: it is such as to affect *us* in such-and-such a way. *Nothing at all* we say about any object describes the object as it is 'in itself', independently of its effect on *us,* on beings with our rational natures and our biological constitutions. It also follows that we cannot assume any similarity ('similitude', in Locke's English) between our idea of an object and whatever mind-independent reality may be ultimately responsible for our experience of that object. Our ideas of objects are not *copies* of mind-independent things.

This is very much the way Kant describes the situation. He does not doubt that there is *some* mind-independent reality; for him this is virtually a postulate of reason. He refers to the elements of this mind-independent reality in various terms: thing-in-itself (*Ding an sich*); the noumenal objects or *noumena;* collectively, *the noumenal world.* But we can form no real conception of these noumenal things; even the notion of a noumenal world is a kind of limit of thought (*Grenz-Begriff*) rather than a clear concept. Today the notion of a noumenal world is perceived to be an unnecessary metaphysical element in Kant's thought. (But perhaps Kant is right: perhaps we can't help think-

---

[6] Kant gives a summary of his own view in precisely this way in the *Prolegomena:*

> Long before Locke's time, but assuredly since him, it has been generally assumed and granted without detriment to the actual existence of external things that many of their predicates may be said to belong, not to the things in themselves, but to their appearances, and to have no proper existence outside our representation. Heat, color, and taste, for instance, are of this kind. Now, if I go farther and, for weighty reasons, rank as mere appearances the remaining qualities of bodies also, which are called primary – such as extension, place, and, in general, space, with all that which belongs to it (impenetrability or materiality, shape, etc.) – no one in the least can adduce the reason of its being inadmissible. As little as the man who admits colors not to be properties of the object in itself, but only as modifications of the sense of sight, should on that account be called an idealist, so little can my thesis be named idealistic merely because I find that more, nay, *all the properties which constitute the intuition of a body belong merely to its appearance.*

ing that there is *somehow* a mind-independent 'ground' for our experience even if attempts to talk about it lead at once to nonsense.)

At the same time, talk of ordinary 'empirical' objects is *not* talk of things-in-themselves but only talk of things-for-us.

The really subtle point is that Kant regards all of these points as applying to sensations ('objects of internal sense') *as well as* to external objects. This may seem strange: what is the problem about whether or not an idea corresponds to a sensation? But Kant is on to something profound.

Suppose I have a sensation *E*. Suppose I *describe E;* say, by asserting '*E* is a sensation of *red.*' If 'red' just means *like this,* then the whole assertion just means '*E* is *like this*' (attending to *E*), i.e. *E is like E* – and no judgment has really been made. As Wittgenstein puts it, one is reduced to virtually a grunt. On the other hand, if 'red' is a true *classifier,* if I am claiming that this sensation *E belongs in the same class* as sensations I call 'red' *at other times,* then my judgment goes beyond what is immediately given, beyond the 'bare thatness', and involves an implicit reference to other sensations, which I am not having at the present instant, and to *time* (which, according to Kant, is not something noumenal but rather a form in which we arrange the 'things-for-us').[7] Whether the sensations I have at different times that I classify as *sensations of red* are all 'really' (noumenally) similar is a question that makes no sense; if they appear to be similar (e.g. if I *remember* the previous sensations as similar to this one, and *anticipate* that future sensations which I will so classify will in their turn seem to be similar to this one, as this one is then remembered) then they are similar-for-me.

Kant says again and again, and in different words, that the objects of inner sense are *not* transcendentally real (noumenal) that they are 'transcendentally ideal' (things-for-us), and that they are no more and no less directly knowable than so-called

---

[7] Here I am being deliberately anachronistic and describing Kant's view by means of an example taken from Wittgenstein's *Philosophical Investigations*. But Wittgenstein's example has deeply Kantian roots: Hegel, writing shortly after Kant, and aware of Kant's doctrine, made precisely the point that any judgment, even of sense impression, has to go beyond what is 'given' to *be* a judgment at all.

'external' objects. The sensations I call 'red' can no more be directly compared with noumenal objects to see if they have the same *noumenal* property than the objects I call 'pieces of gold' can be directly compared with noumenal objects to see if they have the same noumenal property.

The reason that 'All properties are secondary' is only a *first* approximation to Kant's view is this: 'All properties are secondary' (i.e. *all properties are Powers*) suggests that saying of a chair that it is made of pine, or whatever, is attributing a Power (the disposition to appear to be made of pine to us) to a noumenal object; saying of the chair that it is brown is attributing a different Power to that *same* noumenal object; and so on. On such a view there would be one noumenal object corresponding to each object in what Kant calls 'the representation', i.e. one noumenal object corresponding to each thing-for-us. But Kant explicitly *denies* this. This is the point at which he all but says that he is giving up the correspondence theory of truth.

Kant does not, indeed, *say* he is giving up the correspondence theory of truth. On the contrary, he says that truth is the 'correspondence of a judgment to its object'. But this is what Kant called a 'nominal definition of truth'. On my view, identifying this with what the metaphysical realist means by 'the correspondence theory of truth' would be a grave error. To say whether Kant held what a metaphysical realist means by 'the correspondence theory of truth' we have to see whether he had a realist conception of what he called 'the object' of an empirical judgment.

On Kant's view, any judgment about external or internal objects (physical things or mental entities) says that the noumenal world as a whole is such that this is the description that a rational being (one with our rational nature) given the information available to a being with our sense organs (a being with our sensible nature) would construct. In *that* sense, the judgment ascribes a Power. But the Power is ascribed *to the whole noumenal world;* you must *not* think that because there are chairs and horses and sensations in our representation, that there are correspondingly noumenal chairs and noumenal horses and noumenal sensations. *There is not even a one-to-one correspondence between things-for-us and things in themselves.* Kant not only gives up any notion of similitude between our ideas and the things in themselves; he even gives up any notion of an abstract isomorphism. And this means that there is no correspondence theory of truth in his philosophy.

What then is a true judgment? Kant does believe that we have *objective* knowledge: we know laws of mathematics, laws of geometry, laws of physics, and many statements about individual objects – empirical objects, things for us. The use of the term 'knowledge' and the use of the term 'objective' amount to the assertion that *there still is a notion of truth*. But what *is* truth if it is not correspondence to the way things are in themselves?

As I have said, the only answer that one can extract from Kant's writing is this: a piece of knowledge (i.e. a 'true statement') is a statement that a rational being would accept on sufficient experience of the kind that it is actually possible for beings with our nature to have. 'Truth' in any other sense is inaccessible to us and inconceivable by us. *Truth is ultimate goodness of fit.*

The empiricist alternative

So far as our argument has gone, it is still possible for a philosopher to avoid giving up the correspondence theory of truth and the similitude theory of reference by *restricting them to sensations and images*. And many philosophers continued to believe even after Kant that similitude *is* the mechanism by which we are able to have ideas that refer to our own (and, although this was more controversial, other people's) *sensations,* and that this is the primary case of reference from an epistemological point of view.

To see why this doesn't work, recall that the heart of Berkeley's argument was the contention that nothing can resemble an 'idea' (sensation or image) except another 'idea', i.e. there can be no resemblance between the mental and the physical. Our ideas can resemble other mental entities, but they cannot resemble 'matter', according to Berkeley.

At this point, we must stop and realize that this is in an important way false. In fact, *everything is similar to everything else in infinitely many respects.* For example, my sensation of a typewriter at this instant and the quarter in my pocket are both similar in the respect that some of their properties (the sensation's occurring right now and the quarter's being in my pocket right now) are *effects of my past actions;* if I had not sat down to type, I would not be having the sensation; and the quarter would not be in my pocket if I had not put it there. Both the sensation and the quarter exist in the twentieth century. Both the sensation and the quarter have been described in English. And so on and so on. The number of similarities one can find between *any* two objects is limited only by ingenuity and time.

In a particular context, 'similarity' may have a more restricted meaning, of course. But to just ask 'are *A* and *B* similar?' when we have not specified, explicitly or implicitly, what *kind* of similarity is at issue, is to ask an empty question.

From this simple fact it already follows that the idea that similitude is the private mechanism of reference must lead to an infinite regress. Suppose, to use an example due to Wittgenstein, someone is trying to invent a 'private language', a language which refers to his own sensations as they are directly given to him. He focusses his attention on a sensation *X* and introduces a sign *E* which he intends to apply to exactly those entities which are qualitatively identical with *X*. In effect, he intends that *E* should apply to all and only those entities which are *similar* to *X*.

If this is *all* he intends – if he does not specify the *respect* in which something has to be similar to *X* to fall under the classification *E* – then his intention is empty, as we just saw. For *everything* is similar to *X* in *some* respect.

If, on the other hand, he *specifies* the respect; if he thinks the thought that *a sensation is E if and only if it is similar to X in respect R;* then, since he is able to think this thought, he is *already* able to refer to the sensations for which he is trying to introduce a term *E,* and to the relevant property of those sensations! But how did he get to be able to do *this?* (If we answer, 'By focussing his attention on two other sensations, *Z, W,* and thinking the thought that two sensations are similar in respect *R* if and only if they are similar to *Z, W*', then we are involved in a regress to infinity.)

The difficulty with the similitude theory of reference is the same as the difficulty with the 'causal chain of the appropriate kind' theory that we mentioned earlier. If I just say, 'The word "horse" refers to objects which have the property whose occurrence causes me on certain occasions to produce the utterance "there is a horse in front of me" ', then one difficulty is that there are too many such properties. For example, let H-A (for 'Horse Appearance') be that property of total perceptual situations which elicits the response 'there is a horse in front of me' from a competent normal speaker of English. Then the property H-A is present when I say 'there is a horse in front of me' (even when I am experiencing an illusion), but 'horse' does not refer to situations with that property, but rather to certain animals. The presence of an animal with the property of belonging to a particular natural kind and the presence of a perceptual situation with the property H-A are *both* connected to my utterance 'There is a horse in front of me' by causal chains. In fact, the occurrence of horses in the Stone Age is connected with my utterance 'There is a horse in front of me' by a causal chain. Just as there are *too many* similarities for reference to be merely a matter of similarities, so there are *too many* causal chains for reference to be merely a matter of causal chains.

On the other hand, if I say 'the word "horse" refers to objects which have a property which is connected with my production of the utterance "There is a horse in front of me" on certain occasions by *a causal chain of the appropriate type*', then I have the problem that, if I am able to specify what *is* the appropriate type of causal chain, I must *already* be able to refer to the kinds of things and properties that make up that kind of causal chain. But how did I get to be able to do this?

The conclusion is not that there are *no* terms which have the logic ascribed by the similitude theory, any more than the conclusion is that there are *no* terms which refer to things which are connected to us by particular kinds of causal chains. The conclusion is simply that neither similitude nor causal connection can be the only, or the fundamental, mechanism of reference.

Wittgenstein on 'following a rule'

Consider the example I mentioned in passing, of the man who attempts to specify the respect R (the respect in which sensations must be similar to X if they are to be correctly classified as E) by saying or thinking that two things are similar in the respect R just in case they are similar in just the way Z, W are similar. This fails, of course, because any two things Z, W are themselves similar in more than one way (in fact, in infinitely many ways). Trying to specifiy a similarity relation by giving finitely many examples is like trying to specify a function on the natural numbers by giving its first 1,000 (or 1,000,000) values: there are always infinitely many functions which agree with any given table on any finite set of values, but which diverge on values not listed in the table.

This is connected with another point that Wittgenstein makes in *Philosophical Investigations* and that was mentioned at the end of Chapter 1. Whatever introspectible signs or 'presentations' I may be able to call up in connection with a concept cannot specify or constitute the *content* of the concept. Wittgenstein makes this point in a famous section which concerns 'following a rule' – say, the rule 'add one'. Even if two species in two possible worlds (I state the argument in *most* un-Wittgensteinian terminology!) have the same mental signs in connection with the verbal formula 'add one', it is still possible that their *practice* might diverge; and it is the practice that fixes the interpretation: signs do not interpret themselves, as we saw. Even if someone pictures the relation '*A* is the successor of *B*' (i.e. $A = B + 1$) just as we do and has agreed with us on some large finite set of cases (e.g. that 2 is the successor of 1, 3 is the successor of 2, . . ., 999,978 is the successor of 999,977), still he may have a divergent interpretation of 'successor' which will only reveal itself in some future cases. (Even if he agrees with us in his 'theory' – i.e. what he *says* about 'successor of'; he may have a divergent interpretation of the whole theory, as the Skolem–Löwenheim Theorem shows.)

This has immediate relevance to philosophy of mathematics, as well as to philosophy of language. First of all, there is the question of *finitism:* human practice, actual and potential, extends only finitely far. Even if we say we can, we cannot 'go on counting forever'. If there are *possible divergent extensions of our practice, then there are possible divergent interpretations of even the natural number sequence* – our practice, or our mental representations, etc., do not single out a unique 'standard model' of the natural number sequence. We are tempted to think they do because we easily shift from 'we could go on counting' to 'an ideal machine could go on counting' (or, 'an ideal *mind* could go on counting'); but talk of ideal machines (or minds) is very different from talk of *actual* machines and persons. Talk of what an ideal machine could do is talk *within* mathematics, it cannot fix the interpretation *of* mathematics.

In the same way, Wittgenstein holds that talk of 'similarity' and 'the same sensation' or 'the same experience' is talk *within* psychological theory; it cannot fix the interpretation *of* psychological theory. *That,* the interpretation of psychological theory and terminology, is fixed by our actual practice, our actual standards of correctness and incorrectness.

In *Ways of Worldmaking*[8] Nelson Goodman makes a closely related point: it is futile to try to have a notion of what the perceptual facts 'really are' independently of how we conceptualize them, of the descriptions that we give of them and that seem right to us. Thus, after discussing a finding by the psychologist Kolers that a disproportionate number of engineers and physicians are unable to see apparent motion at all, that is 'motion' produced by lights which successively flash at different positions, Goodman comments (p. 92):

> Yet if an observer reports that he sees two distinct flashes, even at distances and intervals so short that most observers see one moving spot, perhaps he means that he sees the two as we might say we see a swarm of molecules when we look at a chair, or as we do when we say we see a round table top even when we look at it from an oblique angle. Since an observer can become adept at distinguishing apparent from real motion, he may take the appearance of motion as a sign that there are two flashes, as we take the oval appearance of the table top as a sign that it is round; and in both cases the signs may be or become so transparent that we look through them to physical events and objects. When the observer visually determines that what is before him is what we agree is before him, we can hardly charge him with an error in visual perception. Shall we say, rather, that he misunderstands the instruction, which is presumably just to tell what he sees? Then how, without prejudicing the outcome, can we so reframe the instruction as to

[8] Published by Hackett, 1978.

prevent such a 'misunderstanding'? Asking him to make no use of prior experience and to avoid all concept-ualization will obviously leave him speechless; for to talk at all he must use words.

Grasp of 'Forms' and empirical association

A Platonist or Neo-Platonist of an antique vintage would have dealt with this issue in a much simpler way. Such a philosopher would have said that when we attend to a particular sensation we also perceive a Universal or a Form, i.e. the mind has the ability to grasp properties in themselves, and not just to attend to instances of those properties. Such a philosopher would say it is the Nominalism of Wittgenstein and Goodman, their refusal to have any truck with Forms and with the direct grasp of Forms, that makes it seem to them that there is any problem with the similitude theory.

While just positing a mysterious power of 'grasping Forms' is hardly a solution, it might seem that an analogue of this power *is* available to us. Properties of things do enter into causal *explanations;* when I have a sensation and it elicits the response 'this is a sensation of red', my response is partly caused by the fact that the sensation had a *property.* True, some philosophers are so nominalistic that they would deny the existence of such enti-ties as 'properties' altogether; but science itself does not hesitate to talk freely of properties. Can we not say that, when Wittgen-stein's privateer (the man who wanted to invent a private lan-guage) attended to X and said 'E' then what *caused* the response 'E' was a causal interaction involving a certain *property,* and *that* property (whatever it was) is the relevant 'similarity' that other sensations must have to X to be correctly classified as E?

The observation that talk of 'properties' is perfectly scientifi-cally legitimate is correct; but this does not help rehabilitate Pla-tonism. We interact with properties only by interacting with their *instances;* and these instances always are instances of *many* properties at the same time. There is no such thing as just inter-acting with a property 'in itself'. Talk of the properties causally associated with a sensation cannot do the work that the notion of the (unique) Form of the sensation did in Platonistic philoso-phy.

To spell this out: when I have a sensation of blue, I have a sensation of *blue,* and I also have a sensation with the complex property of being such as to be classed by me at that instance under that particular verbal label. Merely attending to *this* sensation does not constitute 'grasping' *one* of these properties. To pick out the property associated in just *one* of these ways with my sensation or with the verbal label is our old friend, the problem of the Causal Chain of the Appropriate Type again.

To see this, observe, first of all, that when my total perceptual experience elicits the response 'I am having the sensation of blue', I am not always *right.* I myself have had the experience of referring to 'the man in the blue sweater' two or three times before someone pointed out that the sweater was *green.* I don't mean the sweater *looked* blue; I realized that I had been misdescribing the sweater the instant the other person spoke. (I don't often have occasion to say 'I am having the sensation of blue', but if I did, then in such a case I would probably have said it two or three times until someone – wondering, perhaps, why I would have the sensation of blue when I was looking at something that was obviously green – queried me, whereupon I would have taken back my previous phenomenal report.) This already shows that the property of eliciting the report 'I am having the sensation of blue', or whatever, is *not the same property* as the property of being a sensation of blue, or a sensation of whatever the relevant quality might be.

Philosophers often refer to such a case as a 'slip of the tongue'. This seems to me to be an unfortunate terminology. The word 'green' might have been on my lips, and I might have found myself, frustratingly, *saying* 'blue'. *That* would have been a slip of the tongue. But in the case I described I didn't even notice I was misdescribing until someone questioned my report (and might never have noticed otherwise).

Another explanation which is suggested is that when I said 'blue' I *meant* green. By now it should be clear that when we say things we don't go around 'meaning' things in the sense of holding meanings in mind. To say I 'meant' green is just to say that I instantly accepted the correction (and felt funny when I realized the way I had been speaking). This is just to repeat what happened, not to explain it.

Whatever the explanation may be (perhaps some slip-up in the verbal processing unit of my brain), the point is that, just as the property A-H described a few pages back will elicit the report 'There is a horse in front of me' even on occasions when no horse is present in the environment, so there is a complex property of my total mind-set which will elicit 'I am having a sensation of blue', when I am not having the sensation of blue (or, anyway, would deny that I was if I were queried). No mechanism of empirical association is perfect. If we decide to stipulate that I am having a sensation of blue whenever I am having a sensation which *elicits* that report (or which elicits that report and is such that the report does not seem 'wrong' to me on second thought), then on folk psychological theory, and perhaps on scientific psychological theory as well, there could be occasions when it will be true that I am having a sensation of blue by *this* criterion although, for one of a variety of reasons, the quality of the sensation is not blue. Moreover, as Wittgenstein puts it, on such a criterion, *whatever seems right to me is going to be right* – i.e. the distinction between making a report of my sensation that really is correct and making a report that seems to me to be correct will have been abandoned. Perhaps we *should* abandon or at least qualify it; perhaps, as Goodman seems to be suggesting, the question of whether one is 'really' having the kind of sensation one thinks one is makes no sense, apart from special cases, such as the case in which one would take the report back if queried; but to abandon this distinction is not a possible move for a metaphysical realist, for the sharp distinction between what really is the case and what one judges to be the case is precisely what constitutes metaphysical realism.

Could one always be wrong about the quality of one's past sensations?

Another way to bring out what is involved is to consider the question: 'Could one always be wrong about one's past sensations?' On the similitude theory, the answer is clearly 'yes'. For according to that theory, my previous sensations either are or aren't similar to the sensations I *now* describe by the various verbal labels 'sensation of red', 'pain', etc., and whether they are or aren't is a totally different question from whether I *then* classified them under those same verbal labels. Perhaps the world is such that what we call a 'sensation of red' at an even numbered minute from the beginning of the Christian Era is actually similar in quality to what we call a 'sensation of green' at an odd-numbered minute, but our memory always deceives us in such a way that we never notice. Then the sensation I classified under the verbal label 'sensation of red' one minute ago would *not* be similar to the sensation I now classify under that same label.

There is something very odd about this alleged possibility, however. For one thing, the sense in which 'I would never notice' is very strong: if I treat my 'sensations of red' at different times as reliable signs of the various correlated physical occurrences (such as fire, the signal to stop, etc.) then I will be successful in all my actions. The 'wrong' similarity class (the class that lumps together the sensations I *call* sensations of red, in spite of the fact that they are not 'really' all of the same 'quality') would be the one that I had *better* use in connection with my problem-solving activities. But then is it really the *wrong* similarity class?

If we don't suppose that the notion of similarity is self-interpreting, then this case could be redescribed as a case in which the relation called 'similarity' by the external observer who is telling us about the case simply differs from the relation called 'similarity' by *us*. If we take this view, then the hypothesis that we are 'really' wrong about our past sensations collapses: from an *internalist* point of view there is no intelligible notion of sensations at different times being 'similar' apart from our standards of rational acceptability.

The correspondence theory of truth again

By now the reader may be convinced that the similitude theory of reference is thoroughly dead. But why should we conclude that the correspondence theory of truth must be given up? Even if the notion of a 'similarity' between our concepts and what they refer to doesn't work, couldn't there be some kind of an abstract isomorphism, or, if not literally an isomorphism, some kind of abstract *mapping* of concepts onto things in the (mind-independent) world? Couldn't truth be defined in terms of such an isomorphism or mapping?

The trouble with this suggestion is not that correspondences between words or concepts and other entities don't exist, but that *too many* correspondences exist. To pick out just *one* correspondence between words or mental signs and mind-independent things we would have already to have referential access to the mind-independent things. You can't single out a correspondence between two things by just squeezing *one* of them hard (or doing anything else to just one of them); you cannot single out a correspondence between our concepts and the supposed noumenal objects without access to the noumenal objects.

One way to see this is the following. Sometimes incompatible theories can actually be intertranslatable. For example, if Newtonian physics were true, then every single physical event could be described in two ways: in terms of particles acting at a distance, across empty space (which is how Newton described gravitation as acting), or in terms of particles acting on fields which act on other fields (or other parts of the same field), which finally act 'locally' on other particles. For example, the Maxwell equations, which describe the behavior of the electro-magnetic field, are mathematically equivalent to a theory in which there are only action-at-a-distance forces between particles, attracting and repelling according to the inverse square law, travelling not instantaneously but rather at the speed of light ('retarded potentials'). The Maxwell field theory and the retarded potential theory are incompatible from a metaphysical point of view, since either there are or there aren't causal agencies (the 'fields') which mediate the action of separated particles on each other (a realist would say). But the two theories are mathematically intertranslatable. So if there is a 'correspondence' to the noumenal things which makes one of them true, then one can define another correspondence which makes the other theory true. If all it takes to make a theory true is abstract correspondence (never mind which), then incompatible theories can be true.

To an internalist this is not objectionable: why should there not sometimes be equally coherent but incompatible conceptual schemes which fit our experiential beliefs equally well? If truth is not (unique) correspondence then the possibility of a certain pluralism is opened up. But the motive of the metaphysical realist is to save the notion of the God's Eye Point of View, i.e. the One True Theory.

Not only may there be correspondence between objects and

(what we take to be) incompatible theories (i.e. *the same objects* can be what logicians call a 'model' for incompatible theories), but even if we fix the theory *and* fix the objects there are (if the number of objects is infinite) infinitely many *different* ways in which the same objects can be used to make a model for a given theory. This simply states in mathematical language the intuitive fact that to single out a correspondence between two domains one needs some independent access to both domains.

What we have is the demise of a theory that lasted for over two thousand years. That it persisted so long and in so many forms in spite of the internal contradictions and obscurities which were present from the beginning testifies to the naturalness and the strength of the desire for a God's Eye View. Kant, who first taught us that this desire is unfulfillable, thought that it was nonetheless built into our rational nature itself (he suggested sublimating this 'totalizing' impulse in the project of trying to realize 'the highest good in the world' by reconciling the moral and empirical orders in a perfected system of social institutions and individual relationships). The continued presence of this natural but unfulfillable impulse is, perhaps, a deep cause of the false monisms and false dualisms which proliferate in our culture; be this as it may, we are left without the God's Eye View.

4

Mind and body

Parallelism, interactionism, identity

In the seventeenth century the great philosophers Descartes, Spinoza, and Leibniz all realized that there was a serious problem about the relation of mind to material body. To some extent, the relation was already a problem for Plato, of course, and for all of the philosophers that came after; but it became much more of a problem with the rise of modern *physics*. In the seventeenth century, people became aware that the physical world is *strikingly causally closed*. The way in which it is causally closed is best expressed in terms of Newtonian physics: no body moves except as the result of the action of some *force*. Forces can be completely described by numbers: three numbers suffice to determine the direction, and one number suffices to describe the magnitude of any force. The acceleration produced by a force has exactly the same direction as the force, and the magnitude of the acceleration can be deduced from the mass of the body and the magnitude of the force according to Newton's First Law, $F = ma$. When more than one force acts on a body, the resultant force can be computed by the parallelogram law.

It is important to recognize how very different such a physics, stressing number and precise algorithms for computation as it does, is from the essentially *qualitative* thinking of the middle ages. In medieval thought almost anything could exert an 'influence' on anything else. (Our word 'influenza' is a survival of this medieval way of thinking. Evil spirits were thought to exert an influence – *questa influenza,* in Italian – on the air which in turn influenced the sufferers of the illness.) In such a way of thinking, it is not *so* surprising that mind can 'influence' body.

In the time of the philosophers I mentioned, the mathematical way of thinking was beginning to appear and to push aside this older way of thinking. The new way of thinking did not fully develop until Newton, but in special cases Descartes already had the parallelogram of forces, and in still more primitive cases Leonardo da Vinci already had it. These thinkers saw that physics could be done in something like the way it is done now. They saw that what physics deals with is force and motion, and they rejected the qualitative style of explanation. Rather, they conceived that the mechanical world had a logic of its own, had a 'program', as we would say, and that it followed that program unless something disturbed it.

It seemed to these thinkers that mental events could do one of two things. (1) They could *parallel* physical events, e.g. events in the brain. The model is a pair of synchronized clocks: the body is a clock which has been wound up and which runs its happy or unhappy way until death, and likewise the entire physical world runs its happy or unhappy way from creation to the Last Judgment (or to gravitational collapse, in a modern version). And the mental events run their happy or unhappy way, and somehow, perhaps by divine providence, it has been arranged so that brain event B will always occur just when sensation S is occurring. (2) They could *interact* with physical events. The mental events might actually be causing brain events, and vice versa.

Descartes' rather notorious form of the interactionist view, the suggestion that the mind can influence matter when the matter is very, very ethereal (and that, in fact, it in some way pushes the matter in the pineal gland), was less the crazy speculation that it might seem to be, and more a hangover from a set of medieval doctrines.[1] In the earlier way of thinking, the mind was thought of as acting on the 'spirit' which in turn acted on 'matter', and spirit was not thought of as *totally* immaterial. 'Spirit' was just the in-between sort of stuff that the medieval philosophers' tendency to introduce in-betweens between any two adjacent terms in the series of kinds of being naturally led them to postulate. It

---

[1] See *The Discarded Image,* by C. S. Lewis, especially Chapter VII, sec. F, for a description of the medieval view (Cambridge, 1964).

was like a gas with just a little bit of push. As soon as 'spirit' is dropped out, and the mind is really thought of as totally immaterial, then the push of the mind on even very ethereal matter in the pineal gland appears very strange. One can't quite visualize that.

The most naive version of the interactionist view conceives of the mind as a sort of ghost, capable of inhabiting different bodies (but without change in the way it thinks, feels, remembers, and exhibits personality, judging from the spate of popular books about reincarnation and 'remembering previous lives') or even capable of existing without a body (and continuing to think, feel, remember, and exhibit personality). This version, which amounts to little more than superstition, is vulnerable to the objection that there is enormous evidence (some of which was already known in the seventeenth century) that the functions of thought, feeling, and memory involve the *brain* in an essential way. Indeed, on such a version it is not clear why we should have complicated brains at all. If all that is needed is a 'steering wheel', that could be a lot smaller than the human brain.

To avoid such scientific objections, sophisticated interactionists such as Descartes maintained that the mind and the brain are an *essential unity*. In some way it is the mind–brain unity that thinks, feels, remembers, and exhibits personality. This means that what we ordinarily call the mind is not the mind at all, but the mind–brain unity. What this doctrine means, what it means to say that something can consist of two substances as different as mind and matter are supposed to be and still be an essential unity, is, however, very obscure.

The parallelist alternative is also very strange. What makes the mental event accompany the brain event? One daring seventeenth-century philosopher suggested that mental events might actually be *identical* with brain events and other physical events, and that was Spinoza. The suggestion in a contemporary form is that the event of my being in pain on a particular occasion might be the same event as the event of my brain being in some state B on that occasion. (I will also express this view by saying that, on such a view, the properties of having that particular sort of pain and being in brain state B are identical. I prefer to talk in this way because I think we have more of a logical theory of *properties* at the present time than we do of events, but

I think the idea can be couched in either way. The idea, in this terminology, is that the property of the person, that the person is experiencing sensation Q, could be *the same property* as the property of being in brain state *B*.) In this form the suggestion was put forward by Diderot, for example, in the eighteenth century, and became 'mainstream' in the 1940s and 1950s. Materialism and the identity theory began to be taken seriously for the first time, and the suggestion began to be advanced that something like Spinoza's view (or Spinoza's view *minus* its elaborate theological and metaphysical embellishments) is right: we are really dealing with one world, and the fact that we do not know until we do a great deal of science that the states of having pains, hearing sounds, experiencing visual sensations, and so on, are in reality brain states doesn't mean that they can't be.

The first contemporary form of this identity theory was advanced by several writers, one of the best known being the Australian philosopher J. J. C. Smart. At first the suggestion was that a sensation, say, a particular sensation of blue, is identical with a certain neuro-physiological state. A variant on this, suggested first by myself, I believe, is a view called *functionalism*. [2] On the functionalist view there is indeed an identity here, but Smart was looking at the wrong sort of brain property to figure as the other term in the identity. According to the functionalist, the brain has properties which are in a sense *not* physical.

Now, what do I mean by saying that the *brain* has *non-physical* properties? I mean properties which are *definable in terms that do not mention the brain's physics or chemistry*. If it seems strange that a system which is physical should have properties which are not physical, consider a computing machine. A computing machine has many physical properties. It has a certain weight, for example; it has a certain number of circuit chips, or whatever. It has economic properties, such as having a certain price; and it also has functional properties, such as having a certain program. Now this last kind of property is non-physical *in the sense that it can be realized by a system quite apart from what its, as it were, metaphysical or ontological composition*

---

[2] N. Block's *Readings in Philosophy of Psychology* (Harvard 1980) contains an excellent collection of articles on Functionalism. My own papers are reprinted as Chapters 14 through 22 of my *Mind, Language and Reality, Philosophical Papers, Vol. 2* (Cambridge, 1975).

might be. A disembodied spirit might exhibit a certain program, a brain might exhibit a certain program, a machine might exhibit a certain program and the functional organization of these three, the disembodied spirit, the brain, the machine, could be exactly the same even though their matter, their stuff, is totally different.

Psychological properties exhibit the same characteristic; the same psychological property (e.g. being angry) can be a property of members of thousands of different species which may have quite different physics and chemistry (some of these species might be extraterrestrial; and perhaps robots will someday exhibit anger). The suggestion of the functionalist is that the most plausible 'monistic' theory in the twentieth century, the most plausible theory that avoids treating Mind and Matter as two separate sorts of substance or two separate realms of properties, is that psychological properties are identical with functional properties.

Today I am still inclined to think that that theory is right; or at least that it is the right *naturalistic* description of the mind/body relation. There are other, 'mentalistic', descriptions of this relation which are also correct, but not reducible to the world-picture we call 'Nature' (indeed the notions of 'rationality', 'truth', and 'reference' *belong* to such a 'mentalistic' version). I shall say something about this later (Chapter 6). This fact does not dismay me: for, as Nelson Goodman has emphasized, one of the attractive features of non-realism is that it allows the possibility of alternative right versions of the world. I am, however, attracted to the idea that *one* right version is a naturalistic version, in which thought-forms, images, sensations, etc. *are* functionally characterized physical occurrences; and what I wish to discuss here is a difficulty with the functionalist theory that occurred to me some years ago: that is that the theory has difficulty with the qualitative character of sensations. When one thinks of relatively abstract pure psychological states, e.g. what we called a 'bracketed' belief, i.e. a thought considered only in its 'notional' content, or of such diffuse emotional states as being jealous or being angry, then the identification of these with functional states of the whole system seems very plausible; but when one thinks of having a presented quality, e.g. experiencing a particular shade of blue, the identification is implausible.

An example I have used for many years in lectures is a variant of the famous example of the 'inverted spectrum'. The inverted spectrum example (which appears in the writings of Locke[3]) involves a chap who walks about seeing things so that blue looks red to him and red looks blue to him (or so that his subjective colors resemble the colors on a color negative rather than the colors on a color positive). One's first reaction on hearing of such a case might be to say, 'Poor chap, people must pity him.' But how would anyone ever know? When he sees anything blue, it looks red to him, but he's been taught to call that color *blue* ever since he was an infant, so that if one asked him what color the object is he would say 'blue'. So no one would ever know.

My variation was the following: imagine your spectrum becomes inverted at a particular time in your life and you *remember what it was like before that*. There is no epistemological problem about 'verification'. You wake up one morning and the sky looks red, and your red sweater appears to have turned blue, and all the faces are an awful color, as on a color negative. Oh my God! Now, perhaps you could learn to change your way of talking, and to call things that look red to you 'blue', and perhaps you could get good enough so that if someone asked you what color someone's sweater was you would give the 'normal' answer. But at night, let us imagine that you would moan, 'Oh, I wish the colors looked the way they did when I was a child. The colors just don't look the way they used to.'

In this case, it seems that one even knows what must have happened. Some 'wires' must have gotten 'crossed' in the brain. The inputs from blue light, that used to go to one mechanism in the brain, now go to another, and the inputs from red light go to the first. In other words, something has switched around the *realizations*, the *physical* states. The *physical* state that formerly played the *functional role* of signalling the presence of 'objective' blue in the environment now signals the presence of 'objective' red in the environment.

Now suppose we adopted the following 'functionalist' theory of subjective color: 'a sensation is a sensation of blue (i.e. has the *qualitative character* that I *now* describe in that way) just in

[3] *An Essay Concerning Human Understanding*, Book II, Chapter 32 (sec. 14).

case the sensation (or the corresponding physical event in the brain) has the role of signalling the presence of objective blue in the environment'. This theory captures one sense of the phrase 'sensation of blue', but not the desired 'qualitative' sense. If this functional role were *identical* with the qualitative character, then one couldn't say that the quality of the sensation has changed. (If this is not clear, then imagine that after the spectrum inversion, and after learning to compensate for it linguistically, you experience an attack of amnesia which wipes out all memory of what colors used to look like. In this case it would seem as if the sensation you are *now* calling a 'sensation of blue' could have almost exactly the functional role that the sensation you used to call the 'sensation of blue' used to have, while having a totally different character.) But the quality *has* changed. The quality doesn't seem to be a *functional* state in *this* case.

It seems to me that the most plausible move for a functionalist to make if such cases are really possible is to say, 'Yes, but the "qualitative character" is just the physical realization.' And to say that for this special kind of psychological property, for *qualities,* the older form of the identity theory was the right one. If the reader is fairly materialistically inclined, he or she probably thinks that the property of having the sensation is a brain property. Readers who are not materialistically inclined probably think that the property of having the sensation is *correlated* with a brain state. Probably most people hold one of these two views: the view that sensation-states are correlated with brain-states, or the view that sensation-states are identical with brain-states. As so often happens, the question becomes debated over and over in the same way. The way it is always discussed is, 'given that *B* is correlated with *Q*, is *B* actually identical with *Q*?' We know that this sensation-state parallels this brain-state, is it or is it not the case that 'the sensation-state is identical with the brain-state?' The more the discussion goes on in that way, the more the concept of *correlation* comes to seem unproblematical. *Correlation* isn't (much) discussed because *everyone knows* that there is at least a correlation. *Identity* is discussed because that is what is problematical. But I am going to try to show you that even *correlation* is problematical, not in the sense that there is evidence of *non-correlation,* but in the epistemological sense that *if* there is a correlation, one can never know which it is. The problem will not depend on assuming materialism, but it will depend upon the fact that we think that there is at least a correlation.

Identity theory and the a priori

What made the revival of interest in the identity theory and other 'monist' theories possible, if not initially (not with Smart and some of the early identity theorists), at least starting around 1960, was the change in the epistemological climate. Identity theory was not taken seriously prior to the 1960s for the reason that philosophers 'knew' it was false. And they thought they knew it was false not on the basis of empirical evidence (for what sort of empirical evidence could show that a sensation-state is not a brain-state?), but *a priori*. One thinks about it and one just sees *a priori* that a sensation-state couldn't be a brain-state, or perhaps one sees that it is *meaningless to say* that a sensation-state is a brain-state in the way in which it is meaningless to say that the number three is blue. Prior to 1950 or 1960 people thought they *just knew,* or many people thought they knew, that sensation-states *can't* be physical. Other people thought they knew those people were wrong. But argument was impossible. The majority would say, 'Look, we can't prove to you that it is impossible for a sensation-state to be a neurophysiological state, we can't prove to you that every number has a successor, we can't prove to you that the number three is not blue, but these are things we *just know;* these are *truths of reason.* We know that it is nonsense or an impossibility for a sensation-state to be a neuro-physiological state as clearly as we know anything.' One had the majority that knew that sensation-states couldn't be brain-states and a minority that knew the majority was wrong. Each knew the other was wrong *a priori.* And there was no really significant possibility of argument or movement from this frozen state in the debate.

In 1951 W. V. Quine published a paper titled 'Two Dogmas of Empiricism'.[4] From that time on, there has been a steady erosion in philosophical confidence in the notion of an *'a priori'*

---

[4] 'Two Dogmas of Empiricism' first appeared in *The Philosophical Review,* 1951. It is reprinted in Quine's *From a Logical Point of View.* (New York, 1961).

truth. Quine pointed out that many things we thought we knew *a priori* have had to be revised. Thus, consider the following: suppose someone had suggested to *Euclid* that this could happen: that one could have two *straight* lines which are perpendicular to a third *straight* line and which *meet*. Euclid would have said that it was a necessary truth that this couldn't happen. According to the physical theory we accept today, it *does* happen. Light passing near the sun behaves as it does not because the light travels in curved lines, but because the light continues to travel in straight lines and the straight lines behave in that way in our non-Euclidean world.

Once we accept *that,* then some philosopher was bound to ask the question, 'What is left of the *a priori?*', and Quine did. (Quine also showed convincingly that the standard empiricist *accounts* of *a priority* – e.g. the notion of 'truth by convention' – were incoherent, but I shall not review his arguments.)

In some ways, I think, Quine went too far. Quine's assertion that 'no statement is immune from revision' suggests that for every statement there are circumstances under which it would be *rational* to reject it. But this is pretty clearly false: under what circumstances, after all, would it be rational to reject 'Not every statement is true', i.e. to *accept* 'All statements are true'?[5]

But if Quine does overstate the case against the *a priori,* what he is nonetheless right about is this: our notions of rationality and of rational revisability are not fixed by some immutable book of rules, nor are they written into our transcendental natures, as Kant thought, for the very good reason that the whole idea of a transcendental nature, a nature that we have *noumenally,* apart from any way in which we can conceive of ourselves historically or biologically, is nonsensical. Since our notions of rationality and of rational revisability are the product of our all too limited experience and all too fallible biology, it is to be expected that even principles we regard as 'a priori', or 'conceptual', or whatever, will from time to time turn out to need revision in the light of unexpected experiences or unanticipated theoretical innovations. Such revision cannot be unlimited: otherwise we would no longer have a concept of anything

---

[5] I discuss Quine's attack on the notion of the *a priori* in 'Analyticity and Apriority: Beyond Wittgenstein and Quine', *Midwest Studies in Philosophy,* Vol. IV, 1979 (Minnesota).

we could call *rationality;* but the limits are not in general possible for us to state. Apart from trivial cases (e.g. 'Not every statement is true') we cannot be sure that it would *never* be rational in *any* context to give up a statement that is regarded (and legitimately so, *in a given context*) as a 'necessary' truth. In general, we have to admit that considerations of simplicity, overall utility, and plausibility may lead us to give up something that was formerly regarded as *a priori,* and that this is *reasonable. Philosophy has become anti-aprioristic.* But once we have recognized that most of what we regard as *a priori* truth is of a contextual and relative character, *we have given up the only good 'argument' there was against mind–body identity.* Identity theorists were bound to point this out, and they did. So there was a changed situation.

I have been using the notion of a *property;* but it seems to me that there are at least two notions of a 'property' that have become confused in our minds.[6] There is a very old notion for which the term 'predicate' used to be employed (e.g. in the famous question, 'Is existence a predicate?'), and there is the notion that we use today when we speak of 'physical properties', 'fundamental magnitudes', etc. When a philosopher has the older notion in mind, he frequently regards talk of properties as interchangeable with talk of *concepts.* For such a philosopher, *properties* cannot be the same unless it is a conceptual truth that they are the same; in particular, the *property* of having a sensation with a certain qualitative character cannot be the same as the property of being in a certain brain-state, since the corresponding predicates are not *synonymous* (in the wide sense of 'analytically equivalent'), and the principle of individuation for predicates is just that being P is one and the same predicate as being Q just in case 'is P' is synonymous with 'is Q'.

Consider, however, the situation which arises when a scientist asserts that temperature *is* mean molecular kinetic energy. On the face of it, this is a statement of identity of properties. What is being asserted is that the *property* of having a particular temperature is *really* (in some sense of 'really') the *same property* as the property of having a certain molecular energy; or (more gen-

---

[6] See 'On Properties', Chapter 19 of my *Mathematics, Matter and Method, Philosophical Papers,* Vol. 1 (Cambridge, 1975).

erally) that the *physical magnitude* temperature is one and the same physical magnitude as mean molecular kinetic energy. If this is right, then since '*x* has such-and-such a temperature' is not *synonymous* with '*x* has blah-blah mean molecular kinetic energy', even when 'blah-blah' is the value of molecular energy that corresponds to the value 'such-and-such' of the temperature, it must be that what the physicist means by 'physical magnitude' is something quite other than what philosophers have called a 'predicate' or a 'concept'.

To be specific, the difference is that, whereas synonymy of the expression '*X* is *P*' and '*X* is *Q*' is required for the predicates *P* and *Q* to be the 'same', it is not required for the property *P* to be the same as the property *Q*. Properties, as opposed to predicates, can be 'synthetically identical'.

If there is such a thing as *synthetic identity of properties,* then why shouldn't it be the case that the property of being in a certain brain-state *is the same property* as the property of having a sensation of a certain qualitative character (very much in line with Spinoza's thinking) – even though it is not a conceptual truth that it is, even though, in fact, it seems to many to be *a priori* false? This is the argument that was made. In short, we had a wave of anti-apriorism, we had the new machinery of the *synthetic identity of properties,* and with these two the identity theorist and in particular the functionalist seem automatically to be in business.

Now, I want to consider what happens when to these two things we add a third. What happens if a philosopher is (1) an anti-aprioristic naturalist, who (2) allows that there is such a thing as the synthetic identity of properties, and (3) also has a *hard-line realist* view of truth? I wish to claim that such a philosopher will find himself confronted with serious epistemological difficulties.

Split brains

Let us consider a particular kind of experiment that neurologists have performed in the last twenty years. This is the famous 'split brain', or brain disassociation experiment. I want to discuss the relevance of this kind of experiment to the identity theory and to what has so far been taken for granted in the whole discussion, the notion that there is a *correlation*.

On the model of the brain as a cognitive system resembling a computer, the brain has a language, an internal language (which may be innate, or which may be a mixture of an innate 'language', or system of representation, *and* a public language). Some philosophers have even invented a name for this hypothetical brain language, 'mentalese'. Let us consider what happens when one has a visual sensation on such a model (and I shall make up my neurology, since I don't know enough, but I don't think anyone really knows enough). Here is one possible story:

When one has a sensation a 'judgment' is made; the brain has to 'print' something like 'red presented at 12 o'clock'. So the quality (call it 'Q') corresponds, among other things, to *a record in mentalese*. Also, there is an input to the verbal processing center, the center which is connected with the voice box, which accounts for the brain's ability to report in the *public* language, 'red now'. It may be that the judgment in mentalese has to be transmitted from one location to another before there is an input to the speech center. There are also events in the visual cortex (which have been studied by the neurologists Hubel and Wiesel), which I am imagining as on the road to the 'record in mentalese', and the verbal process. These 'records', 'inputs', and other events may take place in different lobes of the brain: if the *corpus collosum* is split, the person's right lobe (the lobe that doesn't have speech) can see red (or at least it will affirmatively signal in response to a written query visible only to that lobe), but if one asks the subject what color the card is, he will reply 'I can't see the card.' And, finally, there is at some point the formation of a memory trace or of memory traces (one could break this up into *short-term memory* and *long-term memory*). There almost certainly is not a linear causal chain; there are probably branchings and rejoinings, a causal network.

The problem is that psychology divides up mental events in a fairly *discrete* way. Here is a sensation of blue. Now it started; now it stopped. Causal networks are not discrete. There isn't a unique physical event which is *the* correlate of the sensation.

If the identity theory is right, then the sensation-state Q is identical with some brain-state or other. A metaphysical realist cannot regard it as in any way a matter of convention or deci-

sion, or as having a conventional component, *which* brain-state
Q is identical with. The position is that *as a matter of fact* we
live in a world in which what we experience as the qualitative
characters of sensations really are *one and the same properties*
as some of the properties that we encounter in other ways as
physical properties of brain events. (Or better put, in which the
property of having a sensation of a certain qualitative character
is really just the property of being in a certain brain-state.)

Let us stop for a moment and see what the view actually says.
Suppose that *red* is the subjective quality we're attending to (produced, say, by staring at a green disk and then removing the disk
to get an afterimage). Suppose that when I experience this *red*,
the sensation-state I am in is identical to a disjunction of brain
states. It can't be identical to *one* maximally specified brain state,
because we know that one can take away any one neuron, or
whatever, and one can still have the experience. But the property
might be a disjunctive one, say (implausibly), *the even numbered
neurons in area blah-blah are firing or the prime numbered ones
are firing*. Actually, it would be a much bigger disjunction than
that. There would be a huge collection of neurological states
such that their disjunction would be the property of experiencing
red.

But now we go a little further. If the even numbered neurons
in area blah-blah are firing, I experience *red*. If the cerebroscope
says, 'no, the prime numbered neurons in area blah-blah are firing', I still experience *red*. That is, I can't tell *which* of these
brain-states I'm in. If I experience *red* I have to be in *one* of
them. But I can't *distinguish* between them. *The even numbered
neurons in area blah-blah are firing* is not an observable property. Even with the knowledge that the identity theory is true, I
can't tell from my sensations that I have this property. Call this
property 'P_1' and call the property that *the odd numbered neurons are firing* 'P_2'. The sensation-state is identical with the disjunction (P_1 or P_2), where this is, of course, a third property. P_1
is not a sensation-state, and P_2 is not a sensation-state; it is only
their *disjunction* that is a sensation-state. In other words, in this
ontology, the *disjunction* of two properties which are themselves
unobservable can be *observable*. It is a complicated logical function of unobservable properties that I experience as a simple
given. That is the position.

It may be that I have made the view sound silly. Thus, a friend of mine has remarked, 'Suppose the only device we have for detecting muons doesn't distinguish between muons and antimuons. Then *muon* isn't an observable property, and *antimuon* isn't an observable property, but the disjunction of them is. This only seems to be paradoxical to those who take observationality to be less of a pragmatic notion than it is.' My purpose, however, is not to ridicule the view, which, indeed, constitutes a very important and legitimate research program in neurophysiology, but to make clear what it commits one to. What leads to difficulties, I shall argue, is not the identity theory by itself but the identity theory taken in conjunction with metaphysical realism – i.e. taken in conjunction with what I called the 'externalist' perspective on the nature of truth.

One can avoid committing oneself to such a perspective. Thus, Carnap would have said (at least in a certain period) that talk about physical objects is highly derived talk about sensations, and that the decision to say that a particular brain state is identical with a sensation-state *Q* is really a decision to modify the language of talk about physical properties in a certain way, to change our concept of the physical property in question.

Since physical object and physical property talk is only highly derived talk about sensations, we can modify the rules. But that standpoint isn't the standpoint of metaphysical realism, at least with respect to material objects and physical properties. Somebody who thinks like that might be a metaphysical realist about *sensations,* but he is not a metaphysical realist about *material objects,* and since he regards material object talk as somewhat soft, he can adopt the identity theory by simply saying 'I adopt it as a kind of *convention,* as a further meaning stipulation.' Since the meanings were not totally fixed beforehand, since there was some openness of texture, there is no problem about 'how can you know that the sensation-state is identical with this property and not some other?' If what *this* property *is* is somewhat vague, then we're allowed to simply postulate the identity as a meaning specification. But I'm talking to someone who really thinks there is a material world out there, and it is not just highly derived talk about sensations; who really thinks that there are physical properties; and who holds that such expressions as 'the neurons in such and such a channel are firing' predicate definite physical properties of us, and either those properties *are* or *aren't* identical to this sensation-state.

Similarly for a philosopher like Daniel Dennett, who thinks that sensation talk is highly vague, who doesn't think there is a well defined subjective property of being in this sensation-state, of having a sensation with this qualitative character. I think he too could adopt an identity theory as a meaning stipulation, fixing not the meaning of the physical object terms this time, but the meaning of the psychological terms. But again, that wouldn't be the position of a full-blown metaphysical realist.

I am considering a full-blown realist who thinks 'yes, I know what this psychological property (the sensation-state) is. I've had it. I can recognize it. I think it's a definite psychological property to which I refer. I know what P_1 and P_2 are, therefore what (P_1 *or* P_2) is, and either the sensation-state is identical to this or it isn't.' Just in the way that a naive physicist might say, 'there's no element of convention' (I think he'd be wrong by the way); 'there's no element of convention in the decision that *temperature is mean molecular kinetic energy*, either temperature *is* mean molecular kinetic energy, or it's some other property'. That is the standpoint I want to examine.

The problem is that if one takes this metaphysical realist standpoint, then there are many more possibilities than people are wont to consider. The possibility that first comes to mind is that the sensation-state is identical with the property of having the appropriate events take place in the visual cortex *and* having the 'record' in 'mentalese' appropriately registered *and* having the input to the speech center *and* having the memory traces formed – i.e. the sensation-state is thought of as identical to the *conjunction* of these several properties. But as soon as we consider the possibility of disassociation, then we become unsure that we really want the whole conjunction. Perhaps the sensation is just the event in the visual cortex? (I.e. the property of having the sensation is 'really' the property of having the event take place in the visual cortex.)

Let us make the assumption that it is, for the moment. Now let us suppose we can cut off the process that produces the record in mentalese, or at least cut off the input to the speech center. Let us imagine that we have shown the subject a red card on the left side of his visual field (so that the card is only 'visible to the right lobe', as neurologists say). The appropriate event in the visual cortex will then take place in the right lobe, but if we say to the subject, 'Do you see anything red?', the subject will say, 'No'.

Now, by one criterion we employ to decide whether or not someone has a sensation, the criterion of sincere verbal reports, we should have to say that *he didn't have the sensation of red,* and therefore that we have *refuted* the theory that Q (the relevant qualitative character) is identical with the visual cortex property in question. But someone could object, 'No, you haven't refuted that theory at all. Because, what kind of an observer is this? The chap's brain is cut in two.' As far as any observer *in a normal condition* can tell, Q is identical with this property of the visual cortex. And observers who are not in a normal condition don't count. They *can't* count.

The difficulty is that there are identity theories which are *observationally indistinguishable,*[7] by which I mean that they lead to the same predictions with respect to the experience of all *observers in a normal condition.*

Consider the view that one doesn't have the sensation of red unless one has the input to the speech center. How could one prove that or refute it? One might think, if we split the corpus colossum but there is some memory that doesn't go through the verbal processing unit, then there is a way; namely, we first ask the chap whether he has a sensation of red. He says, 'No'. Then we sew the corpus colossum back together (a neat trick if you can do it!), and ask, 'Did you have a sensation of red?' He might say, 'Yes, but it was crazy, you know I had this sensation of red and you asked me whether I had it, and I heard myself sincerely

---

[7] The notion of 'Observational Indistinguishability' was introduced in papers on space–time theory by Clark Glymour and David Malament in *Foundations of Space–Time Theories,* Earman, Glymour, and Stachel (eds.), *Minnesota Studies in the Philosophy of Science,* Vol. VIII (Minnesota University 1977). The analogous problem in space–time theory is the existence of 'possible' space–times (i.e. space–times allowed by relativity theory) which differ in their global topological properties, but in which observers would have exactly the same experiences. Such examples are often dismissed on the grounds that 'simplicity considerations' would tell one which space–time one is living in; the trouble with this (as Malament points out) is that the physical theory (general relativity) doesn't *say* we live in the *simplest* space–time compatible with its laws.

telling you I didn't.' (I am told that actually it is more customary for patients to 'reconcile' or rationalize situations of this kind than to describe them as I have just imagined.) Would such a report show that there *was* a sensation of red without there being an input to the speech center?

It would not. If Daniel Dennett (who at one time held the view that the sensation *is* the input to the speech center, or a view close to this[8]) wished to reconcile this subject's report with his theory, all he would have to say is, 'I don't deny that at the later time the psychological event of *remembering having had the sensation earlier* took place. I deny that the *sensation* took place at the earlier time.' On either theory the subject *later* has the experience of remembering *rightly or wrongly* that he had the sensation of red earlier.

The disagreement here is an actual one. Most neurologists do believe that in the 'split brain' patients the right lobe is 'conscious'. In effect, this amounts to saying that there is sometimes a sensation of red, or whatever, even though there is no input to the speech center. ('There are two loci of consciousness', is the way it is frequently put.) At least one famous neurologist, Eccles, holds, however, that the disassociated right lobe (or left lobe, in the case of patients who have the speech center on the right) is *not* conscious. There is a *unitary* consciousness on Eccles' view; that the disassociated right lobe can 'simulate' conscious behavior does not show that it is a second 'locus of consciousness', he would say.

Nor will it help to appeal to methodological maxims, e.g. 'choose the simpler theory'; for there does not appear to be any relevant kind of 'simplicity' which is possessed by the 'unitary' view and lacked by the 'two loci' view, or possessed by the 'two loci' view and lacked by the 'unitary' view. Perhaps the 'two loci' view is simpler in one respect; it says that certain behavioral capacities (which the right lobe possesses, even if it does not possess speech) are sufficient for consciousness, and this agrees with the fact that we call animals (who do not possess speech either) conscious. But there are many *dissimilarities* between an animal with an intact brain, whose brain processes are still 'integrated',

---

[8] Dennett's model of consciousness is presented in 'Towards a Cognitive theory of Consciousness', reprinted in his *Brainstorms* (Bradford Books, 1978).

even if they do not involve speech, and one piece of a 'split brain'. If the case were not one which touches us so nearly, if we did not have such a strong tendency to metaphysical realism about *sensations,* would it not be in keeping with our best methodological intuitions to regard this as a case to be *legislated* rather than fought over?

In short, there are a number of observationally indistinguishable identity theories. If the identity theorist is right, it would seem that there is no way on earth in which one could know which *way* he is right; know with *which* brain-state a given sensation-state is identical (*or correlated with*). The point is sufficiently important to deserve further illustration.

Thomas Nagel[9] has made the plausible claim that one cannot imagine *what it would be like* to be a bat. But *why* should this be a plausible claim? Some years ago I read a delightful book about bats by Donald Griffin. I came to realize that bats are not basically different from any other mammals. We mostly *do* think we can imagine what sensations our dogs and cats have. What is the difficulty with bats?

Well, bats can hear sounds several octaves higher than we can. I cannot imagine what it would be like to be a bat in the sense of imagining what the echolocation sensation would be. But need this be *so* difficult? I used to be able to hear sounds an octave higher than the highest sounds I can hear in middle age. But the subjective pitches have not changed: the highest sounds I can hear may be an octave lower than the highest sounds I could hear when I was ten years old in *objective* pitch, but the highest sounds I hear now have the same thin, squeaky quality that the sounds on the threshold of being too high to hear always did for me. Perhaps *that's* how a sound five octaves higher than those we hear sounds to a bat: like a short high squeak.

Now, imagine a debate between two philosophers or psychologists, one of whom says *no* bat *quale* is at all like any human *quale.* Bat *qualia* are unimaginably different from human *qualia.* You will never be able to imagine what it feels like to be a bat (or even a dog or cat). The other philosopher, we may imagine, replies, 'Nonsense! Perhaps there are *some* bat sensations I can't imagine. There are some sensations of other humans (e.g. some

---

[9] 'What is it like to be a bat?', reprinted in N. Block, *op. cit.*

sensations of the other sex) I probably can't imagine, but that doesn't mean I regard the psychological space of those other humans as unimaginably different from my own. Why shouldn't I think of the bat's visual field, for example, as very much like my visual field? (N.B. Bats see very well, contrary to folklore.) Allowing for some adjustments for the optics of the bat eye, or the bat's hearing within the range that overlaps with mine, it's like my hearing, and its pains are like my pains.' Now could we *settle* this?

Because the number of neurons is different, and because the arrangement is different (the acoustic center of the bat's brain is enlarged to become 7/8ths of the brain), the properties at the most completely specified neurological level – number of neurons firing where – which are identical with a *quale* in the case of a bat on the assumption that the identity theory is correct, cannot literally be the same as the properties which are identical with any *quale* in the case of a human. Or can they? Suppose that when a bat has a certain visual sensation (produced by seeing red objects), that the bat's brain has the disjunctive property $(P_1 \text{ or } P_2)$, where P_1 and P_2 are maximally specified states of the bat's brain. (It would really be a much more complicated disjunctive property with thousands of cases, but let us simplify.) And let us suppose that when I have a certain visual sensation (produced by seeing red objects), my brain has the disjunctive property $(P_1' \text{ or } P_2')$. Consider the following two theories: (1) that the qualitative character of the bat's sensation (call it, 'red_B') is identical with (*or at least correlated with*) the disjunctive property $(P_1 \text{ or } P_2)$ and the qualitative character of the human sensation (call it, 'red_H') is identical with (*or at least correlated with*) the *different* property $(P_1' \text{ or } P_2')$. (2) That the qualitative character of the bat's sensation is *identical* with the qualitative character of *my* sensation (i.e. $red_B = red_H$) and both are *identical* with (*or correlated with*) the more complex disjunctive property $(P_1 \text{ or } P_2 \text{ or } P_1' \text{ or } P_2')$.

On the first theory the bat and I have different experiences, while on the second we have the same experience; but these two theories lead to the same predictions with respect to what *human* observers, normal and abnormal will experience. Once again, they are observationally indistinguishable.

Will methodological maxims ('choose the simpler theory')

help? Once again, it is not clear that they can. Ned Block has pointed out that the first theory is simpler in one respect (the *quale* is identified with a simpler physical property in *each* case), but the second is simpler in another respect (the second theory is 'non-chauvinist'; it allows that one doesn't have to have *exactly* our physical constitution to have our *qualia*). And once again, we lack principles for determining a unique preferred trade-off. Indeed, what reason is there to think there should or must be such principles? Why should we not, as Wittgenstein urged we do, abandon our metaphysical realism about sensations and about 'same' (as applied to sensations), and treat this too as a case to be legislated rather than fought over?

Finally, I want to present three theories which I am sure are false, but which it is difficult or impossible to rule out if metaphysical realism is right. These are: (1) that red_H is identical with a functional (or quasi-functional) state after all, namely the state of being in whatever material (e.g. physical) state earliest in your life played the functional role of normally signalling the presence of objective red. (2) that rocks have *qualia* (i.e. events qualitatively similar to, as it might be, *visual sensations,* take place in rocks). (3) that nations are conscious.

Let us first consider (1). Recall the argument I used to show that red_H could not be a functional state. That argument was that if we identified red_H with the functional state of *being in whatever material state (e.g. brain-state) normally signals the presence of objective red,* then I would not have undergone a spectrum inversion (at least in the 'amnesia' case), since I am in that functional state when I see something objectively red both *before* the spectrum inversion and *after* the spectrum inversion (allowing time for linguistic adjustment to take place, and, if necessary, postulating an attack of amnesia). But on a metaphysical realist position it is certainly possible that I *have* undergone a spectrum inversion (even though I don't remember it because of the attack of amnesia). The case is even stronger if I don't have an attack of amnesia and *recall* that my spectrum has been inverted; even in this case, if the linguistic adjustments have become automatic, there is a sense in which what used to be 'the sensation of green' now plays the functional role of 'signalling the presence of objective *red* in the environment'.

This argument only shows that red_H is not identical with the functional state mentioned. It does not show that it is not identical with a more complicated functional state, such as *the state of being in whatever material state earliest in your life realized the above functional state.* One might object that this is a funny property, a complicated logical function of functional properties. But why is a complicated logical function of functional properties less likely to be identical with red_H than a disjunction of complicated physical properties? Does the world prefer disjunctions of physical properties to conjunctions of functional properties?

Let us consider (2). Let P_3 be the property of being a rock, and consider the hypothesis that red_H is identical with the disjunctive property (P_1 or P_2 or P_1' or P_2' or P_3). Of course, rocks have this property all the time. So on this hypothesis, events of the qualitative character red_H are taking place in rocks all the time. (They are not experiencing red in the *functional* sense of experiencing red, but an event of the qualitative character of the event that plays the functional role of being the sensation of red in us is taking place in them all the time.) Or consider more complicated hypotheses on which rocks are having different *qualia* at different times. Or just the hypothesis that some one of these hypotheses (which not specified) is correct. We might say 'Well, these hypotheses are crazy.' Yes, they are. But each of them leads to the same predictions with respect to all human observers as the 'sane' theory. None of them can be ruled out on observational or experimental grounds, because each of them is observationally indistinguishable from the more standard view.

We might think that these theories can be ruled out by an appeal to the methodological principle that *one shouldn't attribute a property to an object with no reason.* Of course this principle doesn't say these theories are *false* (sometimes things we have no reason to believe are true), but at least it says we are *justified* in taking them to be false. But is there *really* no reason to hold the least specific of these theories (the theory *that* some such theory is correct, and rocks have *qualia*)? What of the argument that if *we* have *qualia* and physicalism is true (and many philosophers think there are many good reasons for accepting physicalism), then there is at least one physical object in which events with a qualitative character take place: so why shouldn't such events take place in *all* physical objects? If we could show that there is something about the *quale* itself which *requires* that it have the particular functional 'role' that it does in the case of humans then this move would be blocked; but this is just what believers in *qualia* as metaphysically real objects tell us we can't do.

Last but not least, let us consider (3). Consider the hypothesis that pain is identical with an appropriate functional state which can be exhibited by either organisms or nations. In other words, suppose that when the United States announces that 'the United States is pained by . . .' it really *is*. We would, of course, never know. Perhaps the reader is at this moment finding it interesting and mildly amusing that a group can behave in ways which resemble the ways in which something that really does feel pain behaves when it manifests its pain; but the reader does not think that the United States really feels pain. On this hypothesis, the reader would be wrong: the national Geist would really be feeling pain.

This hypothesis connects with an interesting discussion in the philosophy of mind. An argument that functionalists (including me) like to employ is the following 'anti-chauvinism' argument: in principle, the differences between a robot and a human (in functional organization, anyway) could be reduced to small details of the physics and chemistry. One might even have a robot that corresponded to us down to the neuron level. (It could even have a 'flesh and blood' body, apart from the brain.) The difference would be that whereas we have neurons made of carbon and hydrogen and proteins and so on, it would have neurons made of electronics, but from the neuron level up all the circuitry would exactly correspond. Now, unless you are a 'hydrogen–carbon chauvinist' who thinks that carbon and hydrogen are intrinsically more conscious, why shouldn't you say that this robot is a person whose brain happens to have more metal in it and less hydrogen and carbon?

This argument has provoked the following reply: 'Well, instead of these electronic gadgets, electronic neurons wired together in the same circuits that human neurons are wired in, let us suppose you have miniature people, little girl scouts and boy scouts.' We don't even have to imagine that these little people even know what the whole scheme is for, or that they see anything except a dimly lit room, or a lot of dimly lit rooms, in which they pass notes to one another. (Their time would have to pass very fast relative to 'our' time, of course.) They could be alienated workers. 'Now,' the reply continues, 'you wouldn't call that thing "conscious" because you know that it is really only these little people moving the body. And that shows that an appropriate functional organization (one like ours) is not sufficient to justify the application of such predicates as "conscious".'

One reply to this reply (the one I actually made) was to deny that the 'hydra-headed robot' (as this last thing has been called) *does* have the same functional organization we do. But there is a more radical reply I might have made. I might have said, 'Why *shouldn't* we call the hydra-headed robot conscious? If the first argument is right (and I think it is), if the robot with the positronic brain would be conscious, why would the fact that the neurons of the hydra-headed robot are *more* conscious mean that the whole thing is *less* conscious? After all, we are in a sense a society of small animals. Our cells are in a sense individual animals. And perhaps they have some little bit of feeling, who knows? Over and above *our* feeling.' Now, if we move that way, if we decide that the hydra-headed robot is conscious (even though its neurons are boy scouts and girl scouts), then why not the United States?

I don't, of course, claim that the United States has the *same* functional organization as *homo sapiens*. Clearly it doesn't. But there are many similarities. The United States has defensive organs. It has ingesting organs, it eats oil and copper and so on. It excretes (pollution) in vast quantities. Is it not perhaps *as* similar in functional organization to a mammal as is a wriggling fly, to which we *do* attribute pain?

How well-defined is 'qualitative character'?

So far we have not questioned the idea that it is perfectly clear what it means to say that two of one's own sensations have or do not have the same 'qualitative character'. Even at an introspective level, this is not the case, however. For one thing, just what one's experiences seem to one to be is notoriously dependent on antecedent conceptualization, as when we report seeing a round table top even when we view it from an angle.

In the case of the round table top, psychologists and philosophers have argued since the nineteenth century about whether
one has 'eliptical sense data' and *thinks* that they are round
(unless one is a 'trained introspectionist') or has round 'Gestalts'
and only thinks that they are elliptical because of optical theory.
One can have experiences which fit each description; and many
experiences will fit either description. Nor is neurology likely to
settle this dispute: the elliptical image on the retina doubtless
produces events in the brain itself, and if we identify *these* with
the 'visual sensation', then we may well get something like the
classical story of 'elliptical sense-data plus unconscious inferences'; the judged character of the experience ('I see a round
table top') also corresponds to 'records' and 'inputs' in the brain,
and if we identify *these* with the visual sensation, we may well
get a story in which one doesn't have elliptical sense-data unless
one *judges* that something looks elliptical. Why should we not
say that these two versions are both legitimate? As Goodman
says about the case of the subject who is asked to describe apparent motion,

> The best we can do is to specify the sort of terms, the
> vocabulary, he is to use, telling him to describe what he
> sees in perceptual or phenomenal rather than physical
> terms. Whether or not this yields different responses, it
> casts an entirely different light on what is happening.
> That the instrument to be used in fashioning the facts
> must be specified makes pointless any identification of the
> physical with the real and of the perceptual with the
> merely apparent. The perceptual is no more a rather
> distorted version of the physical facts than the physical is
> a highly artificial version of the perceptual facts.[10]

If I see a red tablecloth at two different times during the day,
do I have the *same* sensation of red? Or do I have different sensations and not notice the difference (unless I happen to be a
painter)?

An especially baffling case is the case of *accommodation*. If a
subject is given glasses which turn the image upside down, after
a time things will again look normal to the subject. Have the

---

[10] *Ways of Worldmaking*, pp. 92–3.

sense-data 'flipped back'? Or has he gotten used to altered sense data, and reinterpreted 'up' and 'down'? Very likely the subject himself cannot say at what point things became normal or which of these things happened. (Readers who like me wear bifocals can ask themselves: does the lower half of the visual field look different even when one isn't noticing the difference?) While there are transformations to which subjects *never* accommodate (in fact, it is only relatively simple changes to which one accommodates), and I have assumed that one would *not* accommodate to a color-inversion, the phenomenon of accommodation certainly casts doubt on the extent to which 'same qualitative character' is a well-defined notion.

Realism about qualia

We have considered a set of sceptical difficulties. What they purport to show is not that the identity theory is wrong (or that the correlation theory is wrong – note that they can all be stated as difficulties for a 'correlation' view just as much as for an identity view), but that, if it is true, then there are a vast number of alternative ways of specifying the details such that one can never know which one of them is true. And not knowing which one of them is true means not knowing what the answer is to a great many traditional sceptical questions, such as whether rocks and other inanimate objects have *qualia,* whether bats and other species have the kind of *qualia* we have or don't have the kind of *qualia* we have, whether groups can feel pain, and so on.

But why should any philosopher think it is even a logical possibility that a rock can have a pain (i.e. that an event of the same 'qualitative character' as a human pain can take place 'in' a rock)? Perhaps Russell gives us some clue to the nature of this kind of metaphysical realism. Russell was a realist about *qualia and* a realist about universals. Moreover, he took *qualia* to be paradigmatic universals. A universal is, above all, a way in which things can be *similar;* and to Russell it seemed that the qualitative similarities of one's own sensations are the epistemologically most primitive and most fundamental examples of 'ways in which things can be similar'. *Qualia,* for Russell, are universals *par excellence.*

Universals, however, are thought of as totally well-defined by a traditional realist: *words* may be vague, but universals themselves can't be vague. (A vague word is vague because it stands for a vague set of concepts, Gödel once said in a conversation; but the concepts are perfectly well-defined.)

So, if *qualia* are universals and universals are by nature well-defined, it must be perfectly well-defined whether any given thing or event – including a half of a split brain or some event in it; including a rock or some event in it; including a nation or group or some event in it – does or doesn't exhibit any given *quale*. And if the *quale* is thought of as independent of the functional role it plays, if it is thought to be wholly contingent that the qualitative character of a sensation of red is the qualitative character of something which has that particular functional role, then it does seem to be a logical possibility that the split brain or the rock has that *quale*.

A philosopher like myself who wishes to deny that every one of these possibilities makes sense (although some of them may – there *is* a temptation to treat the right lobe of the split brain as a 'locus of consciousness', and I have suggested that it would be legitimate to decide to do this) has to be careful to make clear that he is not espousing some form of behaviorism. Saying that 'qualia' are not well defined entities is not the same thing as saying they don't exist, that it is all just behavior, or whatever. Many notions are vague and still have some clear referents. The notion of a *house*, for example, is ill-defined in the case of igloos (is an igloo a house?), in the case of hogans, perhaps in other cases as well. But the fact that there is no fact of the matter as to whether or not an igloo is a house doesn't mean that houses don't exist. And, similarly, the fact that there is no fact of the matter as to whether or not the right lobe is 'conscious' doesn't mean that conscious beings don't exist.

Qualitative similarity of sensations is defined to some extent: if I have a sensation of red followed by a sensation of green, I know that I have had dissimilar sensations (and I know this without comparing their functional roles), and if I have a sensation of red followed by the 'same' sensation of red, I know (up to the vagueness we discussed above) that I have had similar sensations. But, for someone with an 'internalist' perspective on truth, it does not follow that there is a fact of the matter in every case as to whether two sensations (let alone two arbitrary events) are qualitatively similar or dissimilar.

Let E be the event of my having a particular sensation at a particular time and E' be some physical event in a rock. The suggestion that the qualitative character of E (say, *red$_H$*) might be identical with or correlated to some such property as (P_1 *or* P_2 *or* P_3) (where P_3 is the property of *being a rock*) offends any sane human sensibility. The suggestion that E and E' might be 'qualitatively similar' events is absurd. We have already discussed one explanation of this absurdity: the explanation that the hypothesis is absurd because it violates the methodological maxim 'do not ascribe properties to an object without a reason'. Even if this explanation worked, what it would yield is far less than the impossibility of rocks having *qualia* (or the incoherence of the notion that they do). If *this* is all that is wrong with the 'hypothesis' that rocks have *qualia* then we are in the position of having to say: *it is possible for all we know that rocks have qualia, but it is a priori highly improbable that they do.*

In fact, the hypothesis that rocks have *qualia* is incoherent in much the way that the Brain in a Vat hypothesis is incoherent: like the Brain in a Vat hypothesis, this 'hypothesis' presupposes a magical theory of reference. Any sane human being regards E and E' as *so* dissimilar that the question of 'qualitative similarity' (in the sense in which two sensations can be qualitatively similar, i.e. feel the same way) does not even arise. But the metaphysical realist, while not denying this at all, thinks that E and E' might (logically possibly) *be* similar in this way, *even though it is 'crazy' to think so.* And he thinks this because he is under the illusion that by having the sensation in question, with its qualitative character, its 'the way it feels', with its functional role, with the accompanying thoughts and judgments, he has somehow brought it about that the expression 'the way this sensation feels' (or some technical substitute, e.g. 'the qualitative character of this sensation', or '*red$_H$*', or 'this *quale*') refers to one definite 'universal', one absolutely well-defined property of metaphysical individual events. But this is not the case.

If there actually were robots functionally isomorphic to us and we worked with them, argued with them, had some of them as friends, we would quickly feel sure that they were conscious. (We might still be puzzled as to whether they had the *same qualia* we do; but we would not think of this any more often than we think of the question whether bats or dogs have the *same qualia* we do.) Suppose, however, we encountered hydra-headed robots. (Imagine that they actually *evolved* by some biological process somewhere, just as animals in symbiotic relationships evolve on earth.) What would we feel about *them?*

While one cannot really feel sure about so bizarre a case, it seems that even here (if we interacted mostly with the whole robot and only rarely with its conscious 'neurons' – the 'boy scouts and girl scouts' of my story) we might begin to attribute consciousness; but probably we would always be divided in our opinions. If we came to be sure that the hydra-headed robots were conscious, then might we begin to be ever-so-slightly queasy about the United States? I do not know.

The perspective I urge with respect to all of these cases is that there is nothing *hidden* here, no noumenal fact of the entities' really being conscious or really not being conscious, or of the qualities' really being the same or really being different. There are only the obvious empirical facts: that rocks and nations are grossly dissimilar from people and animals; that robots of various kinds are in between sorts of objects; and so on. Rocks and nations *aren't* conscious; that is a fact about the notion of consciousness we actually have.

What makes this line seem so disturbing is that it makes our standards of rational acceptability, justification and ultimately of truth, dependent on standards of similarity which are clearly the product of our biological and cultural heritage (e.g. whether we have or haven't interacted with 'intelligent robots'). But something like this is true of most of the language we use in everyday life, of such words as 'person', 'house', 'snow', and 'brown', for example. A realist who accepted this resolution of the puzzles about *qualia* would be likely to express it by saying that '*qualia* don't really exist', or that *qualia* belong to our 'second class conceptual system'; but what is the point of a notion of 'existence' that puts *houses* on the side of the *non-existent*? Our world is a human world, and what is conscious and not conscious, what has sensations and what doesn't, what is qualitatively similar to what and what is dissimilar, are all dependent ultimately on our human judgments of likeness and difference.

5

Two conceptions of rationality

In the preceding chapters I have spoken of rationality and of 'rational acceptability'. But rationality is not an easy thing to give an account of.

The problem is not without analogues in other areas. Some years ago I studied the behavior of natural kind words, for example, *gold,* and I came to the conclusion that the extension of the term is not simply determined by a 'battery of semantical rules', or other institutionalized norms. The norms may determine that certain objects are *paradigmatic examples* of gold; but they do not determine the full extension of the term, nor is it impossible that even a paradigmatic example should turn out not to really be gold, as it would be if the norms simply *defined* what it is to be gold.

We are prepared to count something as belonging to a kind even if our *present* tests do not suffice to show it is a member of the kind if it ever turns out that it has the same essential nature as (or, more vaguely, is 'sufficiently similar' to) the paradigmatic examples (or the great majority of them). What the essential nature is, or what counts as sufficient similarity, depends both on the natural kind and on the context (iced tea may be 'water' in one context but not in another); but for gold what counts is ultimate composition, since this has been thought since the ancient Greeks to determine the lawful behavior of the substance. Unless we say that what the ancient Greeks meant by *chrysos* was *whatever has the same essential nature* as the paradigmatic examples, then neither their search for new methods of detecting counterfeit gold (which led Archimedes to the density test) nor their physical speculations will make sense.

It is tempting to take the same line with rationality itself, and to say that what determines whether a belief is rational is not the norms of rationality of this or that culture, but an *ideal theory* of rationality, a theory which would give necessary and sufficient conditions for a belief to be rational in the relevant circumstances in any possible world. Such a theory would have to *account for* the paradigmatic examples, as an ideal theory of gold accounts for the paradigmatic examples of gold; but it could go beyond them, and provide criteria which would enable us to understand cases we cannot presently see to the bottom of, as our present theory of gold enables us to understand cases the most brilliant ancient Greek could not have understood. A general difficulty with the proposal to treat 'rational', 'reasonable', 'justified', etc., as natural kind terms is that the prospects for actually *finding* powerful generalizations about all rationally acceptable beliefs seem so poor. There are powerful universal laws obeyed by all instances of gold, which is what makes it possible to describe gold as the stuff that will turn out to obey these laws when we know them; but what are the chances that we can find powerful universal generalizations obeyed by all instances of rationally justified belief?

That the chances are poor does not mean that there are *no* analogies between scientific inquiry into the nature of gold and moral inquiry or philosophical inquiry. In ethics, for example, we start with judgments that individual acts are right or wrong, ('observation reports', so to speak) and we gradually formulate maxims (not exceptionless generalizations) based on those judgments, often accompanied by reasons or illustrative examples, as for instance 'Be kind to the stranger among you, because you know what it was like to be a stranger in Egypt' (a 'low level generalization'). These maxims in turn affect and alter our judgments about individual cases, so that new maxims supplementing or modifying the earlier ones may appear. After thousands of years of this dialectic between maxims and judgments about individual cases, a philosopher may come along and propose a moral conception (a 'theory'), which may alter both maxims and singular judgments and so on.

The very same procedure may be found in all of philosophy

(which is almost coextensive with theory of rationality). In a publication a few years[1] ago I described the desiderata for a moral system, following Grice and Baker, and I included (1) the desire that one's basic assumptions, at least, should have *wide appeal;* (2) the desire that one's system should be able to withstand rational criticism; (3) the desire that the morality recommended should be *livable.*

The way to develop a better understanding of the nature of rationality – the only way we know – is, likewise, to develop better philosophical conceptions of rationality. (An unending process; but that is as it should be.) It is striking that the desiderata I listed for a moral system, unchanged, could be listed as the desiderata for a methodology or a system of rational procedure in any major area of human concern. In analytical philosophy the main attempts to better understand the nature of rationality in this way have come from philosophers of science, and two important tendencies have resulted from these efforts.

Logical positivism

In the past fifty years the clearest manifestation of the tendency to think of the methods of 'rational justification' as given by something like a list or canon (although one that philosophers of science have admittedly not yet succeeded in fully formalizing) was the movement known as Logical Positivism. Not only was the list or canon that the positivists hoped 'logicians of science' (their term for philosophers) would one day succeed in writing down supposed to exhaustively describe the 'scientific method'; but, since, according to the logical positivists, the 'scientific method' exhausts rationality itself, and testability by that method exhausts meaningfulness ('The meaning of a sentence is its method of verification'), the list or canon would determine what is and what is not a cognitively meaningful statement. Statements testable by the methods in the list (the methods of mathematics, logic, and the empirical sciences) would count as meaningful; all other statements, the positivists maintained, are 'pseudo-statements', or disguised nonsense.

---

[1] 'Literature, Science, and Reflection', *New Literary History,* vol. VII, 1975–6, reprinted in my *Meaning and the Moral Sciences,* Routledge and Kegan Paul, 1978.

An obvious rejoinder was to say that the Logical Positivist criterion of significance was *self-refuting:* for the criterion itself is neither (a) 'analytic' (a term used by the positivists to account for logic and mathematics), nor (b) empirically testable. Strangely enough this criticism had very little impact on the logical positivists and did little to impede the growth of their movement. I believe that the neglect of this particular philosophical gambit was a great mistake; that the gambit is not only correct, but contains a deep lesson, and not just a lesson about Logical Positivism.

The point I am going to develop will depend on the following observation: the forms of 'verification' allowed by the logical positivists are forms which have been *institutionalized* by modern society. What can be 'verified' in the positivist sense can be verified to be correct (in a non-philosophical or prephilosophical sense of 'correct'), or to be probably correct, or to be highly successful science, as the case may be; and the public recognition of the correctness, or the probable correctness, or the 'highly successful scientific theory' status, exemplifies, celebrates, and reinforces images of knowledge and norms of reasonableness maintained by our culture.

On the face of it, the *original* positivist paradigm of verification was not this publicly institutionalized one. In Carnap's *Der Logische Aufbau der Welt* (The Logical Construction of the World) verification was ultimately private, based on sensations whose subjective quality or 'content' was said to be 'incommunicable'. But, under the urgings of Neurath, Carnap soon shifted to a more public, more 'intersubjective', conception of verification.

Popper has stressed the idea that scientific predictions are confronted with 'basic sentences', sentences such as 'the right pan of the balance is down' which are publicly accepted even if they cannot be 'proved' to the satisfaction of a sceptic. He has been criticized for using 'conventionalist' language here, for speaking as if it were a convention or social decision to accept a basic sentence; but I think that what sounds like a conventionalist element in Popper's thought is simply a recognition of the *institutionalized* nature of the implicit norms to which we appeal in ordinary perceptual judgments. The nature of our response to a sceptic who challenges us to 'prove' such statements as 'I am standing on the floor' testifies to the existence of social norms *requiring* agreement to such statements in the appropriate circumstances.

Wittgenstein argued that without such public norms, norms shared by a group and constituting a 'form of life', language and even thought itself would be impossible. For Wittgenstein it is absurd to ask if the institutionalized verification I have been speaking of is 'really' justificatory. In *On Certainty* Wittgenstein remarks that philosophers can provide one with a hundred epistemological 'justifications' of the statement 'cats don't grow on trees' – but *none* of them starts with anything which is more sure (in just this institutionalized sense of 'sure') than the fact that cats don't grow on trees.

Sceptics have doubted not only perceptual judgments but ordinary inductions. Hume, whose distinction between what is *rational* and what is *reasonable* I am not observing, would have said there is no *rational* proof that it will snow (or even that it will probably snow) in the United States this winter (although he would have added that it would be most unreasonable to doubt that it will). Yet our response to a sceptic who challenges us to 'prove' that it will snow in the United States this winter testifies that there are social norms requiring agreement to such 'inductions' just as much as to ordinary perceptual judgments about people standing on floors and about equal arm balances.

When we come to high-level theories in the exact sciences, people's reactions are somewhat different. Ordinary people cannot 'verify' the special theory of relativity. Indeed, ordinary people do not at the present time even *learn* the special theory, or the (relatively elementary) mathematics needed to understand it, although it is beginning to be taught in freshman physics courses in some of our colleges. Ordinary people defer to scientists for an informed (and socially accepted) appraisal of a theory of this type. And because of the instability of scientific theories, a scientist is not likely to refer to even so successful a theory as special relativity as 'true' *tout court*. But the judgment of the scientific community is that special relativity is a 'successful' – in fact, like quantum electrodynamics, an unprecedentedly successful – scientific theory, which yields 'successful predictions' and which is 'supported by a vast number of experiments'. And these judgments are, in fact, deferred to by other members of the society. The difference between this case and the cases of institutionalized norms of verification previously referred to (apart from the hedging of the adjective 'true') is the special role of experts and the institutionalized deference to experts that such a case involves; but this is no more than an instance of the division of intellectual labor (not to mention intellectual authority relations) in the society. The judgment that special relativity and quantum electrodynamics are 'the most successful physical theories we have' is one which is made by authorities which the society has appointed and whose authority is recognized by a host of practices and ceremonies, and in that sense institutionalized.

Recently it occurred to me that Wittgenstein may well have thought that *only* statements that can be verified in some such 'institutionalized' way can be true (or right, or correct, or justified) at all. I don't mean to suggest that any philosopher ever held the view that *all* things which count in our society as 'justifications' really are such. Philosophers generally distinguish between institutions which are constitutive of our concepts themselves and those which have some other status, although there is much controversy about how to make such a distinction. I mean to suggest that Wittgenstein thought that it was some subset of our institutionalized verification norms that determines what it is right to say in the various 'language games' we play and what is wrong, and that there is no objective rightness or wrongness beyond this. Although such an interpretation does fit much that Wittgenstein says – for instance, the stress on the need for 'agreement in our judgments' in order to have concepts at all – I do not feel sure that it is right. It is just too vague who the 'we' is in Wittgenstein's talk of 'our' judgments; and I don't know whether his 'forms of life' correspond to the institutionalized norms I have mentioned. But this interpretation occurred to me upon reading Wittgenstein's *Lectures and Conversations*. In this Wittgenstein rejects both psychoanalysis and Darwin's theory of evolution (although unlike the positivists he does not regard such language as *meaningless*, and he has admiration for Freud's 'cleverness'). Wittgenstein's view about psychoanalysis (which he calls a 'myth') does not signify much, since so many people have the view – mistakenly in my opinion – that psychoanalysis is more or less nonsense. But his rejection of *evolution* is quite striking.[2] Wittgenstein contrasts Darwin's theory unfavorably with theories in physics ('One of the most important things about an explanation is that it should work, that it should enable us to predict something. Physics is connected with Engineering. The bridge must not fall down' (*Lectures on Aesthetics,* p. 25)). And he says people were persuaded 'on grounds which were extremely thin'. 'In the end you forget entirely every question of verification, you are just sure it must have been like that.'

Again, the great discussions about 'analyticity' that went on in the 1950s seem to me to be connected with the desire of philosophers to find an objective, *uncontroversial* foundation for their arguments. 'Analyticity', i.e. the doctrine of truth by virtue of meaning alone, came under attack because it had been *overused* by philosophers. But why had philosophers been tempted to announce that so many things which are in *no* intelligible sense 'rules of language', or consequences of rules of language, were analytic or 'conceptually necessary', or whatever? The answer, I think, is that the idea that there is a definite set of *rules of language* and that *these* can settle what is and is not rational, had two advantages, as philosophers thought: (1) the 'rules of

---

[2] Concerning evolution what Wittgenstein said was 'People were certain on grounds which were extremely thin. Couldn't there have been an attitude which said: "I don't know. It is an interesting hypothesis which may eventually be well confirmed" ', *Lectures on Aesthetics,* p. 26, in Cyril Burret (ed.) *L. W. Wittgenstein: Lectures and Conversations,* Berkeley, University of California Press, 1967. What it would be like for evolution to be 'well confirmed' Wittgenstein does not say, but the paragraph suggests that actually *seeing* speciation occur is what he has in mind ('Did anyone see this process happening? No. Has anyone seen it happening now? No. The evidence of breeding is just a drop in the bucket.')

It is instructive to contrast Wittgenstein's attitude with Monod's:

> the selective theory of evolution, as Darwin himself had stated it, required the discovery of Mendelian genetics, which of course was made. This is an example, and a most important one, of what is meant by the content of a theory, the content of an idea . . . [A] good theory or a good idea will be much wider and much richer than even the inventor of the idea may know at his time. The theory may be judged precisely on this type of development, when more and more falls into its lap, even though it was not predictable that so much would come of it (J. Monod, 'On the Molecular Theory of Evolution', in Harre, R. (ed.), *Problems of Scientific Revolution: Progress and Obstacles to Progress in the Sciences,* Oxford, 1975).

language' are constitutive institutionalized practices (or norms which underlie such practices), and as such have the 'public' status I have described; (2) at the same time, it was claimed that only philosophers (and not linguists) could discover these mysterious things. It was a nice idea while it lasted, but it was bound to be exploded, and it was.

I shall call any conception according to which there are institutionalized norms which define what is and is not rationally acceptable a *criterial* conception of rationality. The logical positivists, Wittgenstein, at least on the admittedly uncertain interpretation I have essayed, and some though not all of the 'ordinary language' philosophers[3] at Oxford shared a criterial conception of rationality even if they differed on other issues, such as whether to call unverifiable statements 'meaningless', and over whether or not some ethical propositions could be 'conceptually necessary'.

---

[3] One might develop an 'ordinary language' philosophy which was not committed to the public and 'criterial' verification of philosophical theses if one could develop and support a conception in which the norms which govern linguistic practices are not themselves discoverable by ordinary empirical investigation. In *Must We Mean What We Say,* Stanley Cavell took a significant step in this direction, arguing that such norms can be known by a species of 'self knowledge' which he compared to the insight achieved through therapy and also to the transcendental knowledge sought by phenomenology. While I agree with Cavell that my knowledge as a native speaker that certain uses are deviant or non-deviant is not 'external' inductive knowledge – I can know without evidence that in my dialect of English one says 'mice' and not 'mouses' – I am inclined to think this fact of speaker's privileged access does not extend to *generalizations* about correctness and incorrectness. If I say (as Cavell does) that it is part of the rule for the correct use of locutions of the form *X is voluntary* that there should be something 'fishy' about *X*, then I am advancing a *theory* to explain my intuitions about specific cases, not just reporting those intuitions. It is true that something of this sort also goes on in psychotherapy; but I am not inclined to grant self-knowledge any kind of immunity from criticism by others, including criticisms which depend on offering rival *explanations,* in either case. And if one allows the legitimacy of such criticism, then the activity of discovering such norms begins to look like social science or history – areas in which, I have argued, traditional accounts of 'The Scientific Method' shed little light. (See my *Meaning and the Moral Sciences,* Routledge and Kegan Paul, 1978.)

In any case, whatever their status, I see no reason to believe that the norms for the use of *language* are what decide the extension of 'rationally acceptable', 'justified', 'well confirmed', and the like.

The gambit I referred to at the outset, the gambit that refutes the logical positivists' verification principle, is *deep* precisely because it refutes every attempt to argue for a criterial conception of rationality, that is because it refutes the thesis that nothing is rationally verifiable unless it is criterially verifiable.

The point is that although the philosophers I mentioned often spoke as if their arguments had the same kind of *finality* as a mathematical proof or a demonstration experiment in physics; that although the logical positivists called their work *logic* of science; although the Wittgensteinians displayed unbelievable arrogance towards philosophers who could not 'see' that all philosophical activity of a pre-Wittgensteinian or non-Wittgensteinian kind is nonsensical; and although ordinary language philosophers referred to each other's arguments and those of non-ordinary language philosophers as 'howlers' (as if philosophical errors were like mistakes on an arithmetic test); no philosophical position of any importance can be verified in the conclusive and culturally recognized way I have described. In short, if it is true that only statements that can be criterially verified can be rationally acceptable, that statement itself cannot be criterially verified, and hence cannot be rationally acceptable. If there is such a thing as rationality at all – and we commit ourselves to believing in *some* notion of rationality by engaging in the activities of *speaking* and *arguing* – then it is self-refuting to *argue* for the position that it is identical with or properly contained in what the institutionalized norms of the culture determine to be instances of it. For no such argument can be certified to be correct, or even probably correct, by those norms alone.

I don't at all think that rational argumentation and rational justification are impossible in philosophy, but rather I have been driven to recognize something which is probably evident to laymen if not to philosophers, namely that we cannot appeal to *public* norms to decide what is and is not rationally argued and justified in philosophy. The claim which is still often heard that philosophy is 'conceptual analysis', that the *concepts themselves* determine what philosophical arguments are right, is, when combined with the doctrine that concepts are norms or rules underlying *public* linguistic practices, just a covert form of the claim that all rational justification in philosophy is criterial, and that philosophical truth is (barring 'howlers') as *publicly demon-*

strable as scientific truth. Such a view seems to me to be simply unreasonable in the light of the whole history of the subject, including the recent history.

What goes for philosophical argument goes for arguments about religion and about secular ideology as well. An argument between an intelligent liberal and an intelligent Marxist will have the same character as a philosophical dispute at the end, even if more empirical facts are relevant. And we all do have views in religion, or politics, or philosophy, and we all argue them and criticize the arguments of others. Indeed, even in 'science', outside of the exact sciences, we have arguments in history, in sociology and in clinical psychology, of exactly this character. It is true that the logical positivists broadened their description of the 'scientific method' to include these subjects; but so broadened it cannot be shown to clearly *exclude* anything whatsoever. (See Chapter 8.)

The positivists, I will be reminded, *conceded* that the verification principle was 'cognitively meaningless'. They said it was a *proposal* and as such not true or false. But they *argued* for their proposal, and the arguments were (and had to be) non-starters.[4] So the point stands.

---

[4] The weakest argument offered in defense of the Verification Principle construed as a proposal was that it 'explicated' the 'pre-analytic' notion of meaningfulness. (For a discussion of this claim, see my 'How Not to Talk about Meaning', in my *Mind, Language and Reality, Philosophical Papers, Vol. 2,* Cambridge University Press, 1975.) Reichenbach defended a form of the Verification Principle (in *Experience and Prediction*) as *preserving all differences in meaning relevant to behavior*. Against an obvious objection (that the non-empirical belief in a divinity – Reichenbach used the example of Egyptian cat worshippers – could alter behavior) Reichenbach replied by proposing to translate 'Cats are divine animals' as 'cats inspire feelings of awe in cat-worshippers'. Clearly the acceptance of this substitute would *not* leave behavior unchanged in the case of a cat worshipper!
The most interesting view was that of Carnap. According to Carnap, *all* rational reconstructions are proposals. The only factual questions concern the logical and empirical consequences of accepting this or that rational reconstruction. (Carnap compared the 'choice' of a rational reconstruction to the choice of an engine for an airplane.) The conclusion he drew was that in philosophy one should be tolerant of divergent rational reconstructions. However, this principle of Tolerance, as Carnap called it, *presupposes* the Verification Principle. For the doctrine that no rational reconstruction is uniquely *correct* or corresponds to the way things 'really are', the doctrine that all 'external questions' are without cognitive sense *is* just the Verification Principle. To apply the Principle of Tolerance to the Verification Principle itself would be circular.

In sum, what the logical positivists and Wittgenstein (and perhaps the later Quine as well) did was to *produce philosophies which leave no room for a rational activity of philosophy.* This is why these views are self-refuting; and also why the little gambit I have been discussing represents a significant argument of the kind philosophers call a 'transcendental argument': arguing about the nature of rationality (the task of the philosophers *par excellence*) is an activity that presupposes a notion of rational justification wider than the positivist notion, indeed wider than institutionalized criterial rationality.

Anarchism is self-refuting

Let me now discuss a very different philosophical tendency. Thomas Kuhn's *The Structure of Scientific Revolutions (SSR)* enthralled vast numbers of readers, and appalled most philosophers of science because of its emphasis on what seemed to be *irrational* determinants of scientific theory acceptance and by its use of such terms as 'conversion' and 'Gestalt switch'. In fact, Kuhn made a number of important points about scientific theories and about how scientific activity should be viewed. I have expressed a belief in the importance of the notions of *paradigm, normal science,* and *scientific revolution* elsewhere; at this point I want to focus on what I do *not* find sympathetic in Kuhn's book, what I described elsewhere as 'Kuhn's extreme relativism'.

The reading that enthralled Kuhn's more sophomoric readers was one according to which he is saying that there is no such thing as *rational* justification in science, it's *just* Gestalt switches and conversions. Kuhn has rejected this interpretation of the *SSR*, and has since introduced a notion of 'non-paradigmatic rationality' which may be closely related to if not the same as what I just called 'non-criterial rationality'.

The tendency that most readers thought they detected in Kuhn's *SSR* certainly manifested itself in Paul Feyerabend's *Against Method.* Feyerabend, like Kuhn, stressed the manner in which different cultures and historic epochs produce different paradigms of rationality. He suggests that the determinants of *our* conceptions of scientific rationality are largely what *we* would call irrational. In effect, although he does not put it this way, he suggests that the modern scientific–technological conception of rationality is fraudulent by its own standards. (I think I detect a similar strain in Michel Foucault.) And he goes far beyond Kuhn or Foucault in suggesting that even the vaunted instrumental superiority of our science may be somewhat of a hoax. Faith healers can do more to relieve your pain than doctors, Feyerabend claims.

It is not those terrifyingly radical claims that I want to talk about, although they are the reason Feyerabend calls his position 'anarchism'. I wish to discuss a claim Kuhn does make in both the *SSR* and subsequent papers, and that Feyerabend made both in *Against Method* and in technical papers. This is the thesis of *incommensurability*. I want to say that this thesis, like the logical positivist thesis about meaning and verification, is a self-refuting thesis. In short, I want to claim that *both* of the two most influential philosophies of science of the twentieth century, certainly the two that have interested scientists and non-philosophers generally, the only two the educated general reader is likely to have even heard of, are self-refuting. Of course, as a philosopher of science I find it a bit troublesome that this should be the case. We shall shortly come to the question of what to make of this situation.

The incommensurability thesis is the thesis that terms used in another culture, say, the term 'temperature' as used by a seventeenth-century scientist, cannot be equated in meaning or reference with any terms or expressions *we* possess. As Kuhn puts it, scientists with different paradigms inhabit 'different worlds'. 'Electron' as used around 1900 referred to objects in one 'world'; as used today it refers to objects in quite a different 'world'. This thesis is supposed to apply to observational language as well as to so-called 'theoretical language'; indeed, according to Feyerabend, ordinary language *is* simply a false theory.

The rejoinder this time is that if this thesis were really true then we could not translate other languages – or even past stages of our own language – at all. And if we cannot interpret organisms' noises at all, then we have no grounds for regarding them as *thinkers, speakers,* or even *persons.* In short, if Feyerabend (and Kuhn at his most incommensurable) were right, then members of other cultures, including seventeenth-century scientists, would be conceptualizable by us only as animals producing responses to stimuli (including noises that curiously resemble English or Italian). To tell us that Galileo had 'incommensurable' notions *and then to go on to describe them at length* is totally incoherent.

This problem is posed in a sympathetic essay on Feyerabend's view by Smart:[5]

> Surely it is a neutral fact that in order to see Mercury we have to point the telescope over the top of that tree, say, and not, as predicted by Newtonian theory, over the top of that chimney pot. And surely one can talk of trees, chimney pots, and telescopes in a way which is independent of the choice between Newtonian and Einsteinian theory. However Feyerabend could well concede that we use Euclidean geometry and non-relativistic optics for the theory of our telescope. He would say that this is not the real truth about our telescope, the tree, and the chimney pot, but nevertheless it is legitimate to think in this way in order to discuss the observational tests of general relativity, since we know on theoretical grounds that our predictions will be unaffected (up to the limits of observational error) if we avail ourselves of this computational convenience.

But the trouble with Smart's rescue move is that I must understand *some* of the Euclidean non-relativists' language to even say the 'predictions' are the same. If *every word has a different significance,* in what sense can any prediction be 'unaffected'? How can I even translate the logical particles (the words for 'if–then', 'not', and so on) in seventeenth-century Italian, or whatever, if I cannot find a translation manual connecting seventeenth-century Italian and modern English that makes some kind of systematic sense of the seventeenth-century corpus, both in itself and in its extra-linguistic setting? Even if I am the speaker who employs both theories (as Smart envisages) how can I be justified

⁵ J. J. C. Smart, 'Conflicting Views about Explanation', in R. Cohen and M. Wartofsky (eds.), *Boston Studies in the Philosophy of Science, Volume II: in Honor of Philipp Frank* (New York, Humanities Press, Inc., 1965).

in equating any word in my Newtonian theory with any word in my general relativistic theory?

The point I am making comes into even sharper focus when we apply to it some of Quine's and Davidson's observations about meaning and translation practice. Once it is conceded that we can find a translation scheme which 'works' in the case of a seventeenth century text, at least in the context fixed by our interests and the use to which the translation will be put, what sense does it have *in that context* to say that the translation does not 'really' capture the sense or reference of the original? It is not, after all, as if we had or were likely to have criteria for sameness of sense or reference apart from our translation schemes and our explicit or implicit requirements for their empirical adequacy. One can understand the assertion that a translation fails to capture exactly the sense or reference of the original as an admission that a better translation scheme might be found; but it makes only an illusion of sense to say that all possible translation schemes fail to capture the 'real' sense or reference. Synonymy exists only as a relation, or better, as a family of relations, each of them somewhat vague, which we employ to equate different expressions for the purposes of interpretation. The idea that there is some such thing as 'real' synonymy apart from all workable practices of mutual interpretation, has been discarded as a myth.

Suppose someone tells us that the German word 'Rad' can be translated as 'wheel'. If he goes on to say his translation is not perfect, we naturally expect him to indicate how it might be improved, supplemented by a gloss, or whatever. But if he goes on to say that 'Rad' can be translated as 'wheel', but it doesn't actually refer to wheels, or indeed to any objects recognized in your conceptual system, what do we get from this? To say that a word A can be translated as 'wheel', or whatever, is to say that, to the extent that the translation can be relied upon, A *refers* to wheels.

Perhaps the reason that the incommensurability thesis intrigues people so much, apart from the appeal which all incoherent ideas seem to have, is the tendency to confuse or conflate concept and conception. To the extent that the analytic/synthetic distinction is fuzzy, this distinction too is fuzzy; but all interpretation involves such a distinction, even if it is relative to the interpretation itself. When we translate a word as, say, *temperature* we equate the reference and, to the extent that we stick to our translation, the sense of the translated expression with that of our own term 'temperature', at least as we use it in that context. (Of course, there are various devices we can use, such as special glosses, to delimit or delineate the way we are employing 'temperature', or whatever the word may be, in the context.) In this sense we equate the 'concept' in question with our own 'concept' of temperature. But so doing is compatible with the fact that the seventeenth-century scientists, or whoever, may have had a different *conception* of temperature, that is a different set of beliefs about it and its nature than we do, different 'images of knowledge', and different ultimate beliefs about many other matters as well. That conceptions differ does not prove the impossibility of ever translating anyone 'really correctly' as is sometimes supposed; on the contrary, we could not say that conceptions differ and how they differ if we couldn't translate.

But, it may be asked, how do we ever know that a translation scheme 'works' if conceptions always turn out to be different? The answer to this question, as given by various thinkers from Vico down to the present day, is that interpretative success does not require that the translatees' beliefs come out the *same* as our own, but it does require that they come out *intelligible* to us. This is the basis of all the various maxims of interpretative charity or 'benefit of the doubt', such as 'interpret them so they come out believers of truths and lovers of the good', or 'interpret them so that their beliefs come out reasonable in the light of what they have been taught and have experienced', or Vico's own directive to maximize the *humanity* of the person being interpreted. It is a constitutive fact about human experience in a world of different cultures interacting in history while individually undergoing slower or more rapid change that we are, as a matter of universal human experience, able to *do* this; able to interpret one another's beliefs, desires, and utterances so that it all makes some kind of *sense*.

Kuhn and Feyerabend, not surprisingly, reject any idea of *convergence* in scientific knowledge. Since we are not talking about the same things as previous scientists, we are not getting more and more knowledge about the same microscopic or macroscopic objects. Kuhn argues that science 'progresses' only instrumentally; we get better and better able to transport people from one place to another, and so on. But this too is incoherent. Unless such locutions as 'transport people from one place to another' retain some degree of fixity of reference, how can we understand the notion of instrumental success in any stable way?

The argument I have just employed is essentially related to Kant's celebrated arguments about preconditions for empirical knowledge. Replying to the contention that the future might be wholly lawless, might defeat every 'induction' we have made, Kant pointed out that if there is any future at all – any future *for us*, at any rate, any future we can grasp as thinkers and conceptualize to say if our predictions were true or false – then, in fact, many regularities must *not* have been violated. Else why call it a *future?* For example, when we imagine balls coming from an urn in some 'irregular' order, we forget that we *couldn't even tell they were balls,* or tell *what order they came out in,* without depending on many regularities. *Comparison* presupposes there are some commensurabilities.

There is a move Kuhn and Feyerabend could make in reply to all these criticisms, but it is not one they would feel happy making, and that would be to introduce some kind of observational/theoretical dichotomy. They could concede commensurability, translatability, and even convergence with respect to observational facts, and restrict the incommensurability thesis to the theoretical vocabulary. Even then there would be problems (why shouldn't we describe the meanings of the theoretical terms *via* their relations to the observational vocabulary à la Ramsey?) But Kuhn and Feyerabend reject this alternative with reason, for in fact the need for principles of interpretative charity is just as pervasive in 'observational language' as in 'theoretical language'. Consider, for example, the common word 'grass'. Different speakers, depending on where and when they live have different perceptual prototypes of grass (grass has different colors and different shapes in different places) and different conceptions of grass. Even if all speakers must know that grass is a plant, on pain of being said to have a different concept altogether, the conception of a *plant* today involves photosynthesis and the conception of a plant two hundred years ago did not. Without interpretative charity which directs us to equate 'plant' 200 years ago with 'plant' today (at least in ordinary contexts) and 'grass' 200 years ago with 'grass' today, no statement about the reference of this word 200 years ago could be made. Nor is it only natural kind words that are so dependent for interpretation on principles of charity; the artifact word 'bread' would pose exactly the same problems. Indeed, without interpretative charity we could not equate a simple color term such as 'red' across different speakers. We interpret discourse always as a whole; and the interpretation of 'observation' terms is as dependent on the interpretation of 'theoretical' terms as is the interpretation of the latter on the former.

What I have given is, once again, a transcendental argument. We are committed by our fundamental conceptions to treating not just our present time-slices, but also our past selves, our ancestors, and members of other cultures past and present, as *persons;* and that means, I have argued, attributing to them shared references and shared concepts, however different the *conceptions* that we also attribute. Not only do we share objects and concepts with others, to the extent that the interpretative exercise succeeds, but also conceptions of the reasonable, of the natural, and so on. For the whole justification of an interpretative scheme, remember, is that it renders the behavior of others at least minimally reasonable by *our* lights. However different our images of knowledge and conceptions of rationality, we share a huge fund of assumptions and beliefs about what is reasonable with even the most bizarre culture we can succeed in interpreting at all.

Why relativism is inconsistent

That (total) relativism is inconsistent is a truism among philosophers. After all, is it not *obviously* contradictory to *hold* a point of view while at the same time holding that *no* point of view is more justified or right than any other? Alan Garfinkel has put the point very wittily. In talking to his California students he once said, aping their locutions: 'You may not be coming from where I'm coming from, but I know relativism isn't *true for me*' . . . If any point of view is as good as any other, then why isn't *the point of view that relativism is false* as good as any other?

The plethora of relativistic doctrines being marketed today (and marketed by highly intelligent thinkers) indicates this sim-

ple refutation will not suffice. Why should an intelligent relativist concede that every view is as true (*for him*) as any other? He
cannot prevent you (or Alan Garfinkel) from saying that his view
is not *true for you* (or justified for you, or whatever): but if he
has his wits about him, he can retort that truth for you is far less
salient (*for him*) than is truth for him. What concept of anything
is more salient than one's *own*, after all? Is it then *really* inconsistent to treat *true, justified*, etc., as *relative* notions?

The answer is that it *is* inconsistent but it *does* require a more
elaborate argument than the (nonetheless very nice) one-liner
produced by Garfinkel. The important point to notice is that if
all is relative, then the relative is relative too. But this takes a bit
of explaining!

Plato was perhaps the first to employ the sort of argument I
have in mind (against Protagoras). Protagoras (a deep-dyed relativist, apparently) claimed that when I say *X*, I really should say
'I *think* that *X*'. Thus when I say 'Snow is white', Protagoras
would say that I really mean that Hilary Putnam thinks that
snow is white, and that what Robert Nozick means by the same
utterance is that Robert Nozick thinks that snow is white. A
more sophisticated statement of the same idea would be that
when I say 'Snow is white', I am using this utterance to claim
that *snow is white* is true-for-me, whereas when Robert Nozick
says the same words he would normally be claiming that *snow
is white* is true-for-*him* (or at least he would count his statement
as having been correct just in case it turned out to be true-for-
him). It follows (on Protagoras' view) that no utterance has the
same *meaning* for me and for anyone else; there is, as we saw
before, an intimate connection between relativism and incommensurability. Plato's counter-argument was that, if every statement *X* means 'I think that *X*', then I should (on Protagoras'
view) really say

    (1) I think that I think that snow is white.

But the process of adding 'I think' can always be iterated! On
Protagoras' view, the ultimate meaning of 'Snow is white' is then
not (1) but

    (2) I think that I think that I think that I . . . (with
        infinitely many 'I thinks') that snow is white.

This Plato took to be a *reductio ad absurdum*. However, Plato's argument is not a good one as it stands. Why should Protagoras not agree that his analysis applies to itself? It doesn't follow that it *must* be self-applied an infinite number of times, but only that it *can* be self-applied *any finite number of times*. But Plato had noticed something very deep.

When one first encounters relativism, the idea *seems* simple enough. The idea, in a natural first formulation is that every person (or, in a modern 'sociological' formulation, every culture, or sometimes every 'discourse') has his (its) own views, standards, presuppositions, and that truth (and also justification) are relative to *these*. One takes it for granted, of course, that whether X is true (or justified) relative to these is *itself* something 'absolute'.

Modern Structuralists like Foucault write as if justification *relative to a discourse* is itself quite absolute – i.e. not at all relative. But if statements of the form 'X is true (justified) relative to person P' are themselves true or false *absolutely,* then there *is,* after all, an absolute notion of truth (or of justification) and not only of truth-for-me, truth-for-Nozick, truth-for-you, etc. A *total* relativist would have to say that whether or not X is true *relative* to P is *itself* relative. At this point our grasp on what the position even means begins to wobble, as Plato observed.

Plato's line of attack on relativism does not seem to have been followed up until recently. But it was brilliantly extended by Wittgenstein in, of all places, the Private Language Argument (alluded to in Chapter 3).

Most commentators read the Private Language Argument as simply an argument against the 'copy theory' of truth. And Wittgenstein's brilliant demonstration that the similitude theory of reference does not work even for reference to sensations *is* certainly part of a sustained attack on metaphysical realism. But I prefer to read the argument as a *pair* of quite traditional arguments (at least Kant would have approved of both of them!) against *two* positions, one a realist position and one a relativist position: for the attempt to read the whole argument as an antirealist one makes it come out looking rather contrived.

The form of relativism Wittgenstein was concerned to attack is known as 'methodological solipsism'. A 'methodological solipsist' is a non-realist or 'verificationist' who agrees that truth is to be understood as in some way related to rational accept-

ability, but who holds that all justification is ultimately in terms
of experiences that each of us has a *private* knowledge of. Thus,
I have *my* knowledge of what experiences of *mine* would verify
that snow is white and Bob Nozick has *his* knowledge of what
experiences of *his* would verify that snow is white: every statement has a different sense for every thinker.

Wittgenstein's argument seems to me to be an excellent argument against relativism in general. The argument is that the relativist cannot, in the end, make any sense of the distinction
between *being right* and *thinking he is right;* and that means that
there is, in the end, no difference between *asserting* or *thinking,*
on the one hand, and *making noises* (*or producing mental
images*) on the other. But this means that (on this conception) I
am not a *thinker* at all but a *mere* animal. To hold such a view
is to commit a sort of mental suicide.

To see that Wittgenstein was right, let us consider, as Wittgenstein does not, how the relativist might *attempt* to draw the distinction that Wittgenstein denies him, the distinction between
being right and thinking he is right.

The relativist might borrow the idea that truth is an *idealization* of rational acceptability. He might hold that X is true-for-
me if 'X is justified-for-me' *would* be true provided I observed
carefully enough, reasoned long enough, or whatever. But sub-
junctive conditionals of the form 'If I *were* to . . . , then I would
think such-and-such', are, like all statements, interpreted differently by different philosophers.

A metaphysical realist can regard statements about what
would be the case if as themselves true or false in an absolute
sense, independently of whether we ever *will* be justified in
accepting or rejecting them. If the relativist interprets statements
about what he *would* believe under such-and-such conditions in
this realist way, then he has recognized *one* class of absolute
truths, and so has given up being a relativist.

A non-realist or 'internal' realist regards conditional statements as statements which we understand (like all other statements) in large part by grasping their *justification* conditions.
This does not mean that the 'internal' realist *abandons* the distinction between truth and justification, but that truth (*idealized*
justification) is something we grasp as we grasp any other concept, via a (largely implicit) understanding of the factors that

make it rationally acceptable to say that something is true. Can the *relativist* interpret statements about what he *would* believe under ideal conditions in this non-realist or 'internal' realist way?

Let us recall that the non-realist position, as I described it (in Chapter 3), assumes an *objective* notion of rational acceptability. The non-realist rejects the notion that truth is correspondence to a 'ready-made world'. That is what makes him a *non*-(metaphysical)-realist. But rejecting the metaphysical 'correspondence' theory of truth is not at all the same thing as regarding truth or rational acceptability as *subjective*. Nelson Goodman, who regards truth and rational acceptability as species of a more general predicate 'rightness', applicable to works of art as well as to statements, has put the point succinctly:

> Briefly, then, truth of statements and rightness of descriptions, representations, exemplifications, expressions – of design, drawing, diction, rhythm – is primarily a matter of fit: fit to what is referred to in one way or another, or to other renderings, or to modes and manners of organization. The differences between fitting a version to a world, a world to a version, and a version together or to other versions fade when the role of versions in making the worlds they fit is recognized. And knowing or understanding is seen as ranging beyond the acquiring of true beliefs to the discovering and devising of fit of all sorts.

The whole *purpose* of relativism, its very defining characteristic, is, however, to *deny* the existence of any intelligible notion of *objective* 'fit'. Thus the relativist cannot understand talk about truth in terms of *objective* justification-conditions.

The attempt to use *conditionals* to explicate the distinction between *being right* and *thinking one is right* fails, then, because the relativist has no *objective* notion of rightness for these conditionals any more than he does for any other sort of statement.

Finally, if the relativist of today, like the ancient Protagoras, simply decides to bite the bullet and say that there is no difference between 'I am right' and 'I think I am right' – that a distinction between being justified and thinking one is justified cannot be drawn in one's *own* case – then what is speaking, on such a conception – beyond producing noises in the hope that one will have the *feeling* of being right? What is *thinking* – beyond producing images and sentence-analogues in the mind in the hope of having a subjective feeling of being right? The relativist must end by denying that any thought is *about* anything in either a realist or non-realist sense; for he cannot distinguish between thinking one's thought is about something and actually thinking about that thing. In short, what the relativist fails to see is that it is a presupposition of thought itself that some kind of objective 'rightness' exists.

There is an interesting relation between the argument I just analyzed (Plato–Wittgenstein) and the argument against incommensurability I attributed to Quine and Davidson: Quine and Davidson argue, in effect, that a consistent relativist should not treat others as speakers (or thinkers) at all (if their 'noises' are *that* 'incommensurable', then they are *just* noises), while Plato and Wittgenstein argue, in effect, that a consistent relativist cannot treat himself as a speaker or thinker.

What to make of this?

The arguments I just set before you convinced me that the two most widely known philosophies of science produced in this century are both incoherent. (Of course, neither of them is *just* a 'philosophy of science'.) This naturally led me to reflect on the meaning of this situation. How did such views arise?

Logical positivism, I recalled, was both continuous with and different from the Machian positivism which preceded it. Mach's positivism, or 'empirio-criticism', was, in fact, largely a restatement of Humean empiricism in a different jargon. Mach's brilliance, his dogmatic and enthusiastic style, and his scientific eminence made his positivism a large cultural issue (Lenin, afraid that the Bolsheviks would be converted to 'empirio-criticism', wrote a polemic against it). Einstein, whose interpretation of special relativity was operationalist in spirit (in marked contrast to the interpretation he gave to general relativity), acknowledged that his criticism of the notion of simultaneity owed much to Hume and to Mach, although, to his disappointment, Mach totally rejected special relativity.

But the most striking event that led up to the appearance of logical positivism was the revolution in deductive logic. By 1879 Frege had discovered an algorithm, a mechanical proof procedure, that embraces what is today standard 'second order logic'. The procedure is *complete* for the elementary theory of deduction ('first order logic'). The fact that one can write down an algorithm for proving *all* of the valid formulas of first order logic –an algorithm which requires no significant analysis and simulation of full human psychology – is a remarkable fact. It inspired the hope that one might do the same for so called 'inductive logic' – that the 'scientific method' might turn out to be an algorithm, and that these two algorithms – the algorithm for deductive logic (which, of course, turned out to be *incomplete* when extended to higher logic) and the algorithm-to-be-discovered for inductive logic – might exhaustively describe or 'rationally reconstruct' not just *scientific* rationality, but all rationality worthy of the name.

When I was just starting my teaching career at Princeton University I got to know Rudolph Carnap, who was spending two years at the Institute for Advanced Studies. One memorable afternoon, Carnap described to me how he had come to be a philosopher. Carnap explained to me that he had been a graduate student in physics, studying logic in Frege's seminar. The text was *Principia Mathematica* (imagine studying Russell and Whitehead's *Principia* with *Frege!*) Carnap was fascinated with symbolic logic and equally fascinated with the special theory of relativity. So he decided to make his thesis a formalization of special relativity in the notation of *Principia*. It was because the Physics Department at Jena would not accept this that Carnap became a philosopher, he told me.

Today, a host of negative results, including some powerful considerations due to Nelson Goodman, have indicated that there *cannot* be a completely *formal* inductive logic. Some important aspects of inductive logic can be formalized (although the adequacy of the formalization is controversial), but there is always a need for judgments of 'reasonableness', whether these are built in via the choice of vocabulary (or, more precisely, the *division* of the vocabulary into 'projectible' predicates and 'non-projectible' predicates) or however. Today, virtually no one believes that there is a purely formal scientific method (on this, see Chapter 8).

The story Carnap told me supports the idea that it was the sucess of formalization in the special case of deductive logic that played a crucial role. If that success inspired the rise of logical positivism, could it not have been the failure to formalize inductive logic, the discovery that there is no *algorithm* for empirical science, that inspired the rise of 'anarchism'?

I won't press this suggestion; in any case, additional factors are probably at work. While Kuhn has increasingly moderated his view, both Feyerabend and Michel Foucault have tended to push it to extremes. There is something political in their minds: both Feyerabend and Foucault link our present institutionalized criteria of rationality with capitalism, exploitation, and even with sexual repression. Clearly there are many divergent reasons why people are attracted to extreme relativism today, the idea that all existing institutions and traditions are bad being one of them.

Another reason is a certain *scientism*. The scientistic character of logical positivism is quite overt and unashamed; but I think there is also a scientism hidden behind relativism. The theory that all there is to 'rationality' is what your local culture says there is is never quite embraced by any of the 'anarchistic' thinkers, but it is the natural limit of their tendency: and this is a reductionist theory. That rationality is defined by an ideal computer program is a scientistic theory inspired by the exact sciences; that it is simply defined by the local cultural norms is a scientistic theory inspired by anthropology.

I will not discuss here the expectation aroused in some by Chomskian linguistics that cognitive psychology will discover *innate* algorithms which define rationality. I myself think that this is an intellectual fashion which will be disappointed as the logical positivist hope for a symbolic inductive logic was disappointed.

All this suggests that part of the problem with present day philosophy is a scientism inherited from the nineteenth century – a problem that affects more than one intellectual field. I do not deny that logic is important, or that formal studies in confirmation theory, in semantics of natural language, and so on are important. I do tend to think that they are rather peripheral to philosophy, and that as long as we are too much in the grip of formalization we can expect this kind of swinging back and forth between the two sorts of scientism I described. Both sorts of scientism are attempts to evade the issue of giving a sane and human description of the scope of reason.

6

Fact and value

Understood in a sufficiently wide sense, the topic of fact and value is a topic which is of concern to everyone. In this respect, it differs sharply from many philosophical questions. Most educated men and women do not feel it obligatory to have an opinion on the question whether there really is a real world or only appears to be one, for example. Questions in philosophy of language, epistemology, and even in metaphysics may appear to be questions which, however interesting, are somewhat optional from the point of view of most people's lives. But the question of fact and value is a forced choice question. Any reflective person *has* to have a real opinion upon it (which may or may not be the same as their notional opinion). If the question of fact and value is a forced choice question for reflective people, one particular answer to that question, the answer that fact and value are totally disjoint realms, that the dichotomy 'statement of fact *or* value judgment' is an absolute one, has assumed the status of a cultural institution.

By calling the dichotomy a cultural institution, I mean to suggest that it is an unfortunate fact that the received answer will go on being the received answer for quite some time regardless of what philosophers may say about it, and regardless of whether or not the received answer is *right*. Even if I could convince you that the fact–value dichotomy is without rational basis, that it is a rationally indefensible dichotomy, or even if some better philosopher than I could show this by an absolutely conclusive argument (of course there are no such in philosophy), still the next time you went out into the street, or to a cocktail party, or had a discussion at some deliberative body of which you happen to be a member, you would find someone saying to you, 'Is that supposed to be a statement of fact or a value judgment?' The view that there is no fact of the matter as to whether or not things are good or bad or better or worse, etc. has, in a sense, become *institutionalized*.

The strategy of my argument is not going to be a new one. I'm going to rehabilitate a somewhat discredited move in the debate about fact and value, namely the move that consists in arguing that the distinction is at the very least hopelessly fuzzy because factual statements themselves, and the practices of scientific inquiry upon which we rely to decide what is and what is not a fact, presuppose values.

The reason this is a somewhat discredited move is that there is an obvious rejoinder to it. The rejoinder to the view that science presupposes values is a protective concession. The defenders of the fact–value dichotomy concede that science does presuppose some values, for example, science presupposes that we want *truth*, but argue that these values are not *ethical* values. I shall imagine a somewhat strawman opponent who takes the view that science presupposes *one* value, namely the value of truth itself.

As we have seen, truth is not a simple notion. The idea that truth is a passive copy of what is 'really' (mind-independently, discourse-independently) 'there' has collapsed under the critiques of Kant, Wittgenstein, and other philosophers even if it continues to have a deep hold on our thinking.

Some philosophers have appealed to the *equivalence principle,* that is the principle that *to say of a statement that it is true is equivalent to asserting the statement,* to argue that there are no real philosophical problems about truth. Others appeal to the work of Alfred Tarski, the logician who showed how, given a formalized language (a formal notation for expressing certain statements, employing symbolic logic), one can define 'true' *for that language* in a stronger language (a so-called 'meta-language').[1]

Tarski's work was itself based on the equivalence principle: in

---

[1] For a non-technical account of Tarski's work see my *Meaning and the Moral Sciences,* Part I, Lecture I.

fact his criterion for a successful definition of 'true' was that it should yield all sentences of the form '*P*' *is true if and only if P,* e.g.

(*T*) 'Snow is white' is true if and only if snow is white

as theorems of the meta-language (where *P* is a sentence of the formal notation in question).

But the equivalence principle is philosophically neutral, and so is Tarski's work. On *any* theory of truth, 'Snow is white' is equivalent to ' "Snow is white" is true.'

Positivist philosophers would reply that if you know (*T*) above, you *know* what " 'Snow is white" is true' means: it means *snow is white.* And if you don't understand 'snow' and 'white', they would add, you are in trouble indeed! But the problem is not that we don't understand 'Snow is white'; the problem is that we don't understand *what it is to understand* 'Snow is white.' *This* is the philosophical problem. About this (*T*) says nothing.

And indeed does this not accord with our intuitions about these matters? If someone approaches us with a gleam in his eye and says, 'Don't you want to know the "Truth"?', our reaction is generally to be pretty leery of this person. And the reason that we are leery (apart from the gleam in the eye) is precisely because someone's telling us that they want us to know the truth tells us really *nothing* as long as we have no idea what standards of rational acceptability the person adheres to: what they consider a rational way to pursue an inquiry, what their standards of objectivity are, when they consider it rational to terminate an inquiry, what grounds they will regard as providing good reason for accepting one verdict or another on whatever sort of question they may be interested in. Applied to the case of science, I would say that to tell us that science 'seeks to discover the truth' is really a purely formal statement. It is to say no more than that scientists don't want to assert that snow is white if snow is not white, that they don't want to assert that there are electrons flowing through a wire if electrons are not flowing through the wire, and so on. But these purely formal statements are quite empty as long as we don't have some idea what the system of criteria of rational acceptability is which distinguishes scientific ways of attempting to determine whether snow is white from other ways of attempting to determine whether snow is white, scientific ways of attempting to determine whether electrons are flowing through a wire from other ways of attempting to determine whether there are electrons flowing through a wire, and so on.

If the notion of comparing our system of beliefs with unconceptualized reality to see if they match makes no sense, then the claim that science seeks to discover the truth can mean no more than that science seeks to construct a world picture which, in the ideal limit, satisfies certain criteria of rational acceptability. That science seeks to construct a world picture which is *true* is itself a true statement, an almost empty and formal true statement; the aims of science are given material content only by the criteria of rational acceptability implicit in science. In short I am saying that the answer to the 'strawman' position I considered, that the only aim of science is to discover truth (besides pointing out that science has additional aims, which is of course true), is that *truth is not the bottom line:* truth itself gets its life from our criteria of rational acceptability, and these are what we must look at if we wish to discover the values which are really implicit in science.

For the purpose of an example let me now imagine an extreme case of disagreement. The disagreement I'm going to imagine is not an ordinary scientific disagreement, although I hope our response to it will enable us to discover something about the nature of scientific values.

The hypothesis that the disagreement is going to be about, in the case I am about to describe, is just the hypothesis we discussed in Chapter 1, the hypothesis that we are all Brains in a Vat. We have argued that this hypothesis cannot possibly be true; but we shall suppose that our arguments have failed to convince one side in this disagreement (which is not improbable, since philosophical arguments never convince everyone). In short, the hypothesis is that everything is a collective hallucination in the way we described before.

Of course, if it were all one collective hallucination in this way, there are many people to whom this need not make any difference. It would make little or no difference to lovers, for example.[2] And I imagine it would make no difference at all to

---

[2] But I keep changing my mind about whether it would or not.

economists. (Why should an economist care if all the money in the world isn't physically real? Most of it isn't physically real on any theory!)

I want the reader to imagine that this crazy (and, I would claim, incoherent) theory, the theory that we are all brains in a vat, is held not by an isolated lunatic, but by virtually all the people in some large country, say, Australia. Imagine that in Australia only a small minority of the people believe what we do and the great majority believe that we are Brains in a Vat. Perhaps the Australians believe this because they are all disciples of a Guru, the Guru of Sydney, perhaps. Perhaps when we talk to them they say, 'Oh if you could talk to the Guru of Sydney and look into his eyes and see what a good, kind, wise man he is, you too would be convinced.' And if we ask, 'But how does the Guru of Sydney know that we are brains in a vat, if the illusion is as perfect as you say?', they might reply, 'Oh, the Guru of Sydney *just knows.*'

As I said before, this is not a scientific disagreement in the ordinary sense. We can imagine that the Australians are just as good as we are at anticipating experiences, at building bridges that stay up (or seem to stay up), etc. They may even be willing to accept our latest scientific discoveries, not as true, but as correct descriptions of what seems to go on in the image. We may or may not imagine that they disagree with us about some predictions concerning the very distant future (for example, they might expect that some day the automatic machinery will break down and then people will begin to have collective hallucinations of a kind which will give evidence that their view is right),[3] but whether they do make such predictions, or whether they commit themselves to no predictions different from the ones afforded by standard theory, will not affect my argument. The point is that here I've imagined a case where a vast number of people have a self-contained belief system which violently disagrees with ours.

There is no question of a disagreement in 'ethical' values here;

---

[3] If they do make such predictions, then it does make this much difference: their view is no longer incoherent in the way we criticized in Chapter 1, since they are making a claim that could be justified (eventually), and hence one that does not require a view of truth as 'transcendent' (or independent of justification) to be understood.

the Australians can have ethics just as similar to ours as you like. (Although an ancient Greek would have said that being *wise* is an *ethical* value; Judaism and Christianity have, in fact, narrowed the notion of the ethical because of a certain conception of Salvation.)

The first thing I want to observe about the hypothetical Australians is that their world view is *crazy*. Sometimes, to be sure, '*crazy*' is used almost as a term of approval; but I don't mean it in that sense here. I think we would regard a community of human beings who held so insane a world view with great sadness. The Australians would be regarded as crazy in the sense of having *sick* minds; and the characterization of their minds as sick is an ethical one, or verges on the ethical. But how, other than by calling them names, could one argue with the Australians? (Or try to argue with them, for I shall suppose that they are not to be convinced.)

One argument that one can immediately think of has to do with the *incoherence* of their view. I don't just mean the incoherence that we found in the view in Chapter 1. That is a *deep* incoherence, which requires a philosophical (and hence controversial) argument to expose. But the Australian's view is incoherent at a much more superficial level. One of the things that we aim at is that we should be able to give an account of how we know our statements to be true. In part we try to do this by developing a causal theory of perception, so that we can account for what we take to be the reliability of our perceptual knowledge, viewed from within our theory itself, by giving an account within the theory of how our perceptions result from the operation of transducing organs upon the external world. In part we try to do this by a theory of statistics and experimental design, so that we can show, within our theory itself, how the procedures that we take to exclude experimental error really do have a tendency in the majority of cases to exclude experimental error. In short, it is an important and extremely useful constraint on our theory itself that our developing theory of the world taken as a whole should include an account of the very activity and processes by which we are able to know that that theory is correct.

The Australians' system, however, does not have this property of coherence (at least as we judge it, and 'coherence' is not some-

thing that we have an algorithm for, but something that we ultimately judge by 'seat of the pants' feel). The Australians, remember, have themselves postulated an illusion so perfect that there
is no rational way in which the Guru of Sydney can possibly
know that the belief system which he has adopted and persuaded
all the others to adopt is correct. Judged by our standards of
coherence, *their* belief system is totally incoherent.

Other methodological virtues could be listed which their belief
system lacks. Their belief system, as I described it, agrees with
ours concerning what the laws of nature are *in the image;* but
does it tell us whether or not the laws of nature that appear to
hold in the image are the laws of nature that actually hold outside the vat? If it fails to, then it lacks a certain kind of comprehensiveness which we aim after, for it does not, even in its own
terms, tell what the true and ultimate laws of nature are. Certainly it violates Ockham's razor. Again, Ockham's razor seems
difficult or impossible to formalize as an algorithm, but the very
fact that the Brain in a Vatist theory postulates all kinds of
objects outside the vat which play no role in the explanation of
our experiences, according to the theory itself, makes it clear
that this is a case in which we can definitely say that the maxim
. . . 'don't multiply entities without necessity' is violated. Let us
call a theory which obeys Ockham's razor, in spirit as opposed
to just in letter, *functionally simple.*

What I have been saying is that the procedures by which we
decide on the acceptability of a scientific theory have to do with
whether or not the scientific theory as a whole exhibits certain
'virtues'. I am assuming that the procedure of building up scientific theory cannot be correctly analyzed as a procedure of veri-
fying scientific theories *sentence by sentence.* I am assuming that
verification in science is a holistic matter, that it is whole theoretical systems that meet the test of experience 'as a corporate
body', and that the judgment of how well a whole system of
sentences meets the test of experience is ultimately somewhat of
an intuitive matter which could not be formalized short of formalizing total human psychology. But let us come back to our
original question. What are the values implicit in science?

I've been arguing that if we take the values to which we appeal
in our criticism of the Brain-in-a-Vatists, and add, of course,
other values which are not at issue in this case, e.g. our desire for

instrumental efficacy, which we presumably share with the Brain-in-a-Vatists, then we get a picture of science as presupposing a rich system of values. The fact is that, if we consider the ideal of rational acceptability which is revealed by looking at what theories scientists and ordinary people consider rational to accept, then we see that what we are trying to do in science is to construct a representation of the world which has the characteristics of being instrumentally efficacious, coherent, comprehensive, and functionally simple. But why?

I would answer that the reason we want this sort of representation, and not the 'sick' sort of notional world possessed by the Australians, possessed by the Brain-in-a-Vatists, is that having this sort of representation system is *part of our idea of human cognitive flourishing,* and hence part of our idea of total human flourishing, of Eudaemonia.

Of course, if metaphysical realism were right, and one could view the aim of science simply as trying to get our notional world to 'match' the world in itself, then one could contend that we are interested in coherence, comprehensiveness, functional simplicity, and instrumental efficacy only because these are instruments to the end of bringing about this 'match'. But the notion of a transcendental match between our representation and the world in itself is nonsense. To deny that we want this kind of metaphysical match with a noumenal world is not to deny that we want the usual sort of empirical fit (as judged by our criteria of rational acceptability) with an *empirical* world. But the empirical world, as opposed to the noumenal world, depends upon our criteria of rational acceptability (and, of course, vice versa). We use our criteria of rational acceptability to build up a theoretical picture of the 'empirical world' and then as that picture develops we revise our very criteria of rational acceptability in the light of that picture and so on and so on forever. The dependence of our methods on our picture of the world is something I have stressed in my other books; what I wish to stress here is the other side of the dependence, the dependence of the empirical world on our criteria of rational acceptability. What I am saying is that we must have criteria of rational acceptability to even have an empirical world, that these reveal part of our notion of an optimal speculative intelligence. In short, I am saying that the 'real world' depends upon our values (and, again, vice versa).

At least some values must be objective

The fact that science is not 'value neutral', as has been thought, does not, to be sure, show that 'ethical' values are objective, or that ethics could be a science. In fact, there is no prospect of a 'science' of ethics, whether in the sense of a laboratory science or of a deductive science. As Aristotle long ago remarked,[4]

> We must be content, then, in speaking of such subjects and with such premises to indicate the truth roughly and in outline, and in speaking about things which are only for the most part true, and with premises of the same kind, to reach conclusions which are no better. In the same spirit, therefore, should each kind of statement be received, for it is the mark of an educated man to look for precision in each class of things just so far as the nature of the subject admits; it is evidently foolish to accept probable reasoning from a mathematician and to demand from a rhetorician scientific proofs.

But the fact that rational acceptability in the exact sciences (which are certainly central examples of rational thinking) does depend on such cognitive *virtues* as 'coherence' and 'functional simplicity' shows that at least some value terms stand for properties of the things they are applied to, and not just for feelings of the person who uses the terms.

If the terms 'coherent' and 'simple' do not stand for *properties* of theories, not even fuzzy or imperfectly defined ones, but only for 'attitudes' that some people have towards theories, then such terms for rational acceptability as 'justified', 'well confirmed', 'best of the available explanations' must also be entirely subjective: for rational acceptability cannot be more objective than the parameters upon which it depends. But, as we argued in the preceding chapter, the view that rational acceptability itself is simply subjective is a self-refuting one. So we are compelled to con-

[4] *Ethica Nicomachea*, Book I, Ch. 3.

clude that at least *these* value-terms have some sort of objective
application, some sort of objective justification conditions.

Of course, one might attempt to avoid conceding that there
are objective values of any kind by choosing to deny that
'coherent', 'simple', 'justified', and the like are *value* terms. One
might hold that they stand for properties which we do value, but
that there is no objective rightness about our doing so. But this
line runs into difficulties at once. 'Coherent' and 'simple' have
too many characteristics in common with the paradigmatic value
words. Like 'kind', 'beautiful', and 'good', 'coherent' and 'simple' are often used as terms of *praise*. Our conceptions of coherence, simplicity, and justification are just as historically condi-
tioned as our conceptions of kindness, beauty, and goodness;
these epistemic terms figure in the same sorts of perennial
philosophical controversies as do the terms for ethical and aesthetic values. The conception of rationality of a John Cardinal
Newman is obviously quite different from that of a Rudolf Carnap. It is highly unlikely that either could have convinced the
other, had they lived at the same time and been able to meet.
The question: *which is the rational conception of rationality
itself* is difficult in *exactly* the way that the justification of an
ethical system is difficult. There is no *neutral* conception of
rationality to which to appeal.

One might attempt various conventionalist moves here, e.g.
saying that 'justified$_{Carnap}$' is one 'property' and justified$_{Newman}$'
is a different 'property', and that a 'subjective value judgment'
is involved in the decision to mean 'justified$_{Carnap}$' or 'justified $_{Newman}$' by the word 'justified' but that no value judgment
is involved in stating the fact that a given statement S is justified $_{Carnap}$ or justified$_{Newman}$. But from whose standpoint is the
word '*fact*' being used? If there is no conception of rationality one
objectively *ought* to have, then the notion of a 'fact' is empty.
Without the cognitive values of coherence, simplicity, and
instrumental efficacy we have no world and no 'facts', not even
facts about what is so *relative* to what, for those are in the same
boat with all other facts. And these cognitive values are arbitrary
considered as anything but a part of a holistic conception of
human flourishing. Bereft of the old realist idea of truth as 'correspondence' and of the positivist idea of justification as fixed by
public 'criteria', we are left with the necessity of seeing our

search for better conceptions of rationality as an intentional human activity, which, like every activity that rises above habit and the mere following of inclination or obsession, is guided by our idea of the good.

Rationality in other areas

If the values implicit in science, especially in the exact sciences, reveal a part of our idea of the good, I think that the rest of our idea of the good can be read off from our standards of rational acceptability in yet other areas of knowledge. At this point, however, it is necessary to broaden the notion of *standards of rational acceptability.*

So far, we have only considered standards of rational acceptability in the literal sense: standards which tell us when we should and when we should not *accept* statements. But standards of rationality in the wide sense have to do not only with how we judge the truth or falsity of systems of statements, but also with how we judge their *adequacy* and *perspicuousness.* There are ways – purely cognitive ways – in which a system of statements can fall short of giving us a satisfactory description other than by being false.

Had I chosen I could have made this point even in connection with theoretical science. I could have pointed out that the concern of exact science is not just to discover statements which are true, or even statements which are true and universal in form ('laws'), but to find statements that are true and *relevant*. And the notion of *relevance* brings with it a wide set of interests and values. But this would have only been to argue that our *knowledge* of the world presupposes values, and not to make the more radical claim that what *counts* as the real world depends upon our values.

When we come to perceptual rationality, that is to the implicit standards and skills on the basis of which we decide whether someone is able to give a true, adequate, and perspicuous account of even the simplest *perceptual* facts, then we see a large number of factors at play. Recently psychologists have stressed just how much theory construction is involved in even the simplest cases of perception. Not only is this true at the neurophysiological level, but it is also true at the cultural level. Someone from a culture which had no furniture might be able to come into a room and give some kind of description of the room, but, if he did not know what a table or a chair or a desk was, his description would hardly convey the information that a member of this culture would wish to have about the room. His description might consist only of true statements but it would not be adequate.

What this simple example shows is that the requirement that a description be adequate is implicitly a requirement that the describer have available a certain set of *concepts;* we expect rational describers with respect to certain kinds of *descripta* to be capable of acquiring certain concepts and of seeing the need to use them; the fact that the describer did not employ a certain concept may be a ground for criticizing both him and his description.

What is true at the simple level of talk about tables and chairs in a room without people in it is also true at the level of description of interpersonal relations and situations. Consider the terms we use every day in describing what other people are like, e.g. *considerate* or *inconsiderate*. *Considerate* and *inconsiderate* may of course be used to praise or blame; and one of the many distinctions which have gotten confused together under the general heading 'fact–value distinction' is the distinction between using a linguistic expression to describe and using that linguistic expression to praise or blame. But this distinction is not a distinction which can be drawn on the basis of vocabulary. The judgment that someone is inconsiderate may indeed be used to blame; but it may be used simply to describe, and it may also be used to explain or to predict.

For example I may say to you, 'Don't let Jones hurt your feelings. You're likely to think that he's taken a dislike to you from the way he will talk, but that's a common misimpression. No matter what he feels about you he'll likely behave in such a way that your feelings will be hurt. He's just a rather inconsiderate man, but don't think that it has anything to do with you.'

In this little imaginary speech someone is using the word 'inconsiderate' not for the purpose of blaming Jones, but with the intention of predicting and explaining Jones' behavior to someone else. And both the prediction and the explanation may be perfectly *correct*. And similarly, 'jealous' may be a term of blame and may be used without any intention of blaming at all. (Sometimes one has a perfect right to be jealous.)

The use of the word 'inconsiderate' seems to me a very fine example of the way in which the fact/value distinction is hopelessly fuzzy in the real world and in the real language. The importance of terms like 'inconsiderate', 'pert', 'stubborn', 'pesky', etc., in actual moral evaluation, has been emphasized by Iris Murdoch in *The Sovereignty of 'Good'*.[5] Even though each of the statements 'John is a very inconsiderate man', 'John thinks about nobody but himself', 'John would do practically anything for money' may be simply a true description in the most positivistic sense (and notice 'John would do practically anything for money' does not contain any value term), if one has asserted the conjunction of these three statements it is hardly necessary to add 'John is not a very good person'. When we think of facts and values as independent we typically think of 'facts' as stated in some physicalistic or bureaucratic jargon, and the 'values' as being stated in the most abstract value terms, e.g. 'good', 'bad'. The independence of value from fact is harder to maintain when the facts themselves are of the order of 'inconsiderate', 'thinks only about himself', 'would do anything for money'.

Just as we criticize a describer who does not employ the concepts of *table* and *chair* when their use is called for, so also, someone who fails to remark that someone is *considerate* or *spontaneous* may open himself to the criticism that he is imperceptive or superficial; his description is not an adequate one.

The super-Benthamites

Let me go back and modify my previous example of the 'Brain-in-a-Vatists'. This time let us imagine that the continent of Australia is peopled by a culture which agrees with us on history, geography and exact science, but which disagrees with us in ethics. I don't want to take the usual case of super-Nazis or something of that kind, but I want to take rather the more interesting case of super-Benthamites. Let us imagine that the continent of Australia is peopled with people who have some elaborate sci-

---

[5] Routledge and Kegan Paul, 1970.

entific measure of what they take to be 'hedonic tone', and who
believe that one should always act so as to maximize hedonic
tone (taking that to mean the greatest hedonic tone of the greatest number). I will assume that the super-Benthamites are
extremely sophisticated, aware of all the difficulties of predicting
the future and exactly estimating the consequences of actions
and so forth. I will also assume that they are extremely ruthless,
and that while they would not cause someone suffering for the
sake of the greatest happiness of the greatest number if there
were reasonable doubt that *in fact* the consequence of their
action would *be* to bring about the greatest happiness of the
greatest number, that in cases where one knows with certainty
what the consequences of the actions would be, they would be
willing to perform the most horrible actions – willing to torture
small children or to condemn people for crimes which they did
not commit – if the result of these actions would be to increase
the general satisfaction level in the long run (after due allowance
for the suffering of the innocent victim in each case) by any positive ϵ, however small.

I imagine that we would not feel very happy about this sort of
super-Benthamite morality. Most of us would condemn the
super-Benthamites as having a sick system of values, as being
bureaucratic, as being ruthless, etc. They are the 'new man' in
his most horrible manifestation. And they would return our
invective by saying that we are soft-headed, superstitious, pris-
oners of irrational tradition, etc.

The disagreement between us and the super-Benthamites is
just the sort of disagreement that is ordinarily imagined in order
to make the point that two groups of people might agree on all
the facts and still disagree about the 'values'. But let us look at
the case more closely. Every super-Benthamite is familiar with
the fact that sometimes the greatest satisfaction of the greatest
number (measured in 'utils') requires one to tell a lie. And it is
not counted as being 'dishonest' in the pejorative sense to tell lies
out of the motive of maximizing the general pleasure level. So
after a while the use of the description 'honest' among the super-
Benthamites would be extremely different from the use of that
same descriptive term among us. And the same will go for 'considerate', 'good citizen', etc. The vocabulary available to the
super-Benthamites for the description of people-to-people situa-

tions will be quite different from the vocabulary available to us. Not only will they lack, or have altered beyond recognition, many of our descriptive resources, but they will very likely invent new jargon of their own (for example, exact terms for describing hedonic tones) that are unavailable to us. The texture of the human world will begin to change. In the course of time the super-Benthamites and we will end up living in different human worlds.

In short, it will not be the case that we and the super-Benthamites 'agree on the facts and disagree about values'. In the case of almost all interpersonal situations, the description we give of the facts will be quite different from the description they give of the facts. Even if none of the statements they make about the situation are *false*, their description will not be one that we will count as adequate and perspicuous; and the description we give will not be one that they could count as adequate and perspicuous. In short, even if we put aside our 'disagreement about the values', we could not regard their total representation of the human world as fully rationally acceptable. And just as the Brain-in-a-Vatists' inability to get *the way the world is* right is a direct result of their sick standards of rationality – their sick standards of theoretical rationality – so the inability of the super-Benthamites to get the way the human world is right is a direct result of *their* sick conception of human flourishing.

Subjectivism about goodness

It has often been claimed that the step from 'John is considerate, truthful, kind, courageous, responsible, etc.' to 'John is morally good' involves at least one unproved (and unprovable) 'premiss', namely, 'Consideration is morally good.' And it has been held that the need for moral 'premisses' before one can draw moral conclusions from 'factual' statements shows that ethical statements are not rationally justifiable.

This picture of ethics as a sort of inverted pyramid, with the tip (which is itself unsupported) consisting of 'ethical axioms' which support our whole body of moral belief and thinking, is naive. No one has ever succeeded in imposing an axiomatic structure upon ethics (as Aristotle remarked in the passage I cited a few pages ago, such moral maxims as we are able to list are almost always true only 'for the most part'). And the same trick, of picturing a body of thinking one wishes to cast into doubt as resting upon unsupportable 'axioms' is one which sceptics have employed in every area. Sceptics who doubt the existence of material objects, for example, argue that the principle that 'if our sensations occur as they would if there were a material world, then there probably is a material world' is a *rationally unsupportable premiss* which we tacitly invoke whenever we claim to 'observe' a material object, or try otherwise to justify belief in their existence. In fact, ethics and mathematics and talk of material objects presuppose concepts not 'axioms'. Concepts are used in observation and generalization, and are themselves made legitimate by the success we have in using them to describe and generalize.

A more sophisticated attack on the idea of ethical objectivity concedes that our ethical beliefs rest on observations of specific cases, 'intuitions', general maxims, etc., and not on some collection of arbitrary 'ethical axioms', but makes the charge that ethical 'observation' itself is infected with an incurable disease: *projection*.

According to this account, humans are naturally, if intermittently, compassionate. So when we see something terrible happening, as it might be, someone torturing a small child just for his own sadistic pleasure, we are (sometimes) horrified. But the psychological mechanism of 'projection' leads us to experience the feeling quality as a quality of the deed itself: we say 'the act was horrible' when we should really say 'my reaction was to be horrified'. Thus we build up a body of what we take to be 'ethical observations', which are really just observations of our own subjective ethical *feelings*.

This story has more sophisticated forms (like any other). Hume postulated a human tendency he called 'sympathy', which has gradually become wider under the influence of culture. Contemporary sociobiologists postulate an instinct they call 'altruism', and speak of 'altruistic genes'. But the key idea remains the same: there are ethical *feelings*, but no objective value properties.

We have already seen that this is not right: there are at least *some* objective values, for example, *justification*. It could still be claimed that the *ethical* values are subjective while the *cognitive* values are objective; but the argument that there can't be any objective values at all has been refuted.

In order to show what is wrong with arguments for moral subjectivism, I must now recall the arguments that were used against metaphysical realism in Chapter 2. This may seem queer: isn't subjectivism the *opposite* of metaphysical realism? If one thinks so, then it will seem that any argument against metaphysical realism must *support* subjectivism; the strategy I am going to follow of using the *same* argument against both metaphysical realism and subjectivism will seem an impossible one.

But in fact, metaphysical realism and subjectivism are not simple 'opposites'. Today we tend to be too realistic about physics and too subjectivistic about ethics, and these are connected tendencies. It is *because* we are too realistic about physics, because we see physics (or some hypothetical future physics) as the One True Theory, and not simply as a rationally acceptable description suited for certain problems and purposes, that we tend to be subjectivistic about descriptions we cannot 'reduce' to physics. Becoming less realistic about physics and becoming less subjectivistic about ethics are likewise connected.

The argument at the end of Chapter 2 was directed against the 'physicalistic' or naturalistic version of metaphysical realism. To recall it, let us suppose that the standard interpretation I (Under which 'cat' refers to cats, 'cherry' to cherries, etc.) is either coextensive with or identical with physicalistic relation R. So R holds between tokens of 'cat' (or physical events of someone's using those tokens suitably) and cats, etc. The non-standard interpretation J we described will then also be co-extensive with a certain relation R', definable in terms of R and the possible worlds and permutations used in constructing J (see Appendix). So R' holds between tokens of 'cat' (or the physical events of someone's using those tokens in the standard way) and *cherries,* etc. R and R' are *both* 'correspondences': The same sentences are 'true' under both correspondences. The actions called for by the R'-truth of a sentence (i.e. the actions which will 'succeed', from the agent's point of view) are the same as the actions called for when the sentence is R-true. If R is 'identical with reference'; if R, R', and all the other relations which assign extensions to our words in ways which satisfy our operational and theoretical constraints are not equally correct; if R, R' and the others are not equally correct because one of them – R – just *is* reference; then that fact itself is an *inexplicable* fact from a physicalist perspective.

This argument is not just an argument against (the physicalist version of) metaphysical realism, but an argument against *reductionism*. If there is nothing in the physicalist world-picture that corresponds to the obvious fact that 'cat' refers to cats and not to cherries, then that is a decisive reason for rejecting the demand that all the notions we use must be reduced to physical terms. For reference and truth are notions we cannot consistently give up. If I think 'a cat is on a mat', then I am committed to believing that 'cat' refers to something (though not to a metaphysical realist account of 'reference') and to believing that 'a cat is on a mat' is true (though not to a metaphysical realist account of truth).

Having reviewed the argument of Chapter 2, let us now see how it bears on the arguments for moral subjectivism. The 'projection' theory gave one account of moral experience: moral experience is, so to speak, mislocated subjective feeling. Contrast the 'projection' theory with the following account: 'all humans have, to some extent, a sense of justice and some idea of the good. So we respond (intermittently) to such appeals as "be kind to the stranger among you, *because you know what it was like to be a stranger in Egypt*". Our sympathy becomes broader, partly because we are persuaded that it *ought* to be broader; we feel that an atrocity is wrong (sometimes) even when we don't easily or spontaneously find the victim a person we can sympathize with. We come to see similarities between injuries to others and injuries to ourselves, and between benefits to others and benefits to ourselves. We invent moral words for morally relevant features of situations, and we gradually begin to make explicit moral generalizations, which lead to still further refinement of our moral notions, and so on.'

This account is, on the face of it, simpler and more sophisticated than the 'projection' theory. (For one thing, it acknowledges the role of *argument* in shaping moral attitudes.) Nevertheless, many intelligent people feel that today we must reject talk of a 'sense of justice' and talk of 'having an idea of the good' (where this is not taken in a purely subjective sense), as 'unscientific'. So moral knowledge becomes problematical; perhaps downright impossible.

But what does 'unscientific' mean here? A belief that there is such a thing as justice is not a belief in *ghosts,* nor is a 'sense of justice' a para-normal sense which enables us to perceive such ghosts. Justice is not something anyone proposes to *add to* the list of objects recognized by physics as eighteenth-century chemists proposed to add 'phlogiston' to the list of objects recognized by chemical theory. Ethics does not *conflict with* physics, as the term 'unscientific' suggests; it is simply that 'just' and 'good' and 'sense of justice' are concepts in a discourse which is not *reducible to* physical discourse. As we have just seen, *other* kinds of essential discourse are not reducible to physical discourse and are not for that reason illegitimate. Talk of 'justice', like talk of 'reference', can be *non*-scientific without being *un*scientific.

As a way of seeing what is going on, let us consider any basic principle of logic or mathematics, say, the principle that the series of whole numbers can always be continued ('every number has a successor'), or the principle that a non-empty set of whole numbers must contain a smallest member. Suppose someone put forward the following view: 'These principles are true for the numbers and sets of numbers we deal with in practice. So they come to seem necessary. By the mechanism called "projection", we attach this *feeling of necessity* to the principles themselves; we feel the *statements* have a mysterious "necessity". But in reality this has no justification. For all we know, these principles may not even be true.'

Virtually no one would agree with this. Virtually every mathematician would say, instead, something like this: 'Most humans have mathematical intuition to some extent. So we intuitively "see", or can be brought by examples (or by skillful questioning, like the slave-boy in Plato's dialogue) to "see" that the principles are necessarily true.'

Kurt Gödel believed that 'mathematical intuition' was analogous to *perception:* mathematical objects (which he called 'concepts') are *out there,* and our intuition enables us to intellectually perceive these Platonic entities; but few mathematicians would commit themselves to such a Platonic metaphysics. Gödel's comparison of mathematical intuition to perception reveals an over-simple idea of perception. Vision does not really give us direct access to a ready made world, but gives us a description of objects which are partly structured and constituted by vision itself. If we take the physicist's rainbow to be the rainbow 'in itself', then the rainbow 'in itself' has no *bands* (a spectroscopic analysis yields a smooth distribution of frequencies); the red, orange, yellow, green, blue and violet bands are a feature of the *perceptual* rainbow, not the physicist's rainbow. The perceptual rainbow depends on the nature of our perceptual aparatus itself, on our visual 'world making' as Nelson Goodman has termed it. (The physicist's 'objects' also depend on our worldmaking, as is shown by the plethora of radically different versions physics constructs of the 'same' objects.) Yet we do not consider vision as *defective* because it sees bands in the rainbow; someone who *couldn't* see them would have defective vision. Vision is certified as good by its ability to deliver a description which fits the objects *for us,* not metaphysical things-in-themselves. Vision is good when it enables us to see the world 'as it is' – that is, the human, functional world which is partly created by vision itself.

A proposed new axiom of set theory, such as the 'Axiom of choice', may be adopted partly because of its agreement with the 'intuition' of expert mathematicians, and partly for its yield. If the axiom of choice did not deliver results which count as successful mathematics the fact that some people find it 'intuitive' would have little interest. Mathematical intuition itself is demonstrated or tested by grasping mathematical principles and by following proofs. In short, mathematical intuition is good when it enables us to see mathematical facts 'as they are' – that is, as they are in the mathematical world which is constructed by human mathematical practice (including the application of mathematics to other subject matters).

A physiological or psychological description of vision cannot tell us whether seeing bands in the rainbow counts as seeing 'correctly' or not. Even less could a physiological or psychological description of the brain-process which goes on when one 'grasps' the Principle of Mathematical Induction tell us whether that principle is *true* or not. Once one sees this, it should be no surprise that a description of the brain process which goes on when one 'sees' that an action is unjust cannot tell us whether the action really *is* unjust.

Talk of moral 'perception', like talk of mathematical intuition, or of reference and understanding, is not reducible to the language or the world-picture of physics. That does not mean physics is 'incomplete'. Physics can be 'complete' – that is, complete for physical purposes. The completeness physics *lacks* is a completeness all particular theories, pictures, and discourses lack. For no theory or picture is complete for *all* purposes. If the irreducibility of ethics to physics shows that values are projections, then *colors* are also projections. So are the natural numbers. So, for that matter, is 'the physical world'. But being a projection in *this* sense is not the same thing as being *subjective*.[6]

Authoritarianism and pluralism

I have been arguing that it is necessary to have standards of rational acceptability in order to have a world at all; either a world of 'empirical facts' or a world of 'value facts' (a world in which there is beauty and tragedy). It should go without saying that it is not possible both to have standards of rational acceptability and not to accept them, or to stand at arm's length from them. (The kind of scepticism which consists in refusing to have any standards of rational acceptability commits one to not having any concepts at all. As Sextus Empiricus recognized, that kind of empiricism ultimately is unexpressible in language.) We have just as much right to regard some 'evaluational' casts of mind as sick (and we all do) as we do to regard some 'cognitional' casts of mind as sick. But to say this is not to reject pluralism or to commit oneself to authoritarianism.

Even in science, holding that science is an objective enterprise (by a standard of 'objectivity' which is admittedly anthropocentric, but, as David Wiggins once remarked, the only standard of

---

6 An unintentionally funny version of the projection theory is cited by C. S. Lewis in *The Abolition of Man* (Macmillan, 1947). Lewis quotes a secondary school English text (which he does not identify, out of charity). 'You remember that there were two tourists present [*Lewis is talking about the well known story of Coleridge at the waterfall*]: that one called it "sublime" and the other "pretty"; and that Coleridge mentally endorsed the first judgment and rejected the second with disgust. Gaius and Titius [*Lewis' pseudonyms for the unidentified authors of the text*] comment as follows: "When the man said *That is sublime*, he appeared to be making a remark about the waterfall . . . Actually he was not making a remark about the waterfall, but about his own feelings. What he was saying was really *I have feelings in my mind associated with the word 'Sublime'*, or shortly, I have sublime feelings." '

objectivity available to us) is not to hold that every scientific question has a determinate answer. Some scientific questions may have *objectively indeterminate* answers, i.e. there may be no convergence with respect to an answer to them even in the ideal limit of scientific inquiry; and some scientific questions may have determinate but context-relative answers (e.g. 'What was the cause of John's heart attack?' may have different correct answers depending on who asks the question and why). And, similarly, holding that ethical inquiry is objective in the sense that some 'value judgments' are definitely true and some are definitely false, and more generally that some value positions (and some 'ideologies') are definitely wrong, and some are definitely inferior to some others, is not the same thing as holding the silly position that there are no indeterminate cases at all. (One especially important kind of indeterminate case has been emphasized by Bernard Williams: this is the case where all the alternatives are so horrible that there is no one of the alternatives that would clearly be chosen by an ideally rational and wise person.) And that there are context relativities in ethics goes without saying.

If today we differ with Aristotle it is in being much more pluralistic than Aristotle was. Aristotle recognized that different ideas of Eudaemonia, different conceptions of human flourishing, might be appropriate for different individuals on account of the difference in their constitution. But he seemed to think that ideally there was some sort of constitution that every one ought to have; that in an ideal world (overlooking the mundane question of who would grow the crops and who would bake the bread) everyone would be a philosopher. We agree with Aristotle that different ideas of human flourishing are appropriate for individuals with different constitutions, but we go further and believe that even in the ideal world there would be different constitutions, that diversity is part of the ideal. And we see some degree of tragic tension between ideals, that the fulfillment of some ideals always excludes the fulfillment of some others. But to emphasize the point again, belief in a pluralistic ideal is not the same thing as belief that every ideal of human flourishing is as good as every other. We reject ideals of human flourishing as wrong, as infantile, as sick, as one-sided.

Nor should commitment to ethical objectivity be confused with what is a very different matter, commitment to ethical or moral authoritarianism. It is perhaps this confusion that has lead one outstanding philosopher[7] to espouse what he himself regards as a limited version of 'non-cognitivism', and to say 'Concerning what "living most fully" is for each man, the final authority must be the man himself.' (Notice the ambiguity in 'the final authority': does he mean the final *political* authority? The final *epistemological* authority? Or does he mean that *there is no fact of the matter*, as his use of the term 'non-cognitivism' suggests?) Respect for persons as autonomous moral agents requires that we accord them the right to choose a moral standpoint for themselves, however repulsive we may find their choice. According to the philosophy of political liberalism, it also requires that we also insist the government not preempt individual moral choices by setting up a state religion or a state morality. But diehard opposition to all forms of political and moral authoritarianism should not commit one to moral relativism or moral scepticism. The reason that it is wrong for the government to dictate a morality to the individual citizen is not that there is no fact of the matter about what forms of life are fulfilling and what forms of life are not fulfilling, or morally wrong in some other way. (If there were no such thing as moral wrong, then it would not be *wrong* for the government to impose moral choices.) The fact that many people fear that if they concede any sort of moral objectivity out loud then they will find some government shoving *its* notion of moral objectivity down their throats is without question one of the reasons why so many people subscribe to a moral subjectivism to which they give no real assent.

[7] David Wiggins in 'Truth, Invention, and the Meaning of Life', *Proceedings of the British Academy*, vol. LXII, 1976.

7

Reason and history

With the rise of science has come the realization that many questions cannot be settled by the methods of the exact sciences, ideological and ethical questions being the most obvious examples. And with the increase in our admiration and respect for the physicist, the cosmologist, the molecular biologist, has come a decrease in respect and trust for the political thinker, the moralist, the economist, the musician, the psychiatrist, etc.

In this situation some have gone with the cultural tide and argued that, indeed, there is no knowledge to be found outside of the exact sciences (and the social sciences to the extent that they succeed in aping the exact sciences, and only to this extent). This view may take the form of positivism or materialism, or some combination of these. Others have tried to argue that science too is 'subjective' and arbitrary – this is the popular reading of Kuhn's immensely successful book *The Structure of Scientific Revolutions,* even if it is not the one Kuhn now says he intended. Others – e.g. the Marxist philosophers and the religious philosophers – adopt a sort of *double-entry* bookkeeping, leaving technical questions to the exact sciences and engineering and ideological or ethical questions to a different tribunal: the Party, the Utopian future, the church. But few can feel comfortable with any of these stances – with extreme scientism in either its positivist or materialist forms, with subjectivism and radical relativism, or with any of the species of double-entry bookkeeping. It is just because we feel uncomfortable that there is a real problem for us in this area.

To be sure, the problem is in one way *un*real. The same person who argues that ethical and political opinions are unverifiable argues with passion for *his* ethical and political opinions. Hume said that he left his scepticism whenever he left his study; and relativists are likely to do the same with their relativism. But this only shows that no one can consistently live by relativism; if this is all that can be said in response to relativism, then we are just pushed from relativism to 1945 style existentialism ('it's all absurd, but you have to choose'). And is *that* so different?

In order to fix our ideas, let us recall a remark by a philosopher of the last century whose Utilitarianism actually covered a good bit of relativism. I am thinking of Bentham, and of Bentham's challenging judgment that 'prejudice aside, the game of pushpin is of equal value with the arts and sciences of music and of poetry'. *Prejudice aside, pushpin is as good as poetry.*

What makes this so shocking to the modern reader is how deeply it conflicts with our current cultural values. The arts have been exalted by us to a place much higher than any they occupied in Plato's day or in the middle ages. As a number of authors have remarked, for a certain sort of educated person, art today is religion, i.e. the closest thing to salvation available.

Bentham is saying that a preference for 'the arts and sciences of music and poetry' over the childish game of pushpin is merely subjective, like a preference for vanilla ice cream over chocolate ice cream. He does not wish to deny that music and poetry do have greater value than pushpin ('prejudice aside' is an important part of the sentence); in the context of his Utilitarianism, the very fact that a large majority *do* prefer music and poetry to pushpin *gives* music and poetry greater 'utility' and hence greater value. But the value is, as it were, the *product* of 'prejudice' (i.e. purely subjective interest); there is no fact of the matter about the relative value of pushpin and poetry apart from the fact that people prefer poetry to pushpin. We don't prefer poetry to pushpin *because* poetry has greater value than pushpin, Bentham is saying, rather, it's the other way around, and poetry has greater value than pushpin because people prefer poetry to pushpin. (For *no* reason apparently.)

Stating the position so baldly already makes it look implausible. Let us consider for the moment a really 'subjective' preference.

One model that people sometimes seem to have in mind for

subjective preference is this. There is something C which is the taste of chocolate ice cream; there is something V which is the taste of vanilla ice cream. There are two feelings L, D which are 'liking' and 'disliking'. And what goes on and *all* that goes on, when Jones likes and Smith dislikes vanilla (and Smith likes and Jones dislikes chocolate), is that Jones experiences V + L when he eats vanilla and C + D when he eats chocolate whereas Smith experiences V + D when he eats vanilla and C + L when he eats chocolate.

Such an account is naive psychologically, however, as Köhler long ago argued. What vanilla tastes like to Jones, who likes vanilla ice cream, is not what it tastes like to Smith, who can't stand vanilla ice cream. Rather it's like this: Call the quality vanilla has for Smith V_s. V_s is an 'unpleasant' taste; it may be imaginable that one could experience V_s and like it, but just barely, and, even if one did, there would be some kind of disassociation or repression. In short, psychologically if not metaphysically, V_s is 'intrinsically' unpleasant. And Smith feels D (dislike for the taste) when he eats vanilla because vanilla has the taste quality V_s (for him). Similarly, V_j, the taste quality of vanilla for Jones is intrinsically 'pleasant' (which is why Jones feels L, liking). In the language of G. E. Moore, the taste V_j and the positive value are an organic unity for Jones, and the taste V_s and the negative value are an organic unity for Smith. Phenomenologically, they cannot really ever be separated into two parts in the way the notation '$V_s + D$', '$V_j + L$' suggests. Almost certainly (barring special factors of repression or disassociation), Smith would like vanilla ice cream too if it evoked V_j in his mouth and not V_s, and Jones would dislike vanilla ice cream too if it evoked V_s in his mouth and not V_j.

Why do we regard the preference for vanilla over chocolate as 'subjective' then? I mean, why do we regard it as subjective even when we don't think *all* value judgments are subjective or agree with Bentham that, prejudice aside, pushpin is as good as poetry? Obviously, if we think all preferences are subjective, we will think this one is too, but the interesting question is why this judgment doesn't even seem objective to us unless, perhaps, we *are* Smith or Jones, why it doesn't have the kind of objectivity that many value judgments do undeniably have.

It isn't just that there is disagreement. If we think there are objective (or warranted) value judgments at all, very likely we think some hotly disputed judgments are objectively right. The Nazis disputed the judgment that *wanton killing of Jews just because of their racial affiliation is wrong*, but anti-Nazis did not regard their disagreement with the Nazis over this judgment as 'subjective'. Those who think homosexuals should have full rights in our society violently disagree with those who think homosexual activity or civil rights of homosexuals should be legally proscribed; but neither side in this dispute regards its own position as 'subjective'. Indeed, disagreement frequently makes people more sure that their moral position is warranted. So it isn't just the fact that 'some people prefer chocolate and some people prefer vanilla' that makes the Smith/Jones disagreement in preference subjective.

Part of the story may be that most people don't have strong preferences between vanilla and chocolate, but this cannot be decisive. If half of the population couldn't stand chocolate but liked vanilla, and the other half couldn't stand vanilla but liked chocolate, we would still (if we were reasonable about our preferences) regard this as a 'matter of taste', i.e. as subjective. It isn't the existence of 'neutrals' that is decisive.

What *is* decisive, in my opinion, is that whatever biological or psychological idiosyncrasies are responsible for Smith's and Jones' preferences are not correlated with important traits of mind and character. If we try the thought experiment of imagining the contrary, of imagining that there was a caste of character that we regarded as good, both for its own sake and because of its effects on feeling, judgment and action, and another caste of character that we regarded as bad, both in itself and for its effects, and that everyone knew that the good caste of mind and character always revealed itself in a preference for vanilla and the bad in a preference for chocolate, then I think we will find that the more vividly we can succeed in making this case real to ourselves, the more we will feel that in such a world the first preference would be seen as 'normal' and 'right' and the second as 'perverse' or 'monstrous' or something of that sort.

I don't mean to claim that *all* preferences are judged morally by the traits of character they are thought to express. Some 'preferences' are terribly important in themselves: someone who thought it was just wonderful to torture small children for the fun of it would (if he was serious) be condemned on the basis of that one attitude. But if the matter preferred is not regarded as important in itself, then whether we make an issue of the preference or take it to be 'a matter of taste' will generally depend on *what*, if anything, we think the preference *shows*. Value judgments often come in clumps; and clumps of value judgments frequently express durable traits of mind, personality, and character. The *independence* of 'I prefer vanilla to chocolate ice cream' from any interesting and significant 'clump' of this kind is just what makes it 'subjective' (along, of course, with the absence of any intrinsic importance to the choice itself).

Even if Smith's preference for vanilla is 'subjective', that does not make it irrational or arbitrary. Smith has a reason – the best possible reason – for liking vanilla, namely *the way it tastes to him*. Values can be 'subjective' in the sense of being relative and still be objective; it is objective that vanilla tastes *better* than chocolate *to* Smith. In *The Sovereignty of Good*, Iris Murdoch pointed out that philosophers as different as the French Existentialists and the logical positivists actually shared a common model of value judgment, the model of reason as supplying the mind with neutral 'facts' on the basis of which the will must arbitrarily choose 'values' – the choice of values must be arbitrary, precisely because 'facts' are (by definition) neutral. But, since the will is given no clues by reason as to how to judge (reason only supplies 'facts', on this picture) it has no *reason* for its arbitrary choice; which is why the French philosophers called it 'absurd', and why more naturalistically inclined philosophers see instinct and emotion (the historic successors to Bentham's all-purpose category of pleasure) as the ultimate basis of moral choice.

In the case we have just examined, the Existentialist–Positivist model does not fit however. The 'fact' – the *taste* itself – and the 'value' – the goodness of the taste – are one, at least psychologically. Presented experiential qualities aren't, in general, neutral and they frequently seem to demand responses and attitudes. One may override these felt demands for good and sufficient reason, as when a child learns to bear the pain of an injection for the sake of the benefits conferred by the immunizing agent injected, but the *prima facie* goodness and badness of particular experiences can hardly be denied. (Interestingly enough, this point was recognized by Plato and the medievals – we are perhaps the first culture to conceive of experience as neutral).

The non-neutrality of experience also bears on the pushpin/poetry case. We find it virtually impossible to imagine that someone who really appreciates poetry, someone who is capable of distinguishing real poetry from mere verse, capable of responding to great poetry, *should* prefer a childish game to arts which enrich our lives as poetry and music do. We *have* a reason for preferring poetry to pushpin, and that reason lies in the felt experience of great poetry, and of the after effects of great poetry – the enlargement of the imagination and the sensibility through the enlargement of our repertoire of images and metaphors, and the integration of poetic images and metaphors with mundane perceptions and attitudes that takes place when a poem has lived in us for a number of years. These experiences too are *prima facie* good – and not just good, but enobling, to use an old fashioned word.

That there can be *reasons* for value judgments – reasons which really are good reasons for particular people to make particular value judgments – does not mean that all value judgments are rational, of course. Value judgments, judgments that people have cared passionately about, and in whose name people have killed and tortured other people, have often enough been based on an unwholesome mixture of aggressive impulses and narcissistic ideas. Not surprisingly, when a relativist historian/philosopher like Michel Foucault writes about the past, he often focusses our attention on these irrational ideas and value judgments. But it is important to see why he does this.

Foucault writes about the early modern era (the sixteenth and seventeenth centuries) and about ideology and culture in general. His knowledge of fact is legendary, even though many specialists dispute Foucault's 'facts'. While some of his books are highly abstract (e.g. *The Archeology of Knowledge*), some are rather specific, e.g. *The Birth of the Clinic* and *The Birth of the Prison*. *The Birth of the Clinic* is perhaps Foucault's best book, and it makes an important part of the case for Foucault's more abstract theories.

What Foucault tries to show is that the 'clinic', i.e. the institution of the hospital and the related medical institutions, was the reflection of the growth of a certain ideology about disease and health as much as the result of any increase in scientific knowledge and technique. This ideology, in turn, was connected with wider ideological changes, especially with the growth of individualism in the seventeenth century. And he suggests both that the 'clinic' is not a very good way of treating most patients and that our belief that it is is a kind of ideological prejudice, in short, a kind of folly.

The wider suggestion that emerges is that ideological convictions and the associated value judgments are a rather arbitrary affair.[1] There is no objective place to stand in ideological matters (except of course, for the mysterious standpoint of Foucault's own allegedly objective 'Archeology of Knowledge').

To see what Foucault is driving at, let us consider a more familiar and less controversial example. In the Middle Ages, it was believed that monarchy was the natural and proper form of government. This belief was based partly on factual beliefs now thought to be unwarranted (e.g. that democracy would inevitably lead to anarchy and tyranny), and partly on the authority of the Church. The view of the Church was in fact based partly on political considerations (the Church was the state religion), but this was not perceived because the Church itself was thought to be the divinely inspired and divinely appointed interpreter of the word and will of God. What Foucault is suggesting is that beliefs held in the recent past, and, by implication, the beliefs we hold right now, are no more rational than the medieval belief in the Divine Right of Kings.

Let us consider the belief in the Divine Right of Kings for a moment. If we don't think there is a *good reason* to believe in the existence of a personal God, one who commands that we live by certain kinds of social forms and structures, then this belief will be immediately stamped as irrational (which is not to deny that the belief answered to real psychological needs). Even if we

---

[1] And also that we are determined in our thinking by the very language we use. Foucault speaks of 'implicit systems which determine our most familiar behavior without our knowing it' (see J. Simon, 'A Conversation with Michel Foucault', *Partisan Review*, No. 2, 1971, p. 201). French Structuralism, at least as represented by Foucault, Althusser, Lacan, Deleuze, etc., often seems to amount to (1) determinism; (2) relativism; and (3) claims that Structuralism is 'linguistic science'.

believe in God, if we don't believe that the Church has special access to his wishes, we will think the Divine Right of Kings was and is an irrational doctrine. And finally, even believing Catholics will concede that the Church's support for monarchy in the Middle Ages was based as much on political considerations as on revelation or sound theology. In short, the belief in the Divine Right of Kings lacks, and always lacked, an adequate rational basis.

How, then, did the belief arise? The usual answer would appeal partly to political and economic factors (one does not have to be a Marxist to concede that these factors are among the determinants of ideology) and partly to psychological factors. The comfort provided by belief in a personal God and a hereafter is obvious, and so, perhaps, is the comfort provided to the believer in an infallible Church and a divinely appointed social order. In short, narcissistic ego-gratification and social conditioning were the real determinants of this belief. And, if this belief is really *typical*, if it is really representative of *all* our 'ideological' beliefs, then such factors are the real determinants of *all* ideology.

It is because they believe something like this that so many modern French thinkers hold Marx, Freud, and Nietzsche in such high esteem. Marx, Freud, and Nietzsche have this in common: they see our cherished religious and ethical ideas as reflections of the *irrational*, of class interest (in the case of Marx), of the unconscious (Freud and Nietzsche), of the Will to Power (Nietzsche).[2] Below what we are pleased to regard as our most profound spiritual and moral insights lies a seething cauldron of power drives, economic interests, and selfish fantasies. This is the view that is the cutting edge of relativism today.

At the same time, no relativist can himself use the term 'irrational' in the way I have just used it in describing the relativist view. Such a use is ruled out by relativism itself. When I showed these pages to a relativist friend he was indignant at my statements about the Divine Right of Kings. Was I not aware that intelligent men had been convinced by philosophical arguments

[2] I am not accusing Marx, Freud, or Nietzsche of drawing relativist conclusions from this.

that this doctrine was correct? Was I offering a cheap Marxist or Freudian explanation? Of course, belief in the Divine Right of Kings was *rational!*

My reply to him was that there may be a sense of 'rational' in which any view that can be intelligently and persuasively defended from the shared assumptions of a culture is a 'rational' view, but *that* sense cannot be the only or the normatively important one. The Jews accepted Moses as lawgiver and prophet because his doctrine filled real religious, cultural, and national *needs;* that is not the same thing as being convinced by rational argument. Later, prophets anointed Jewish kings (after trying to dissuade the Jews from having kings at all); that hardly proves that later Christian kings are divinely appointed. Christianity, which shared the Jewish bible, became the religion of the Roman Empire – hardly because the population or the Emperor had rational proof that Christianity was true. Roman emperors were then anointed (as Jewish Kings had been); that hardly proves that they were divinely appointed. Finally, after the assumptions of Christianity had been accepted, one could give 'rational arguments' for the Divine Rights of Kings *from those assumptions.* But to express this by saying that in the late Roman Empire or the Middle Ages, 'belief in the Divine Right of Kings was perfectly rational' is to debase the notion of rationality.

Hegel, who introduced the idea that Reason itself changes in history, operated with two notions of rationality: there is a sense in which what is rational is measured by the level to which Spirit has developed in the historical process at a given time; it is in something like this sense that it is claimed by some that 'belief in the Divine Right of Kings was rational at the time'. And there is a limit notion of rationality in Hegel's system; the notion of that which is destined to be stable, the final self-awareness of Spirit which will not itself be transcended. When present day relativists 'naturalize' Hegel by throwing away the limit-concept of true rationality, they turn the doctrine into a self-defeating cultural relativism.

No relativist wants to be a relativist about *everything* however. How do these French thinkers put limits on their own relativism? The answer varies with the thinker. In the case of a Marxist like Althusser, the answer adopted is a version of the 'class interest' theory: all 'ideologies' are the product of non-rational factors, but those ideologies that are the product of the interests of the working class are (in the present era) 'just', and tend in the direction of human liberation, while those ideologies that spring from the interests of the exploiting class are 'unjust' and produce misery. But Althusser distinguishes himself from previous expounders of this class-relativist view by refusing to say that even Marxist ideology ('working class' ideology) is *true* or *closer to the truth* than bourgeois ideology. Ideologies can be 'just' or 'unjust' according to Althusser, but not true or false.[3] ('True' and 'false' apply, he says, in 'laboratory science', and, presumably, to those ordinary empirical statements that have clear empirical test conditions.) Foucault also seems to be moving towards a class-interest view in his most recent work, although it is hard to be sure. The point of such a view, at least in its radical Althusserian form, is that it seeks to preserve the radical relativist claim that no 'ideology' can be rational while saving the idea that some ideologies (the preferred one – Marxism–Leninism in the case of Althusser) can be good by distinguishing between good and bad or 'just' and 'unjust' ideologies on grounds other than rational acceptability. The idea is that although all ideologies are adopted for irrational or non-rational causes, some non-rational causes (working class interests) are good, and produce good ideologies (by definition?) and some non-rational causes are bad and produce bad ideologies. Instead of judging ideologies by their *reasons* (which are always *rationalizations*) we should judge them by their causes.

This way of limiting one's own relativism is clearly unworkable however. For on what is the judgment based that the victory of 'working class interests' will lead to such manifestly desirable consequences as a world free from war and racism, and not to totalitarianism and imperialism disguised as 'socialism'? If the

---

[3] According to Althusser, 'Philosophical propositions are Theses.'
'Philosophical Theses can be held *negatively* as dogmatic propositions, insofar as they are not susceptible of demonstration in *strict* scientific sense of the term (in which one talks of demonstration in mathematics or in logic), nor of proof in the *strict* scientific sense (in which one talks of proof in the experimental sciences) . . . Philosophical Theses, since they can neither be demonstrated nor scientifically proved, cannot be said to be "true" (demonstrated or proved, as in mathematics and in physics). They can only be said to be "just" ', *Philosophie et Philosophie Spontanee des Savants,* pp. 13–14, Maspero (1967).

answer is that the latter wouldn't be 'true' socialism, or reflect 'true' working class interests, then on what is the judgment based that any particular institution (e.g. the French Communist Party, of which Althusser is a leading member) or policy will promote 'true' working class interests and 'true' socialism? If these beliefs can be rationally justified, then not every ideology is irrational; if they cannot be, then the claim that any institution or policy is 'just' must be as utterly irrational as every other 'ideological' claim is asserted to be. If all human thought about ideological questions is self-serving folly, then thought about which beliefs spring from 'working class interests' and which do not must also be self-serving folly.

Coming back to Foucault, however, and ignoring the signs in Foucault's most recent work that he too is becoming radicalized, his motive for focussing on the cases he chooses is *precisely* to suggest the utterly non-rational (and, in fact, *irrational*) character of the real *reasons* that people have for adopting ideological positions. And the notion of the ideological here is very wide; it is not just Communism, Fascism, Democracy, the Divine Right of Kings, etc., that are under discussion. The belief that someone is 'diseased' and needs a 'cure', the belief that someone is a 'criminal' and should, if possible, be 'rehabilitated', and many, many more of our everyday beliefs are 'ideological' in the sense of these thinkers. Indeed, to the eagle eye of the Marxist sociologist or the French philosopher, almost *every* belief is 'ideological'. Perhaps, 'if I drop this glass, it will break' is ideologically neutral, but little else is.

It may seem that I have missed the real point of what Foucault is saying. His real point, he himself would say, is not that the ideological perspectives of the past were foolish or irrational at all, but rather that all ideology in the very wide sense in which he uses the term, including our present ideology, is culture-relative. He is trying to show us how every culture lives, thinks, sees, makes love, by a set of unconscious guiding assumptions with non-rational determinants. If previous ideologies now seem 'irrational' it is because we judge them by our culture-bound notion of rationality.

What is troubling about Foucault's account is that the determinants he and other French thinkers point to are *irrational by our present lights.* If our present ideology is the product of forces that are irrational *by its own lights,* then it is internally incoherent. The French thinkers are not *just* cultural relativists; they are attacking our present notion of rationality from within, and this is what the reader feels and is troubled by.

Cultural relativism is not a new doctrine at all. Anthropologists have been preaching cultural relativism to us as long as there have been anthropologists. But it would be a mistake to assimilate the relativism of Foucault to the older relativism.

When an anthropologist preaches relativism to us, normally he cites practices and beliefs of an exotic tribe which initially strike us as irrational or repulsive or both, and proceeds to show that these actually promote welfare and social cohesion. In short, he shows (to the extent that the example is a reasonable one) that what is considered wrong or irrational in our society may actually be reasonable and right in different natural and social circumstances.

Of course, the wrong conclusion is frequently drawn by anthropologists from their own examples (and some of the examples are rather less clear than the anthropologist thinks). Very often an anthropologist will say 'it's all relative', meaning that there is no fact of the matter as to what is right and wrong at all. And Richard Boyd has suggested to me that very often the motive is a political one; to convince us to stop destroying primitive cultures by attacking our belief in the superior rationality and morality of our own. Unfortunately, the argument is very confused. The anthropologist's examples (when they are good ones) show that right and wrong, for example, are relative to circumstances, *not* that there is no right and wrong at all, even in specified circumstances. His argument against cultural imperialism amounts to this: other cultures are not objectively worse than ours (because there is no such thing as objective better and worse, according to him); therefore they are *just as good* as *ours;* therefore it is wrong to destroy them.

This argument equivocates. The conclusion requires that 'just as good as' means *objectively* just as good as (at least by our lights); but what follows from the non-existence of objective values cannot be that everything is (in the required sense) 'just as good' as anything else, but rather that there is no such thing as 'just as good as'. If values really *were* arbitrary, then why should we not destroy whatever cultures we please?

Fortunately, there are better grounds for criticizing cultural imperialism than the denial of objective values. The anthropologist's motive may be a good one, but he has chosen the wrong argument. Another term on which he equivocates is the notion of being 'relative'. What his examples actually confirm is Dewey's 'objective relativism'. Certain things are right – *objectively right* – in certain circumstances and wrong – *objectively wrong* – in others, and the culture and the environment constitute relevant circumstances. About this the anthropologist is right. But this is not the same thing as values being 'relative' in the sense of being mere matters of opinion or taste.

Still, freed of its conceptual confusions, the anthropologist's argument should not trouble us. We should welcome his observations, for they tend to widen our sensibilities and attack our smug assumption of cultural superiority. But the very comparison of Foucault's argument with the anthropologist's brings out their difference: Foucault is not arguing that past practices were *more* rational than they look to be, but that all practices are *less* rational, are, in fact, mainly determined by unreason and selfish power. The similarity of this doctrine to the older cultural relativism is a superficial one.

The fact is that the position we have been discussing caters to an intellectual temptation which is the product of our increased knowledge about and sensitivity to psychological and sociological mechanisms. The knowledge and the sensitivity are in part pretense and in part real; the temptation is to fall into the trap of concluding that all rational argument is mere rationalization and then proceeding to try to *argue rationally* for this position.

If *all* 'rational argument' *were* mere rationalization, then not only would it make no sense to try to argue rationally for any view, but it would make no sense to *hold* any view. If I view my own assent and dissent as crazy behavior, then I should stop assenting and dissenting – something to which there can be no rational assent or dissent, only crazy parody of rational discussion, cannot be called a *statement*. Like Sextus Empiricus, who eventually concluded that his own scepticism could not be expressed by a statement (because even the statement, 'I do not know' could not be one he *knew*), the modern relativist, were he consistent (and *how* could one *consistently* hold a doctrine which makes nonsense of the notion of consistency?) should end by regarding his own utterances as mere expression of feeling.

To say this is not to deny that we can rationally and correctly think that *some* of our beliefs are irrational. It is to say that there are limits to how far this insistence that we are all intellectually damned can go without becoming unintelligible. We *do,* for example, *discuss* just such doctrines as those advanced by Foucault; we make an effort to be impartial; we try to adopt what Popper calls 'the critical attitude', and actively to seek evidence and argumentation we might overlook, even when it bears against our own views. None of this would make the slightest sense if we did not think that these practices of discussion and communication, and these virtues of criticism and impartiality tend to weed out irrational beliefs, if not at once, then gradually, over time, and to improve the warranted assertibility of our final conclusions. Rationality may not be defined by a 'canon' or set of principles, *but* we do have an evolving conception of the cognitive virtues to guide us.

It will be objected that this conception does not 'get us very far'. Rudolf Carnap and John Cardinal Newman were both careful and responsible thinkers, and both were committed to the cognitive virtues just mentioned, but no one thinks that one could have convinced the other, had they lived at the same time and been able to meet. But the fact that there is no way to resolve all disputes to everyone's satisfaction does not show that there is no better and worse in such a case. Most of us think that Newman's Catholicism was somewhat obsessive; and most philosophers think that, brilliant as he was, Carnap employed many weak arguments. That we make these judgments shows that we *do* have a regulative idea of a just, attentive, balanced intellect, and we do think that there is a fact of the matter about why and how particular thinkers fall short of that ideal. Some will say, 'So what; we are no better off when it comes to resolving an actual dispute than if there were *no* notion of rational acceptability external to the views under debate to which we could appeal!' This is true when it comes to any one unresolvable dispute such as the Carnap–Newman dispute just imagined; but it is not true that we would be just as well off in the long run if we abandoned the idea that there are really such things as impartiality, consistency, and reasonableness, even if we only approximate them in our lives and practice, and came to the view that there are only subjective beliefs about these things, and no fact of the matter as to which of these 'subjective beliefs' is right.

Perhaps the analogy I have (occasionally) drawn between philosophical discussion and political discussion may be of help. One of my colleagues is a well-known advocate of the view that all government spending on 'welfare' is morally impermissible. On his view, even the public school system is morally wrong. If the public school system were abolished, along with the compulsory education law (which, I believe, he also regards as an impermissible government interference with individual liberty), then the poorer families could not afford to send their children to school and would opt for letting the children grow up illiterate; but this, on his view, is a problem to be solved by private charity. If people would not be charitable enough to prevent mass illiteracy (or mass starvation of old people, etc.) that is very bad, but it does not legitimize government action.

In *my* view, *his* fundamental premises – the absoluteness of the right to property, for example – are counterintuitive and not supported by sufficient argument. On *his* view I am in the grip of a 'paternalistic' philosophy which he regards as insensitive to individual rights. This is an extreme disagreement, and it is a disagreement in 'political philosophy' rather than merely a 'political disagreement'. But much political disagreement involves disagreements in political philosophy, although they are rarely as stark as this.

What happens in such disagreements? When they are intelligently conducted on both sides, sometimes all that can happen is that one sensitively diagnoses and delineates the source of the disagreement. Often, when the disagreement is less fundamental than the one I described, both sides may modify their view to a larger or smaller extent. If actual agreement does not result, perhaps possible compromises may be classed as more or less acceptable to one or another of the parties.

Such intelligent political discussion between people of different outlooks is, unfortunately, rare nowadays; but it is all the more enjoyable when it does happen. And one's attitude toward one's co-disputant in such a discussion is interestingly mixed. On the one hand, one recognizes and appreciates certain intellectual virtues of the highest importance: open-mindedness, willingness to consider reasons and arguments, the capacity to accept good criticisms, etc. But what of the fundamentals on which one cannot *agree?* It would be quite dishonest to pretend that one thinks there are no better and worse reasons and views *here.* I don't think it is just a matter of *taste* whether one thinks that the obligation of the community to treat its members with compassion takes precedence over property rights; nor does my co-disputant. Each of us regards the other as lacking, at this level, a certain kind of sensitivity and perception. To be perfectly honest, there is in each of us something akin to *contempt,* not for the other's *mind* – for we each have the highest regard for each other's minds – nor for the other as a *person* –, for I have more respect for my colleague's honesty, integrity, kindness, etc., than I do for that of many people who agree with my 'liberal' political views – but for a certain complex of emotions and judgments in the other.

But am I not being less than honest here? I say I respect Bob Nozick's mind, and I certainly do. I say I respect his character, and I certainly do. But, if I feel contempt (or something in that ballpark) for a certain complex of emotions and judgments in him, is that not contempt (or something like it) for *him?*

This is a painful thing to explore, and politeness normally keeps us from examining with any justice what exactly our attitudes are towards those whom we love and disagree with. The fact is that none of us who is at all grown up likes and respects *everything* about *anyone* (least of all one's own self). There is no contradiction between having a fundamental liking and respect for someone and still regarding something in him as an intellectual and moral weakness, just as there is no contradiction between having a fundamental liking and respect for oneself and regarding something in oneself as an intellectual and moral (or emotional, etc.) weakness.

I want to urge that there is all the difference in the world between an opponent who has the fundamental intellectual virtues of open-mindedness, respect for reason, and self-criticism, and one who does not; between an opponent who has an impressive and pertinent store of factual knowledge, and one who does not; between an opponent who merely gives vent to his feelings and fantasies (which is all people commonly do in what passes for political discussion), and one who reasons carefully. And the ambivalent attitude of respectful contempt is an honest one: respect for the intellectual virtues in the other; contempt for the intellectual or emotional weaknesses (according to one's own lights, of course, for one always starts with them). 'Respectful contempt' may sound almost *nasty* (especially if one confuses it with contemptuous respect, which is something quite different). And it *would* be nasty if the 'contempt' were for the other as a person, and not just for one complex of feelings and judgments in him. But it is a far more honest attitude than *false relativism;* that is, the pretense that there is no giving reasons, or such a thing as better or worse reasons on a subject, when one really does feel that one view is reasonable and the other is irrational.

It may be helpful to descend from the abstract level at which we have been discussing and consider once more a relatively simple example. Consider the judgment that most ordinary people are prepared to make at most times, that peace is preferable to war. (Such judgments are never discussed by Foucault, just as they are never described by Swift, and for the same reason: both are *satirists.* Only social folly interests them, not – when it exists – social sanity.) There are no doubts about the sources of such a judgment. We are too familiar with the horrors of war, with what war does to adults and children, to combatant and non-combatant, to the very land and foliage. Even if this judgment springs partly from self-interest, that does *not* make it irrational, quite the contrary.

Yet whole populations can make the opposite judgment, that war is preferable to peace, and not for reasons of legitimate self-defense. Aggression and fantasy can whip people up to a national blood thirst. But, again, what this shows is not that *all* value judgments are irrational, but only that some are; and that it is very hard to tell which are which when one is not able to put aside partisanship or criticize one's own beliefs (which is why we assign so much importance to impartiality and the critical attitude among the cognitive virtues).

That some value judgments are rational and objective does not mean that our abstract talk about Capitalism, Democracy,

Socialism, Rights, Autonomy, and so on, is not frequently non-sense. Even when what we mean to say about some general issue is right, frequently we have trouble expressing it well, especially if we are not trained in the expression of abstract ideas. The case of the anthropologist who says there are no objective values when what he means is that values are relative to circumstances is a case in point. Even when we do succeed in expressing what we mean to say effectively, there *are* powerful forces of a non-rational kind tending to sway our judgment. My purpose here is not to deny that power can corrupt our judgment and narcissism seduce it; it is to deny that we are helpless in the face of these powerful forces, so helpless that it would be idle (and in fact, self-deception) to attempt to judge with intelligence and justice. To say we *can* be rational is different from saying we can be infallible. On the contrary, as Iris Murdoch points out, the striving for a reasoned and rational stance is essentially something progressive, something 'infinitely perfectible'.[4]

What I have said so far might, perhaps, be conceded by an intelligent moral relativist. A relativist need not be concerned to undermine the rationality of all 'value' judgments, or to defend Foucault's picture of history as a discontinuous series of 'discourses' or 'ideologies' which succeed one another for no rational reason. A more modest relativist might be happy to agree with Dewey[5] that some values are objectively relative – i.e. rational *given the circumstances,* the nature and history, of those who make them. What is important, such a modest relativist maintains, is precisely the *relativity* of all values. The 'objectivity' he is denying is not the objectivity Dewey was affirming, which is simply the objectivity of any judgment that is warranted in its actual existential setting, but it is rather the objectivity a Plato would affirm, the spurious objectivity (the relativist would say) that purports to speak from an absolute point of view, apart *from* all circumstances and valid *for* all circumstances.

If we are not content to accept such a modest relativism, if we feel troubled by Dewey's own ethical writings, it is not, I think, because we really do hanker for Absolutes. When I claim that

---

[4] *The Sovereignty of Good,* p. 23.
[5] See Dewey's Theory of Valuation, in *The Encyclopedia of Unified Science,* vol. II, no. 4, University of Chicago (1939).

the murder and suffering of innocent people is wrong, I do not, I think, really care about the question whether this judgment would be valid for a being of a *totally* alien constitution and psychology. If there are beings on, say, Alpha Centauri, who cannot feel pain and who do not mind individual death, then very likely our fuss about 'murder and suffering' will seem to them to be much ado about nothing. But the very alienness of such a life form means that they cannot understand the moral issues involved. If our 'objectivity' is objectivity humanly speaking, it is still objectivity enough.

What *is* of concern is that Dewey's doctrine of 'objective relativism' cannot handle the case of the Nazi (although Dewey would have disputed this). We want to say that the Nazi's goals were deeply wrong; and the claim that 'this is true relative to your interests and false relative to the Nazi's interests' is just the kind of 'moral relativism' we find repulsive. Objective relativism seems the *right* doctrine for many moral cases; but not for cases where rights and duties are manifest and sharp and the choice seems to us to be between right and wrong, good and evil.

Indeed, there is a sense in which the modern instrumental notion of rationality is itself 'objective relativist'. The core of this notion is a deceptively simple dichotomy: the idea is that the choice of 'ends' or 'goals' is *neither rational nor irrational* (provided some minimal consistency requirements are met); while the choice of means is *rational to the extent that it is efficient*. Rationality is a predicate of means, not ends, and it is totally conflated with efficiency. Thus, Jones' preference for vanilla over chocolate ice cream is neither rational or irrational, but the action of choosing vanilla over chocolate on a particular occasion would be rational for Jones, given his 'preference ordering'. This conception, which goes back to Hume's dictum that 'reason is and ought to be the slave of the passions', and which deeply influenced Bentham, is widely assumed to be the right one by modern social scientists. It has played a role in welfare economics and in many other areas. The modern economist's notion of a *Pareto optimum* is an attempt to have a notion of economic optimality which considers only efficiency of means, and involves no 'value judgments' concerning the goals of the various economic agents; this notion is of contemporary interest precisely *because* the assumption is made that the choice of means is subject to rational criticism, while the choice of ends is not.

This whole conception loses much of its persuasive appeal, however, when we see what an oversimplified psychological theory it rests upon. In the Benthamite scheme, goals, ends, preferences are treated either as fixed individual parameters (i.e. the individual's learning is pictured as a process of learning to better estimate consequences and probable consequences of actions and to attain ends more efficiently, but not as a process of acquiring new ends) or as individual parameters which, if not actually *fixed,* change only as a result of factors which have no rational status and which the theorist cannot take account of.

Bernard Williams[6] has pointed out that there are a number of ways in which an individual's goals, and not just the means he chooses to attain them, can be rationally criticized; ways which become apparent the moment we pass beyond this narrow 'Benthamite' psychology.

The 'Benthamite' conception does allow *one* case in which an individual can be persuaded to abandon a goal (or, at any rate, to abandon *pursuit* of the goal) by rational criticism: this is the case in which he had misestimated consequences in the direction of badly underestimating the *costs* of attaining the goal (relative to other goals he has). This opens the door to a question which has to do as much with imagination as with propositional intelligence: the question of what it would *actually be like,* experientially, to attain the goal. Many human beings pursue goals they would not actually enjoy attaining or would not enjoy nearly as long or nearly as much as they think. Even within a Benthamite framework, it would be possible to improve the account of rational decision making by taking into account the possibility of misestimating the actual existential *feel* of various goals. And this begins to introduce a sense in which goals themselves can be criticized as irrational, and not just means.

Again, people often *overlook* goals they might pursue if they thought of them. Or, even if they think of them (or someone suggests them) they may lack the imagination (imagination again!) to visualize what the attainment of these goals would

---

[6] I am here summarizing a lecture titled 'Internal and External Reasons', given at Harvard, Nov. 1978.

really be like – all the more if these goals are long-term traits of character, such as developing an appreciation of poetry. The man who prefers pushpin to poetry may not actually be able to imagine what it would be like to have a developed sensitivity to the nuances of real poetry, and if his intelligence could be raised or his imagination improved he might be brought to see that he is making a *mistake*.

It is significant that the ability to rationally criticize one's own goals (and those of others) may depend just as much on one's imagination as on one's ability to accept true statements and disbelieve false ones. And it is significant that one's goal may be a long-term trait of mind or character, and not a thing or event.

There are still further ways besides misestimating the real experiential significance of one's goals or of possible alternative goals in which one may make errors in the choice of goals. Williams points out (reviving an observation that goes back to Aristotle) that very often a goal is *general* (e.g. 'having a good time this evening') and the problem is not so much to find a *means* to the 'end', but to find an overall pattern of activity that will constitute an acceptable *specification* of the goal (e.g. 'going to a movie' or 'staying home and reading a book'). Whether one can think of creative and novel specifications of one's goal or only of commonplace and banal specifications will depend again on imagination and not just propositional intelligence.

The problem, as Williams pointed out, is that even if one replaces the narrow Benthamite psychology with an account that does justice to all of these things, one still seems to be left with a certain relativism. Williams' example was a hypothetical case of a young man whose father wished him to undertake a military career. The old man appeals to family traditions (the males have been army officers for generations) and patriotism, but in vain. Even when the young man makes as vivid to himself as he can what it would be like to be an army officer, there is nothing in this goal which appeals to him. It just is not *his* end; and not because of some failure of intelligence or imagination.

Even the case of the Nazi could be like this. Suppose the Nazis had won the war, so that we could not appeal to Germany's defeat as a practical reason for not being a Nazi. Perhaps some Nazis were simply lacking in knowledge of the actual consequences of Nazism, the suffering brought about, and so on. Perhaps some Nazis would not have been Nazis if they had had the intelligence and imagination to appreciate these consequences, or to appreciate more vividly the alternative life, the life of a good man. But doubtless many Nazis would still have been Nazis, because they did not care about the suffering their actions caused and because no matter how vivid they might make the alternative life seem to their imaginations, it would no more speak to anything in them than the military life did to the young man in Bernard Williams' story. There is no end *in them* to which we can appeal, neither an actual end or even a potential one, one which they would come to realize if they were more intelligent and more imaginative. Even without 'Benthamite psychology', we are faced again with the problem of moral relativism.

Let us consider a case less inflammatory than the Nazi case. Imagine a society of farmers who, for some reason, have a total disinterest in the arts, in science (except in such products as assist them in farming), in religion, in short, in everything spiritual or cultural. (I don't mean to suggest that actual peasant societies are or ever have been like this.) These people need not be imagined as being *bad* people; imagine them as cooperative, pacific, reasonably kind to one another, if you like. What I wish the reader to imagine is that their *interests* are limited to such minimal goals as getting enough to eat, warm shelter, and such simple pleasures as getting drunk together in the evenings. In short, imagine them as living a relatively 'animal' existence, and as not wishing to live any other kind of existence.

Such people are not *immoral*. There is nothing impermissible about their way of life. But our natural tendency (unless we are entranced with Ethical Relativism) is to say that their way of life is in some way contemptible. It is totally lacking in what Aristotle called 'nobility'. They are living the lives of swine – amiable swine, perhaps, but still swine, and a pig's life is no life for a man.

At the same time – and this is the rub – we are disinclined to say the pig-men are in any way *irrational*. This may be the result of our long acculturation in the Benthamite use of 'rational' and 'irrational', but, be that as it may, it is our present disposition. The lives of the pig-men are not as *good* as they might be, we want to say, but they are not *irrational*.

We do not want to say that it is just a matter of *taste* whether one lives a better or worse life. We don't see how we can say that it is *rational* to choose the better life and *irrational* to choose the worse. Yet *not* saying some such things seems *precisely* to be saying that 'it's all relative'; the ground crumbles beneath our feet.

Perhaps some of the corrections to Benthamite psychology suggested by Bernard Williams will help with *this* case. Let us assume the pig-men are born with normal human *potential* (if they aren't, then their lives *aren't* 'worse than they might be', and we are not justified in feeling contempt, but only, at most, pity). Then they might be led to appreciate artistic, scientific, and spiritual aspects of life; to live more truly human lives, so to speak. And if any of them did this, they would doubtless *prefer* those lives (even though they might be less *fun*) to the lives they are now living. People who live swinish lives feel *shame* when they come to live more human lives; people who live more human lives do not feel *ashamed that they did* when they sink into swinishness. These facts give one grounds for thinking that the pig-men are making the sort of error, the sort of *cognitive* short-fall, that Williams discussed; grounds for thinking that they have *overlooked* alternative goals, and certainly grounds for thinking that they have never made vivid to themselves what realization of those alternative goals would be like. In short, one cannot really say that they have *chosen* the worse life; for they never had an adequate conception of the better.

While this might give us a handle on the notion that *those* peoples' lives are open to rational criticism, it is not evident how to apply it to the case of the Nazi. (One could make it a tautology that anyone who doesn't actually *choose* the better life hasn't 'adequately conceived' it; but such a maneuver would clearly be no help.) Even in the case of the pig-men, if they were *ideologically fanatic* pig-men, as opposed to mere pig-men, then our point about the direction of shame might not hold. There might not, in such a case, be any end that is *theirs,* even latently, to which we could appeal.

Our reluctance to accuse the pig-men of a defect in *reason* (unless we can point to some end that is *theirs,* at least latently, which they are failing to achieve) is the product of the recent vicissitudes of the notion of reason in our culture, as is easy to establish. For neither ancient philosophers nor the medievals saw anything strange about saying that if *A* is a *better* life than *B* then that fact is a *reason*, the best possible reason, for *choosing A* over *B*. We have lost the ability to see how the goodness of an end can make it *rational* to choose that end.

Of course, this is very largely explained by the fact that we don't regard 'goodness' as anything objective. But now we are confronted with a circle, or rather two curves. There is the modern circle: the instrumentalist conception of rationality supports the claim that the goodness of an end doesn't particularly make it irrational *not* to choose that end, or to choose an end which is downright bad, which in turn supports the claim that goodness and badness are not objective, which in turn supports the claim that the instrumentalist notion of rationality is the only intelligible one. And there is the traditional arch: reason is a faculty which chooses ends on the basis of their *goodness* (as opposed to the 'passions', which try to dictate ends on the basis of the appetites; or 'inclination'); a claim which supports the view that it is *rational* to choose the good, which in turn supports the claim that goodness and badness are objective. Clearly we cannot simply go back to the ancient or medieval world-view, whatever conservatives might wish; but is the Benthamite circle really the only alternative left to us?

8

The impact of science on modern conceptions of rationality

If the discussion that we have reviewed – and it is a discussion that has been going on for many decades – seems inconclusive, it is perhaps because the discussion always assumes a kind of priority of rationality over goodness. The question is always whether there is any sense in which it can be called *irrational* to choose a bad end, as if goodness were on trial and rationality were the judge. To assume this stance, especially when one's assumptions about rationality are a largely unexamined collection of cultural myths and prejudices, is to prejudge the question of the status of value judgments in advance. In the remainder of this essay I propose to reverse the terms of the comparison and to ask not how rational is goodness, but why is it good to be rational? Asking what value rationality itself has will both force us to become clearer about the nature of rationality itself and about the assumptions we are prone to make concerning rationality and may enable us to see what is wrong with the way we think about the former question.

Let us recall that when Max Weber introduced the modern fact–value distinction, his argument against the objectivity of value judgments was precisely that it is not possible to establish the truth of a value judgment to the satisfaction of *all possible rational persons*.[1] From the very beginning it was the impossi-

[1] Cf. especially 'Die Objektivität sozialwissenschaftlicher Erkenntnis', in *Archiv für Sozialwiss. und Sozialpolitik*, vol. 19 (1904), pp. 24–87, and 'Der Sinn der Wertfreiheit der soziologischen und ökonomischen Wissenschaften', in *Logos*, VII (1917), pp. 49–88 and 'Wissenschaft als Beruf', Vortrag, 1919. All three texts were reprinted in *The Methodology of the Social Sciences*, Glencoe, Illinois, 1949.

bility, or alleged impossibility, of rational proof that cast value judgments into a somewhat suspect light. Rationality has been putting value on trial for a long time. And in this context, rationality always means scientific rationality;[2] it is the results of 'positive science' that are said to be such that they can be established to the satisfaction of all rational persons. One reason for valuing rationality is obvious. Scientific rationality undeniably aids us in achieving various practical goals. While few educated people would subscribe to the view that we ought to pursue science solely for the sake of technological success, there is no doubt that the technological success of science is overwhelming in the most literal sense of the word. We live in an apparently endless

[2] K. O. Apel reads Weber as I do in 'The Common Presuppositions of Hermeneutics and Ethics: Types of Rationality Beyond Science and Technology', *Research in Phenomenology*, No. IX, 1979. Thus Apel writes (p. 36):

> Max Weber, however, also proposed a strictly negative answer with regard to my question as to possible types of rationality beyond value-free science and technology. And this answer has become paradigmatic, I suggest, for the present system of Western ideology. Weber restricted the scope of methodical understanding to 'value-free' understanding which he centered around the 'ideal type' of 'purposive–rational understanding' of 'purposive–rational actions'. Now 'purposive–rational actions' may also be called 'instrumental actions'; and in those cases where these actions are successful, they may be analyzed or reconstructed as being based on successful transpositions of the if–then-rules of nomological science into the if–then-rules of technological prescriptions. Hence Max Weber thus restricted the business of methodical understanding to the attempt of grasping the (value-free) *technological means–ends-rationality* beyond the human actions. And it is this idea of *instrumental rationality* which indeed constituted Weber's paradigm of rationality in a restrictive sense.
>
> It has to be pointed out, though, that for a *purposive–rational understanding* in sociology it is not necessary to fulfill the maximal requirement of making sure that the agent succeeded in transposing nomological rules into his technological maxims about means–ends-relations. In order to understand his actions in the light of that type of instrumental rationality, it is enough to make sure that it was rational for the agent to act as he did under the presupposition of *his* aims and *his* beliefs about means or ways or strategies as being suited to reaching his aims. Thus it becomes the empiric–hermeneutic business of understanding to hypothetically find out and verify those goal-intentions and means-beliefs on the side of the agent, in the light of which his actions can be understood as being rational in the sense of technological means–ends rationality.

series of technological revolutions – 'the Industrial Revolution', 'the Electronic Revolution' – which constantly remind us how momentous a force science is in shaping our lives. Even before the Industrial Revolution the apparently unique success of Newtonian physics impressed a number of minds. For example, when the notion of 'progress' first began to be discussed in the seventeenth century, the progressivists clinched their case with the claim that 'Newton knew more than Aristotle.' No one could argue convincingly that Shakespeare is a better dramatist than any of the ancient tragedians, or a better poet than Homer; but it seemed undeniable that the scientist Newton had made a real and undeniable advance in knowledge upon the scientist Aristotle.

Although the encyclopedists and others were quick to generalize the notion of progress from science to political institutions and morality, that generalization has appeared as dubious to the twentieth century as it appeared evident to the nineteenth.

Auguste Comte built a philosophy, positivism, celebrating the success of science. History, as Comte tells it, is a success story: we start with primitive myths, these become refined and purified until eventually the high religions appear, the high religions in turn give way to the metaphysical theories of a Plato or a Kant, and finally in our own day metaphysics itself has to give way to 'positive science'. Evidently, there is no doubt who the hero of this success story is: the hero is Science. And if what impressed the Few about science from the start was its stunning intellectual success, there is no doubt that what has impressed the Many is its overwhelming material and technological success. We are impressed by this even when it threatens our very lives.

One reason, then, for doubting that value judgments have any cognitive status is that they cannot be 'verified by the methods of science', as it gets put over and over again. Then too there is the fact, that we have already seen play a central role in Foucault's discussion, that one cannot get universal, or even majority, agreement on ethical matters. Whether abortion is right or wrong or whether homosexuality is right or wrong do not seem to be questions on which some answer can be demonstrated to everyone's satisfaction; whereas it is widely believed that the correctness of a scientific theory can be demonstrated to everyone's satisfaction. The very rationality of science itself is sometimes thought to consist, or to consist in part, in the fact that at least the predictions of science can be publicly demonstrated; that everyone can be brought to agree that these results do obtain, that the phenomena predicted by the theory do occur. Of course there is a threat of circularity here: if we *identify* rational procedures as those which lead to conclusions on which we can get majority assent, then Weber's argument, even if correct, that in ethical matters one cannot get the consent of all rational people, would mean that one cannot get consent of all those who use methods which are guaranteed to produce the assent of the majority or the overwhelming majority. That is, the way in which we determine that value judgments cannot be verified to the satisfaction of all *rational* people is simply by observing that they cannot be verified to the satisfaction of the overwhelming majority of *all* people. It is not, after all, as if we had a *test* for rationality; Weber's formulation suggests that somehow we first take a headcount of those members of the population who are rational and then see whether or not they can all be brought to agree on whether or not some value judgment is true. But nothing like this really goes on. All that Weber's examples (Chinese Mandarins and so on) really show is that value judgments cannot be verified to the satisfaction of all educated people or all intelligent people (which is by no means the same thing as all *rational* people). In a disguised form Weber's argument is a Majoritarian argument; he is appealing to the fact that we can get the agreement of educated people on 'positive science' whereas we cannot get such an agreement on ethical values. It is interesting to contrast this stance with Aristotle's: Aristotle said that of course in ethics we should always try to get the agreement of the Many, but very often we know that realistically we cannot. Sometimes, elitist as it sounds to present day ears to say it, we are only able to convince the wise; and of course we have to rely on our own judgment to tell who are and who are not the wise.

Of course it is not really true that one can get overwhelming agreement on the truth of an arbitrary accepted scientific theory. The fact is that most people are woefully ignorant of science and many theories, especially in the exact sciences, require so much mathematics for their comprehension that most people are not even capable of understanding them. While this is of course conceded, to most people it does not seem to affect the point. For, according to the watered-down operationism which seems to have become the working philosophy of most scientists, the content of the scientific theory consists in testable consequences, and these can be expressed by statements of the form *if we perform such and such actions, then we will get such and such observable results*. Statements of this form, if true, can be demonstrated to be true by repeating the appropriate experiment often enough. It is true that there are many difficulties with this account: experiments are much harder to design, perform, and evaluate than the layman may think. But there is no doubt that as a matter of fact it has been possible to achieve widespread agreement on the experimental adequacy of certain theories in the exact sciences. The layman's acceptance of these theories may be a matter of his deference to experts, but at least the experts seem to be in agreement.

Intellectually, of course, Instrumentalism does not simply in and of itself constitute a tenable conception of rationality. No doubt scientific results have enormous practical value; but, as we have already said, no educated person thinks that science is valuable solely for the sake of its practical applications. And even if science were valued solely for the sake of its applications, why should *rationality* be valuable solely for the sake of applications? To be sure it is of value to have an instrument that helps us select efficient means for the attainment of our various ends; but it is also valuable to know what ends we should choose. It is not surprising that the truth of value judgments cannot be 'rationally demonstrated' if 'rational verification' is by definition limited to the establishment of means–ends connections. But why should we have such a narrow conception of rationality in the first place?[3]

---

[3] Attributing just such a narrow conception of rationality to Weber, Apel writes (*loc. cit.*, p. 37):

> This issue of Weber's methodology of 'understanding' was in perfect accordance with his (more or less implicit) philosophy of history. For in the context of his own reconstruction of the history of Western civilization, he started out from the heuristic hypothesis that at least this part of history could be conceived of as a continuous progress of 'rationalization' and at the same time, as a process of disillusionment or, as he liked to say, 'disenchant-

Majoritarianism is also intenable. To be sure it is nice to get agreement on what one takes to be true. And it is always nice to avoid conflict with one's fellows. But people have lived for centuries with the uncomfortable knowledge that on some matters one has to rely on one's judgment even when it differs from the judgment of the majority. Many have gloried in relying on their judgment when it differed from the judgment of the majority. The idea that on some matters, ethical matters among them, the considerations to be weighed are just so complex, and so imprecise, that we cannot hope to rely on anything like scientific proof or scientific definitions but have to rely on perception and judgment is an old one. And it is plausible that one of the highest manifestations of rationality should be the ability to judge correctly in precisely those cases where one cannot hope to 'prove' things to the satisfaction of the majority. It seems strange indeed that the fact that some things should be impossible to prove to everyone's satisfaction should become an argument for the irrationality of beliefs about those things.[4]

Even if these conceptions are intellectually weak however, it seems to be the case that both Instrumentalism and Majoritarianism are powerfully appealing to the contemporary mind. The contemporary mind likes demonstrable success; and the contemporary mind is uncomfortable with the very notions of judgment and wisdom. I am not a sociologist, and I will not attempt to explore the question why industrial society, in both its capi-

ment' ['Entzäuberung']. By 'rationalization' he understood the progress in putting into force means–end-rationality in all sectors of the socio-cultural system, especially in the sphere of economics and bureaucratic administration, under the constant influence of the progress in science and technology. By the process of 'disillusionment' or 'disenchantment,' on the other hand, Weber understood, among other things, the dissolution of a commonly accepted religious or philosophical value-order or world-view. And he was prepared to draw practical consequences from this development for his personal world-view in so far as he suggested that a rigorous and sincere thinker had to accept the following insight: Human progress in the sense of 'rationalization' has its complement in giving up the idea of a rational assessment of last values or norms in favor of taking recourse to ultimate pre-rational decisions of conscience in face of a pluralism, or, as Weber said, 'polytheism' of last norms or values.

[4] Indeed, we saw in Chapter 5 that the consensus theory of rational acceptability is self-refuting!

talist and its socialist versions, should be so taken with the themes of instrumental success and majority consent. But doubtless the sociological fact has something to do with the ever increasing prominence of the conception that rationality equals scientific rationality, and the conception of scientific rationality as itself based on the demonstration of instrumental connections to the (potential) satisfaction of the overwhelming majority.

If the conception of rationality we have just described, the conception of rationality as consisting in methods (whose nature is usually left rather vague) which, whatever their nature, result in the discovery of effective means/ends connections and the establishment of these connections 'publicly', is not as it stands intellectually tenable, philosophical attempts to make it respectable have not been lacking. One of these attempts grows out of the older empiricism of Locke, Berkeley and Hume. By the time of Mill this empiricism had solidified into what philosophers call phenomenalism: that is the doctrine that all we can really talk about are *sensations*. Even everyday objects, e.g. tables and chairs, are really just sets of objective regularities in actual and possible human sensations, on this conception. As Mill put it, physical objects are 'permanent possibilities of sensation'. Another way to put the same idea is to say that all talk that appears to be about the physical world, or whatever, is really just highly derived talk about sensations.

The virtue of this point of view, in the eyes of its holders, was that it enabled them to say clearly what the content was, not only of science, but of all cognitively meaningful talk whatsoever. Any scientific theory is really just an 'economical' way of stating a number of facts of the form: *if you perform such and such actions, then you will have such and such experiences*. The holder of this view does not have to defend the untenable claim that scientists are interested only in applications, or only in the attainment of practical goals, and disinterested in knowledge for its own sake. The phenomenalist does not have to deny that we want to know the nature of black holes, that we want to know whether or not there was a Big Bang, what the true origin of homo-sapiens was, etc. We do want to know all these things and not just because knowing them might enable us to build better machines. But knowing these things is, although it takes refined philosophical analysis to show it, just knowing a great many facts of the form *if you perform such and such actions, then you will have such and such experiences.* Whatever our reason for being interested in them, *all facts are ultimately instrumental.* At the same time, there seems to be no way of making out the claim that to call something good is to make any prediction of the form: *if you perform such and such actions then you will have such and such experiences.* Thus statements about the goodness or badness of anything have no cognitive meaning on this conception; in the words of the twentieth-century Logical Empiricists such statements are purely 'emotive'. Phenomenalism came to grief on two points, however. In the first place the claim that statements about material objects are translatable into statements about actual and possible sensations seems as a matter of fact to be false. Careful logical investigation of this claim, starting with the work of Carnap and the Vienna Circle in the 1930s, convinced the phenomenalists themselves that the claim was unfounded. Scientific theories as a whole undoubtedly lead us to expect that we will have certain experiences if we perform certain actions; but the idea that the statements of science are translatable one by one into statements about what experiences we will have if we perform certain actions has now been given up as an unacceptable kind of reductionism. In the second place sensations are necessarily private objects; although we may be able in practice to decide whether or not someone had a sensation by simply asking them, we are immediately in some kind of epistemological trouble if someone raises the question 'how do you know that the person associates the same sensations with his descriptions that you do?' If the content of science consists in predictions about what sensations any rational being will have if that rational being performs certain actions, then to know what that content itself means we would have to be able to tell, for example, whether extraterrestrials if we encounter any, have the same sensations that we do or not, etc. For this reason, philosophers like Rudolph Carnap and Sir Karl Popper insisted that the observational predictions of science should be stated in the form *if anyone performs such and such actions, then such and such publicly observable events will take place* – where both the actions to be performed and the observable events that should be expected must be described in terms of 'public' objects, e.g. meter readings, and not in terms of such private objects as sensations.

To sum up, the older empiricism, or phenomenalism, seemed to provide us with a tidy criterion of cognitive significance: a statement is cognitively significant if it is translatable into a statement about sensations. But it turned out that either the notion of 'translation' is hopelessly vague, or else that statements of science itself failed to satisfy this criterion of cognitive significance. The trouble with drawing a sharp line between factual statements and value judgments on the grounds that the former but not the latter are 'translatable' into statements about sensations is that the alleged translatability of the first class of statements has not been, and apparently cannot be, demonstrated. Empiricist reductionism drew a sharp line between the factual and the evaluational, but at the price of giving a wholly distorted picture of the factual.

Our original purpose, however, was to consider answers to the question 'why is it good to be rational?' The first answer we considered, and rejected as too narrow, was that rationality enables us to discover reliable means/ends connections. Phenomenalism came into the story because if phenomenalism were true then the apparent conflict between being interested in a scientific theory for the sake of its instrumental consequences, and being interested in the theory in order to learn what it tells us about natural processes would dissolve. The conflict between instrumental interests and purely theoretical interests could in a sense be finessed. Of course there would still be some kind of difference between these interests; but even purely theoretical interests would be interests in facts which, in the ultimate logical analysis, would have been revealed to be of an instrumental nature. *All* knowledge worthy of the name would have been shown to be knowledge of means/ends connections; it is just that when we are interested in the means/ends connection because we hope to exploit it for the attainment of some goal, then we call our interests 'practical', and when we are interested in knowing the means/ends connection out of pure curiosity then we call it a theoretical interest. This attempt to reduce all the statements of science to statements of the form *if you perform action A then you will get result B* has, as we remarked, failed.

The contention of Carnap and Popper, that the observation statements of science are couched in physical thing language and not in sensation language, is obviously correct if taken as a generalization about the practice of scientists. When it is erected into an epistemological absolute, however, its import becomes rather momentous. For one thing, if no observation statement at all is allowed to talk about sensations, then introspection is ruled out as a mode of scientific observation. Although many psychologists would agree that it should be ruled out, the fact is that some psychologists, undeterred by both philosophical and psychological dogma, have gone on performing experiments which involve at least in part reliance on introspective reports. In fact, Carnap would not have been as dogmatic in prohibiting this as some behaviorist psychologists were; he would have permitted the use of sensation reports, provided that they were construed not as observation reports but as behavioral data, the 'behavior' being the making of the verbal reports themselves. But what it means to construe the acceptance of an introspective report as an 'inference from verbal behavior' is not altogether clear. Even in the case of reports which are not about sensations but about physical objects, e.g. 'there is a table in front of me', we do not normally accept the report unless we have some theory according to which the person was in a position to observe the fact that he reports. In this sense it is a part of our whole demand for coherence in our world picture that observations should themselves be theoretically explainable; if someone claims to have observed that there was a table in a certain place by *clairvoyance* we do not accept this 'observation report' because it does not cohere with our total body of theory. In this sense *every* observation report has some component which could be described as 'inferential'. On the other hand, when, say, a doctor accepts the report of a patient that the patient feels pain, it is hard to know on the basis of what 'scientific theory' the doctor infers that the patient feels pain from the patient's verbal report; if the general assumption that people are in a good position to tell whether or not they have a pain counts as a theory, then the general assumption that people are in a good position to tell whether or not there is a table in front of them also counts as a theory; but it is hard to see that there is any fundamental methodological difference between accepting someone's say so that there was a table in front of them and accepting someone's say so that they had a pain.

Popper and Carnap would reply that the methodological difference is that the former statement but not the latter is publicly checkable; but they both exaggerate the extent to which observation reports about physical objects are always publicly checkable. Many such reports are made with the aid of instruments which it takes a good deal of training to use. (It is notorious that learning to 'see' through a very high-powered microscope requires a good deal of specialized training and skill and that not everyone is capable of acquiring the skill.) What accepting this epistemological dogma does is make it a part of the definition of rationality that rational beliefs are capable of being *publicly* checked. Making it part of the definition of rationality is very convenient; it makes it unnecessary to provide any argument for this contention. Perhaps the argument is, at bottom, that whatever is not publicly checkable may become a matter of disagreement, and that wherever there is unsettleable disagreement there is no being right or wrong. But this would assume what I have called Majoritarianism, that is the idea that it is built into the very notion of rationality that what is rationally verifiable is verifiable to the satisfaction of the overwhelming majority.

The fact that Logical Empiricism was fundamentally a sophisticated expression of the broad cultural tendencies to instrumentalism and majoritarianism becomes evident, I think, in the later history of this movement. Although the Logical Empiricists had abandoned phenomenalism as early as 1936, for the next twenty years, that is until the movement began to break up and disappear as a recognizable philosophical tendency, Logical Empiricist philosophers of science were fond of talking about 'the aim of science' and fond of identifying the aim of science with *prediction* (with some additions and qualifications which I shall discuss in a moment). The idea that the aim of science is prediction was the fundamental idea of positivism from its beginnings in the writings of Auguste Comte. As we saw, this idea had at least some kind of serious philosophical rationale as long as phenomenalism was in vogue; for then one could argue that all cognitively meaningful statements were predictions in disguise, or infinite sets of predictions in disguise. The reappearance of this doctrine, after the disappearance of phenomenalism, is like the appearance of 'primitive' material in a patient's associations in therapy, after the 'defenses' have been stripped away. To say that the aim of science is successful prediction (or successful prediction plus something simply described as 'simplicity'), seems dangerously close to saying that science is pursued only for practical goals; and this is something that no philosopher has wanted to be put in the position of maintaining. Indeed, the philosophers who defended a purely instrumentalist conception of science did so not because they were themselves worshippers of the practical, or narrow minded men who could not appreciate the beauty of abstract scientific knowledge for its own sake, but they did so rather because they felt that by identifying what is 'cognitively significant' with what has value for the making of predictions they could once and for all rule out all forms of obscurantism and metaphysics. 'Metaphysics' was for these philosophers simply another name for various kinds of transcendental speculation; it was religious and 'metaphysical' speculations (in their sense of 'metaphysical') that they were afraid of.

I am suggesting that the appearance in the culture of a philosophical tendency which was hypnotized by the success of science to such an extent that it could not conceive of the possibility of knowledge and reason outside of what we are pleased to call the sciences is something that was to be expected given the enormously high prestige that science has in the general culture, and given the declining prestige of religion, absolute ethics, and transcendental metaphysics. And I am suggesting that the high prestige of science *in the general culture* is very much due to the enormous instrumental success of science, together with the fact that science seems free from the interminable and unsettleable debates that we find in religion, ethics and metaphysics.

Since, however, the professional philosophers who, as it were, rationalized the instrumentalist tendency in the culture were not themselves vulgar-minded or purely practical persons, it is not surprising that they themselves felt inclined to widen the description of 'the aim of science' somewhat, so as more explicitly to leave room for aims other than just successful prediction. And so we find other aims being listed by Logical Empiricist writers in the 1940s and 1950s: the discovery of laws, retrodiction (i.e.

the prediction of past as opposed to future events), and the discovery of 'explanations', by which these writers meant simply the deduction of predictions and retrodictions from laws.

What happened here is interesting. In order to make it explicit that science is interested in discovering laws of nature for their own sake, and not merely for the sake of the predictions to which those laws lead, these writers replaced the simple formula 'the aim of science is successful prediction' with a *list*. The list is in fact open-ended: laws of nature turn out to include not only laws of nature in the strict sense, i.e. statements which it is physically impossible to falsify, but also the so-called 'laws' of evolutionary theory, which are really descriptions of general tendencies which may at some time, owing to the action of intelligent life, cease to hold, and even statements about the purely contingent dispositions of individual groups and even individual organisms. To say that scientists are trying to discover 'laws of nature', including physically contingent generalizations which hold for long periods of time and which have wide explanatory significance, such as those upon which evolutionary theory is based, or those upon which the science of economics is based, and seek to discover significant truths concerning the dispositions of groups and individual organisms, and seek to organize all of these into a deductive (and inductive) structure, is, of course, quite correct. But why this particular list?

The reason for the list is that it is thought to be embracing enough to include all of the kinds of truths that scientists seek to discover, certainly in physical science, and narrow enough not to include any of the objectionable ('cognitively insignificant') material. The old search for a 'criterion of cognitive significance', such as 'a sentence is meaningful if and only if it is possible to verify or falsify it', has been replaced by a list of types of statements, such that a statement is to be admitted if it is of one of these types and otherwise to be rejected. But why was this at all a plausible move for a philosopher to make? Even if it is true that all of the statements in the disciplines that we call 'sciences' are of these types (and it is not at all clear that this is the case – is historical explanation really just subsumption of retrodictions under 'laws'?), does it follow that the verification of these types of statements and just these types of statements is the aim of reason itself, and not just the aim of the special applications of reason that we call the sciences? The answer, of course, is that these philosophers did not seriously doubt that 'science' exhausts reason. But why did they not doubt this? They did not doubt this because for them the opposition was not between science, in the sense of knowledge proceeding by essentially the methods of the empirical and mathematical sciences, and informal reason, proceeding by methods which might be adapted to interests different than those of the sciences, but no less capable of having genuine standards. Rather the opposition was between knowledge proceeding by the methods of the sciences, and pseudo knowledge pretending to proceed by revelation, or some kind of funny transcendental faculties. Reason had to be co-extensive with science because *What Else Could It Be?* Nevertheless the claim of these philosophers that reason is co-extensive with science landed them in some peculiar predicaments. Since they did not wish to deny that there is such a thing as historical knowledge, for example, they were committed to the position that history is a science, and even to the position that what the historian is really trying to do is to subsume individual statements about the past under *laws* – a claim about history that seems false on the face of it.

It is, perhaps, not surprising that the Logical Empiricist tendency began to disintegrate by 1950. We have been looking at this tendency solely from the point of view of one question; the Logical Empiricists had a great many different philosophical interests, and they made many valuable contributions. Nevertheless, from the point of view of the question we have been asking, which is 'what good is rationality?', the Logical Empiricist movement represented a reasoned philosophical defense of the view that the answer, and the sole answer, to the question is that rationality is good for the discovery of means/ends connections. The philosophical doctrine of phenomenalism provided the Logical Empiricists with an interesting philosophical defense of this claim. When the phenomenalism was given up, and the philosophical *defense* of the claim was replaced by the bare claim, and even more when the bare claim was made more 'reasonable' by allowing exceptions, modifications, etc., the whole cutting power of the movement disappeared. The trouble with the position that the aims of reason itself are the discovery of predictions, retrodictions, laws of nature, and the systematization of all of these, and that these are *all* the aims of reason, is that there is simply no reason to believe it, I don't mean to say that there is reason to believe that it is false; if the notion of a law of nature is widened so that the discovery of laws of nature includes the discovery of dispositional statements about individual organisms, and the notion of a disposition is so wide (or so vague) that the statement that a certain scientist is envious of his colleague's reputation counts as a statement of a 'disposition', and the statement that that scientist told a certain joke because he was jealous of his colleague's reputation is a 'subsumption of a particular event under law', then it may be that everything one says can be interpreted as either stating general laws or as subsuming descriptions under general laws. Perhaps even saying of someone that he is *morally good* can be construed as ascribing a 'disposition' to that someone. No, the trouble with trying to specify the aims of cognitive inquiry in general by means of a list of this kind is that the list itself has to be *construed:* if the terms in the list are construed in a more or less literal way, then the kinds of statements in the list would not even include all of the sorts of statements that scientists are interested in discovering, certainly not if 'scientist' includes *historian, psychiatrist,* and *sociologist;* while if the terms in the list are construed so leniently that there is no difficulty in construing the statements made by historians (and descriptive statements in the language of everyday psychology) as belonging to types included in the list, then the list becomes worthless. In any case, in the absence of any epistemological explanation of why statements of *these kinds* and only statements of these kinds should be capable of rational verification such a list would only be a mere hypothesis about the limits of rational inquiry. A mere hypothesis, whether in the form of a list or in some other form, could not have the exclusionary force that the Logical Empiricists wanted 'criteria of cognitive significance' to have.

'Method' fetishism

Since the answer to the question 'Why is it good to be rational?' cannot be simply that rationality enables one to attain practical goals, and cannot be simply that rationality enables one to discover means/ends connections, we may consider another possible answer which has had a considerable amount of appeal at different times. Many philosophers have believed that science proceeds by following a distinctive *method;* if there is in fact a method with the property that by using that method one can reliably discover truths, and if no other method has any real chance of discovering truths, and if what *explains* the extraordinary success of science, and the persistence of controversy in fields other than science, is that science and science alone has consistently employed this *method,* then perhaps rationality, to the extent that there is such a thing, *should* be identified with the possession and employment of this method. The answer to the question 'Why is it good to be rational?' would then be that it is good to be rational because if one is rational one can discover truths (of whatever kind one is interested in), whereas if one is not rational one has no real chance of discovering truths, save by luck. Like the instrumentalists' view this view went through a philosophical history of rise, stagnation, and decline. From the publication of Mill's *Logic* in the 1840s until the publication of Carnap's *Logical Foundations of Probability,* influential philosophers of science continued to believe that something like a formal method (*'inductive logic'*) underlies empirical science, and that continued work might result in an explicit statement of this method, a formalization of inductive logic comparable to the formalization of deductive logic that was achieved starting with the work of Frege in 1879. If such a method *had* been discovered, then even if this did not by itself *prove* that the method exhausts rationality, still the burden of proof would have been very much upon those who claimed that there were truths which could be justified or shown to be rationally acceptable by any other method.

According to the most influential school, the so-called 'Bayesian' school, the general character of this inductive method that philosophers have been trying to formalize is as follows: we assume or pretend that the language of science has been formalized and that scientists have available a certain number of reliable observations expressible by 'observation sentences' in this formalized language. We also assume that the various hypotheses under consideration are expressed by formulas of this language. The problem of inductive logic is taken to be the problem of defining a 'confirmation function', that is a probability function which will determine the mathematical probability of each one of the hypotheses relative to the observational evidence or, in another terminology, the 'degree of support' the evidence lends to each of the alternative hypotheses. Usually one assumes that one knows the probability that the given evidence would have been obtained if each of the alternative hypotheses were true; this is the so-called 'forward probability', i.e. the probability of the evidence *given* the hypothesis. What we wish to calculate is the so-called 'inverse probability', that is the probability of the hypothesis *given* the evidence. Bayes' theorem gives this 'inverse probability' as a simple function of the forward probabilities and certain other probabilities, the so-called 'prior probabilities' of the alternative hypotheses, i.e. the probabilities or 'subjective degrees of belief' assigned by scientists to those alternative hypotheses prior to examining the observational evidence.

The 'forward probabilities' are indeed easy to calculate in the two most common cases: they are easy to calculate when (a) the hypothesis actually implies the evidence (in this case the 'forward probability' of the evidence given the hypothesis is *one*); or when (b) the hypothesis is itself a statistical or stochastic hypothesis part of whose content is that the particular evidence obtained should occur with a certain probability r. The difficulty in applying Bayes' theorem – a difficulty so serious that both philosophers and statisticians are deeply divided over the importance and usefulness of Bayes' theorem in the case of the confirmation of theories – is the need for a prior probability metric, a set of 'subjective degrees of belief', in the terminology of De Finetti and Savage.

Let us confine ourselves for the moment to hypotheses which are such that the 'forward probabilities' can really be computed. For hypotheses of this kind the method just described is indeed a purely formal method; that is we could program a computing machine to compute the degrees of support of the various hypotheses given the appropriate 'inputs'. But the inputs would have to include not only the computable 'forward probabilities', but also the prior probability metric in the given context. If we think of this prior probability metric as representing the scientists' antecedent beliefs about the world, as the term 'subjective probability function' suggests, then it looks as if one of the inputs to the method itself is a set of substantive factual beliefs (or degrees of belief) about the world. This is the way in which many philosophers of science today view the matter; increasingly it is coming to be believed it is not possible to draw a sharp line between the *content* of science and the *method* of science; that the method of science in fact changes constantly as the content of science changes. Bayes' theorem, if it really does capture the logic of theory confirmation, provides a way of formalizing this dependence of the method of science upon the content of science, through the need for a prior probability function.

To put the matter somewhat more abstractly, we might say that the 'method' fetishist assumes that rationality is *inseparable*. But Bayes' theorem indicates that this is not the case; that we can separate rationality, even in the area of science, even in the special area where we are dealing with theories for which the forward probabilities are computable, into two parts: a *formal* part, which can be schematized mathematically and programmed on a computer, and an *informal* part which cannot be so schematized and which depends on the actual changing beliefs of scientists. Now it would be nice, to put it mildly, if the formal part of rationality sufficed to guarantee good results. If we could say that provided scientists make their observations carefully, gather sufficient observations, and calculate degrees of support according to Bayes' theorem, then eventually they will come into agreement even if they disagree at the beginning, owing to the difference in their subjective degrees of belief, then all would be well. But there are two things wrong with this happy picture.

The first thing wrong is that even if we could show that in the long run the 'prior probability function' cancels out, or that scientists with different prior probability functions eventually come into agreement provided they continue to gather more evidence and to use Bayes' theorem, it would still be necessary that this convergence be reasonably rapid. If scientists with different prior probability functions will not come into agreement until the phenomenon to be predicted has already taken place, or until millions of years have passed, then, in the short run, the fact that there is some mathematical guarantee of eventual convergence is useless; the trouble with long-run justifications is that the long run may be much too long. In the famous words of John Maynard Keynes, 'in the long run we'll all be dead'. The second thing wrong is that it does turn out, as a matter of fact, that differences in the prior probability function can lead to violent differences in the actual degrees of support assigned to theories, and that these differences can amount to what would ordinarily be considered as gross irrationalities.

To put this last point in another way, a scientist will only assign degrees of support to hypotheses that look 'reasonable' if he starts out with a 'reasonable' prior probability function. If a person only obeys the formal part of the description of rationality, if he is logically consistent and assigns degrees of support in accordance with Bayes' theorem, but his prior probability function is extremely 'unreasonable', then his judgments of the extent to which various hypotheses are supported by the evidence will be (as scientists and ordinary people actually judge these matters) wildly 'irrational'. Formal rationality, commitment to the formal part of the scientific method, does not guarantee real and actual rationality.

The extent to which this is true is in fact rather shocking. Arthur Burks has in fact shown that there are even 'counter inductive prior probability functions'. That is, there is a certain logically possible prior probability metric such that if a scientist had that metric then as more evidence came in for a hypothesis (using the term more evidence on the basis of our normal inductive judgments) then the scientist would assign lower and lower weight to the hypothesis for a very long time.

One way out of the difficulty might be to try to supplement the present formal account of scientific method by a further set of formal rules which would determine which priors are reasonable (henceforth, I shall refer to a prior probability function simply as a 'prior', in conformity with common statistical usage), and which priors are unreasonable. But there does not seem to be any good reason to think that there would be a set of rules which could distinguish between reasonable and unreasonable priors and which would be any simpler than a complete description of the total psychology of an ideally rational human being. The hope for a formal method, capable of being isolated from actual human judgments about the content of science (that is, about the nature of the world), and from human values seems to have evaporated. And even if we widen the notion of a method so that a formalization of the psychology of an ideally rational human scientist would count as a 'method', there is no reason to think that a 'method' in *this* sense would be independent of judgments about aesthetics, judgments about ethics, judgments about whatever you please. The whole reason for believing that the scientific method would not apply to or presuppose beliefs about ethical, aesthetic, etc., matters was the belief that the scientific method was a *formal* method, after all.

My discussion has depended on assuming the correctness of one particular approach to formalizing the scientific method, the so-called 'Bayesian' approach. But similar problems arise in each of the other approaches that have been attempted. Even if one tries to isolate some small part of the inductive method which would not be as 'high-powered' as the confirmation of theories, and which would be more in line with what Bacon understood by 'induction', that is, even if one tries to isolate a method for confirming simple generalizations by examining a sufficient number of instances and 'projecting' the truth of the generalization, similar problems arise. Nelson Goodman[5] has shown that no *purely formal* rule for inductive projection can even be free from inconsistencies; before a formal rule can even hope to yield consistent results one has to have *in advance* segregated the predicates of the language into those one is willing to regard as 'projectable' and those which one will treat as 'non-projectable'. The fact that even the most elementary part of induction turns out to have a part (namely the division of the vocabulary into a projectable and a non-projectable part) which is informal, again, strongly supports the conclusion suggested by our discussion of Bayes' theorem, that one cannot draw a sharp line between the actual beliefs of scientists and the scientific method. What Goodman did was to invent a predicate 'grue' which applies to things just in case they are *observed prior to the year 2000 and green or not observed prior to the year 2000 and blue.* Prior to the year 2000, everything which is examined and seen to be green is also examined and seen to be grue. Any formal rule of projection which told us that when we've examined a certain number of things, say emeralds, with a property P then we are allowed to infer that 'all emeralds are P' would permit us to make the con-

---

[5] See his *Fact, Fiction and Forecast,* 2nd ed., Hackett (1977), first published in 1954.

tradictory inferences that 'all emeralds are green' and 'all emeralds are grue'. And Goodman convincingly shows that all attempts to rule out 'bizarre' predicates like 'grue' on purely formal grounds cannot work.[6]

There is actually a close connection between Goodman's difficulty in the case of Baconian induction and the need for a prior in connection with Bayes' theorem. Suppose the two hypotheses the scientist has to choose between (at some time prior to the year 2000) are 'all emeralds are green' and 'all emeralds are grue'. Let us suppose that the relevant evidence is that a great many emeralds have been examined and all found to be green (and hence all found to be grue as well). If the scientist computes the degree of support of the two hypotheses using Bayes' theorem then it turns out that he can either find a much higher degree of support for the normal hypothesis ('all emeralds are green') or a much higher degree of support for the abnormal hypothesis ('all emeralds are grue') or an equal degree of support for both hypotheses, depending on his prior. If one's subjective probability metric assigns a much higher prior probability to 'all emeralds are green' than to 'all emeralds are grue', then one will, in fact, behave as if one were projecting 'green' and not projecting 'grue'. From a Bayesian point of view the need for a decision as to which predicates are projectable and which are not before one can make an induction is just a special case of the need for a prior.

Karl Popper has suggested that one should accept *the most falsifiable* of the alternative hypotheses; but it turns out that his formal measures of falsifiability will yield different results depending on which predicates of the language one chooses to take as primitive. Whether one thinks of the scientist, as Popper does, as trying to find *the most falsifiable hypothesis that has not*

---

[6] Goodman's own solution is to consider form *plus* the history of prior projection of the predicates involved in the inference (along with certain related matters, e.g. 'entrenchment' and 'over-riding'). On Goodman's proposal it would follow that a culture which had *always* projected such 'crazy' predicates as his celebrated predicate 'grue' would now be perfectly justified in doing so – their inferences would now be inductively valid'!

While I agree with Goodman that fit with past practice is an important principle in science, Goodman's version of this principle is too simple and too relativistic.

yet been ruled out, or thinks in the more conventional way that one is trying to compute *degrees of support for hypotheses,* the need for an informal element corresponding to a Goodmanian decision that certain predicates are projectable and others are not, or corresponding to the acceptance of a Bayesian prior, is still necessary.

At this point the reader may wonder, if there is no such thing as the scientific method, or if the method, in so far as it can be formalized, depends on inputs which are not formalizable, then how do we account for the success of science? It is undeniable that science has been an astoundingly successful institution. We tend to feel that the reason for its success must have something to do with the differences between the ways in which scientists proceed to gather knowledge and the way in which people traditionally proceeded to gather knowledge in the prescientific ages. Is this wholly wrong? The answer is that it is not. The alternatives that we have to choose between are not that science succeeds because it follows some kind of rigorous formal algorithm, on the one hand, and that science succeeds by pure luck. Starting in the fifteenth century, and reaching a kind of peak in the seventeenth century, scientists and philosophers began to put forward a new set of methodological maxims. These maxims are not rigorous formal rules; they do require informal rationality, i.e. intelligence and common sense, to apply; but nevertheless they did and do shape scientific inquiry. In short, there is a scientific method; but it presupposes prior notions of rationality.[7] It is not a method *de novo* which can serve as the be all and end all, the very definition of rationality.

One of the most important methodologists of the seventeenth century was the physicist Boyle. Prior to the seventeenth century, physicists did not sharply distinguish between actually performing experiments and simply describing thought experiments which would confirm theories that they believed on more or less a priori grounds. Moreover, physicists did not see the need to publish descriptions of experiments which failed. In short, experiments were conceived of largely as *illustrations* for doc-

---

[7] Mill himself concedes this (in a remarkably grudging tone of voice) when he writes that we cannot expect the inductive method to work 'if we suppose universal idiocy to be conjoined with it' (*Utilitarianism,* Chapter 2).

trines believed on deductive and a priori grounds; not as evidence for and against theories. Boyle wrote manuals of experimental procedure, he emphasized the need for a sharp distinction between thought experiments and actual experiments, and he emphasized the need to give a complete description of all the experiments one performed, especially including the experiments that failed. Boyle was himself a disciple of the philosopher Francis Bacon, and Boyle was undoubtedly led to an appreciation of the importance of these rules by Bacon's inductive outlook; in fact, however, the specific instructions given by Boyle may have been more important or as important in shaping the course of physical inquiry as the more abstract and schematic defense of inductive procedure given by Bacon.

Turning away from trying to establish theories a priori towards trying to test theories by deriving testable conclusions from them and performing experiments certainly was a methodological shift. As we have seen, however, we cannot simply identify *being rational* with *believing theories solely because they are supported by carefully performed experiments*. For one thing, even in science it is not always possible to perform controlled experiments. Sometimes one has to rely on passive observation rather than on the kind of active intervention which is implied by the term 'experiment'. And, as we saw before, even when one has carefully performed experiments for the purpose of choosing among alternative theories, the estimation of the degree to which the experimental results support the various alternative theories is still a wholly informal matter.

Against what we have been urging, Karl Popper has repeatedly argued that there *is* a distinctive scientific method, it can be stated, and we should rely only on it for discovering the nature of the world.

Popper does think, however, that there are notions of rationality which are wider than scientific rationality and which do apply to the making of ethical decisions.

In Popper's conception, set forth in his influential book, *The Logic of Scientific Inquiry (Logik der Forschung)*, and in subsequent publications, Popper has argued that the scientific method consists in putting forward 'highly falsifiable' theories; theories that imply risky predictions. We then proceed to test all of the theories until only one survives. We then accept the surviving

hypothesis as the one to go on for the time being, and repeat the
entire procedure. Since the elimination of all the theories but one
is made on deductive grounds – a theory is eliminated when it
implies a prediction which is definitely falsified – no use of
Bayes' theorem is required, and no estimation of degrees of support is involved, Popper claims.

One problem with Popper's view is that it is not possible to
test all strongly falsifiable theories. For example, the theory that
if I put a flour sack on my head and rap the table 99 times a
demon will appear is strongly falsifiable, but I am certainly not
going to bother to test it. Even if I were willing to test it I could
think of 10^{100} similar theories, and a human lifetime, or even the
lifetime of the human species, would not suffice to test them all.
For logical reasons, then, it is necessary to select, on methodological grounds, a very small number of theories that we will
actually bother to test; and this means that something like a
prior selection is involved even in the Popperian method. As I
remarked above, even Popper's computations of degrees of falsifiability are sensitive to which predicates one considers as
primitive in one's language, and in that sense even the notion of
falsifiability requires a prior decision analogous to Goodman's
decision that certain predicates are 'projectable' and others are
not. Let us waive these technical points, however, which are not
of interest to us in our present discussion, in any case. Even if
the Popperian method is incomplete, and requires to be supplemented by a more intuitive method which we are not able to
formalize at the present time, could it not be that it describes a
necessary condition, if not a sufficient condition, for scientific
rationality? Could it not be, in short, that a necessary condition
for the acceptability of a scientific theory be that it have survived
a Popperian test? The Popperian test itself may involve a prior
selection of theories to test which is itself informal and for which
we do not have an algorithm; the calculation of which theories
are most strongly falsifiable may involve informal decisions for
which we do not have an algorithm; but we could still insist that
no theory be accepted unless a set of theories has first been
selected all of which are *intuitively* 'highly falsifiable', and unless
all those theories except the one which we accept have been sub-
sequently refuted by carefully performed experiments. In short,
could it not be that the advice we ought to give the scientist is:

proceed as Popper advises you should proceed, and, where Popper's methods are not capable of being formalized, rely on your intuition as to how the Popperian maxims should be interpreted? And might it not be the case that the Popperian method, vague and informal as it is in part, exhausts not only the notion of *scientific* rationality, but all of *cognitive rationality*, that is, might it not be the case that a statement is warrantedly assertible, or rationally acceptable, if and only if it is implied by a theory which can be accepted on the basis of a Popperian test? The answer is that such a conception of rationality is too narrow *even for science*. For one thing it would rule out the acceptance of one of the most successful and widely admired of all scientific theories, Darwin's theory of evolution by natural selection. This is a consequence which Popper himself is willing to accept with equanimity, but certainly the scientific community is not. The theory of natural selection is not highly falsifiable; it does not imply definite predictions such that if they come out wrong then the theory is refuted. We accept the theory of natural selection not because it has survived a Popperian test, but because it provides a *plausible explanation* of an enormous amount of data, because it has been fruitful in suggesting new theories and in linking up with developments in genetics, molecular biology, etc., and because the alternative theories actually suggested have either been falsified or seem wholly implausible in terms of background knowledge. In short, we accept the Darwinian theory of evolution by natural selection as what Peirce called an 'abduction', or what has recently been called an 'inference to the best explanation'. This is exactly the kind of inference that Popper wanted to *drive out* of science; but scientists are not going to be persuaded by Popper that they should give up theories which are not strongly falsifiable in cases where those theories provide good explanations of vast quantities of data, and in cases where no plausible alternative explanation is in the field. Indeed, as I have pointed out in another publication,[8] Popper exaggerates the extent to which even the theories of classical physics are themselves strongly falsifiable.

We weaken our description of the scientific method still further, then, by allowing the 'inference to the best explanation' as

---

[8] See 'The Corroboration of Theories', in my *Mathematics, Matter and Method*.

a legitimate form of scientific inference-drawing, even when the 'best explanation' inferred to is not strongly falsifiable in Popper's sense. The scientific method has now become a tremendously vague thing;[9] but this we expected to happen, anyway, in view of the formal results in inductive logic we described above. Could it be that the 'scientific method', described *this* vaguely is now exhaustive? And could it be that given even such a vague description, it is clearly the case that no value judgment is capable of being verified or confirmed by this method? The answer is that if the scientific method is described simply as 'make experiments and observations as carefully as you can, and then make inferences to the best explanation and eliminate theories which can be falsified by crucial experiments', then it is impossible to see what *cannot* be verified by a method so vaguely described. Suppose, for example, I want to verify the statement 'John is a bad man.' I might argue as follows: 'The following are observed facts, that John is inconsiderate, that John is extremely selfish, and that John is a very cruel person. Someone who is inconsiderate, selfish and cruel is *prima facie* a bad person; therefore John is a bad man.' There are two points at which a defender of the view that 'value judgments' cannot be 'scientifically verified' might object to this argument. He might object to the last step; that is the step from *John is cruel, John is inconsiderate, John is extremely selfish, to John is a bad man.* Admittedly this is a *conceptual* step; the claim is that there is a conceptual link between being cruel, inconsiderate, and selfish and being morally bad.[10]

---

9 Alternatively, we could restrict the term 'scientific method' to refer to the conscious application of maxims of experimental procedure, as I recommended in *Meaning and the Moral Sciences,* and just stop trying to make it so elastic that it can cover everything we call 'knowledge'.

10 The fact that a truth or an inference is of the sort we call 'conceptual' does not mean that it must be purely *linguistic* in character (i.e. true by virtue of *arbitrary* linguistic conventions). Philosophers of many different tendencies have seen that concepts, fact, and observations are interdependent. As we remarked in Chapter 6, concepts are shaped by what we observe or intuit and in turn shape what we are able to observe and intuit. In these respects, the inference in the text involving 'good' is exactly analogous to the following inference involving 'conscious'. 'John is speaking intelligently, acting appropriately, and responding to what goes on; therefore John is conscious.' The conceptual link here is that 'speaking *intelligently*', 'acting *appropriately*', '*responding* to what goes on' are *prima facie* reasons for attributing consciousness, in just the way that inconsiderateness, selfishness, and cruelty are *prima facie* reasons for attributing moral badness.

Of course, if there are no conceptual links among the moral predicates then this is an invalid step; but why should one believe that there are no conceptual links among the moral predicates? It might be argued that the use of steps described as 'conceptual' in an argument is itself unscientific; but it surely cannot be maintained that there are no such steps in science itself. For example, if I make the inference from Newton's description of the solar system to the statement that 'it is the gravitational attraction of the moon that causes the tides' then I am employing my informal knowledge that there is a conceptual link between statements about forces and statements of the form *A caused B*. The word 'cause' does not even appear in Newton's description of the solar system and of the tides; but I know that the gravitational force that *A* exerts on *B* can be described as caused by (the mass of) *A* simply by virtue of understanding Newton's theory.

Of course, if we describe the scientific method as consisting in the drawing of 'inferences to the best explanation', or whatever, from 'observational statements' which are *themselves in value-neutral language,* then we can rule out 'John is inconsiderate' and 'John is selfish' as 'observation statements' (although, in particular cases, it might be easier to get agreement on these than on, say, whether an object is *mauve*). But such statements occur constantly in the writings of, for example, *historians.* That history, clinical psychology and ordinary language description can really avoid words like 'considerate' and 'selfish' altogether is doubtful (and where to draw the line would be an immense problem: is 'stubborn' value-neutral? is 'angry' value-neutral? for that matter, is 'twisted her arm savagely' value-neutral?). But, in any case, to identify *rationality* with scientific rationality so described would be to beg the question of the cognitive status of value judgments; it would be to say these judgments are not rationally confirmable because *they are* value judgments, for rationality has been *defined* as consisting exclusively of raw and neutral observation and the drawing of inferences from value-neutral premisses. But why should one accept such a definition?

9

Values, facts and cognition

I argued in Chapter 6 that 'every fact is value loaded and every one of our values loads some fact'. The argument in a nutshell was that *fact* (or truth) and *rationality* are interdependent notions. A fact is something that it is rational to believe, or, more precisely, the notion of a fact (or a true statement) is an idealization of the notion of a statement that it is rational to believe. 'Rationally acceptable' and 'true' are notions that take in each other's wash. And I argued that being rational involves having criteria of *relevance* as well as criteria of rational acceptability, and that all of our values are involved in our criteria of relevance. The decision that a picture of the world is true (or true by our present lights, or 'as true as anything is') and *answers the relevant questions* (as well as we are able to answer them) rests on and reveals our total system of value commitments. A being with no values would have no facts either.

The way in which criteria of relevance involve values, at least indirectly, may be seen by examining the simplest statement. Take the sentence 'the cat is on the mat'. If someone actually makes this judgment in a particular context, then he employs conceptual resources – the notions 'cat', 'on', and 'mat' – which are provided by a particular culture, and whose presence and ubiquity reveal something about the interests and values of that culture, and of almost every culture. We have the category 'cat' because we regard the division of the world into *animals* and *non-animals* as significant, and we are further interested in what *species* a given animal belongs to. It is *relevant* that there is a *cat* on that mat and not just a *thing*. We have the category 'mat' because we regard the division of inanimate things into *artifacts* and *non-artifacts* as significant, and we are further interested in the *purpose* and *nature* a particular artifact has. It is relevant that it is a *mat* that the cat is on and not just a *something*. We have the category 'on' because we are interested in *spatial relations*.

Notice what we have: we took the most banal statement imaginable, 'the cat is on the mat', and we found that the presuppositions which make this statement a *relevant* one in certain contexts include the significance of the categories *animate/inanimate, purpose,* and *space.* To a mind with no disposition to regard these as *relevant* categories, 'the cat is on the mat' would be as *irrational* a remark as 'the number of hexagonal objects in this room is 76' would be, uttered in the middle of a tete-à-tete between young lovers.

Not only do very general facts about our value system show themselves in our categories (*artifacts, species name, term for a spatial relation*) but, as we saw in Chapter 6, our more specific values (for example, sensitivity and compassion) also show up in the use we make of specific classificatory words ('considerate', 'selfish'). To repeat, our criteria of relevance rest on and reveal our whole system of values.

The relevance of this discussion of relevance to the question raised in the preceding chapter ('What is the value of rationality?') is immediate. If 'rationality' is an ability (or better, an integrated system of abilities) which enables the possessor to determine what *questions* are relevant questions to ask and what *answers* it is warranted to accept, then its value is on its sleeve. But it needs no argument that *such* a conception of rationality is as value loaded as the notion of relevance itself.

It may be objected that I have lumped together factors that belong apart, however, and thereby masked a sort of sleight of hand. The very fact that I have spoken of two factors, rational acceptability and relevance, testifies, it may be claimed, to the persistence and permanence of something like the fact/value dichotomy. A rational person, on the conception the objector has in mind, would be one who could tell what was and what was not warrantedly assertible; what a person chose to regard as *interesting,* or *important,* or *relevant* might have bearing in evaluating his character or even his mental health, but not his *cognitive* rationality, the objector would say.

Acceptability and relevance are interdependent in any real context, however. Using any word – whether the word be 'good', or 'conscious', or 'red', or 'magnetic' – involves one in a history, a tradition of observation, generalization, practice and theory.

It also involves one in the activity of *interpreting* that tradition, and of adapting it to new contexts, extending and criticizing it. One can interpret traditions variously, but one cannot apply a word at all if one places oneself entirely outside of the tradition to which it belongs. And standing inside a tradition certainly affects what one counts as 'rational acceptability'. If there were one method one could use to verify any statement at all, no matter what concepts it contained, then the proposed separation of the ability to verify statements from the mastery of a *relevant* set of concepts might be tenable; but we have already seen that there is no reason to accept the myth of the one Method.

The two-components theory

Our present intuitions about rationality seem to be in conflict; certainly no one philosophical theory seems to reconcile them all. On the one hand, it is simply not true that we *never* judge ends as rational or irrational; on the other hand, when we are confronted with a case like that of the hypothetical 'rational Nazi' we do not see how to justify criticizing such an intelligently elaborated and considered system of ends as *irrational* even if we find it morally repellant.

One way in which it has been suggested we might resolve these problems is the following: assuming a sharp fact/value dichotomy, we can justify condemning the man who is only interested in knowing the number of hairs on people's heads as irrational on the ground that he has an inadequate perception of *facts* (what 'adequate' means is a problem, of course). The Nazi only disagrees with us about *values*, which is why *he* is not irrational. In between cases can be handled, perhaps, along the lines suggested by Bernard Williams. In particular, then, our argument against the method fetishist, that we cannot, without circularity, rule out of the 'observational evidence' such descriptive judgments as 'John is considerate', can be met by advancing the theory that the ordinary language moral–descriptive vocabulary has two 'meaning components' simultaneously. One component is a *factual* component; there are certain generally accepted *standards* for considerateness, and 'John is considerate' conveys the information that John meets those standards.[1] But there is also an *emotive* meaning component: 'John is considerate' conveys a 'pro-attitude' towards a certain aspect of John's conduct. What can be rational, it is claimed, is the acceptance of the *factual* component of the statement 'John is considerate'; acceptance of the emotive meaning component, sharing the 'pro-attitude', is what is neither rational nor irrational.

The notion of the 'factual' here comes from the individual philosopher's preferred view of the Furniture of the World. For a materialist philosopher, the 'factual' component in the meaning of any statement has to consist in a statement expressible in the vocabulary of *physical science*. But a difficulty comparable to the difficulty that plagued phenomenalism at once arises.

Phenomenalism, we recall, was the doctrine that all meaningful statements are translatable without residue into statements about sensations. 'Physicalism' (as the type of Materialism we are discussing came to be called) was the doctrine that the whole 'factual' meaning of any statement can be translated without residue into the language of physics. And, once again, the doctrine seems to be false.

To see why, consider not a moral–descriptive statement but a psychological statement, say 'X is thinking about Vienna.' It is obvious that even if there are necessary and sufficient conditions expressible in terms of brain states or whatever for an arbitrary organism to be thinking about Vienna, it would take an unimaginably perfected neurological (or, perhaps, functionalist–psychological) theory to say what these are. The conditions for

---

[1] What 'standards' means here is a problem however. If the claim is that 'John is considerate' is descriptively true (i.e. the 'factual component' is true) if and only if *most speakers would agree that John is considerate,* then it would follow from *this* analysis of the 'factual component' that there cannot be a person whom a sensitive judge would *correctly* classify as 'considerate' even though *most* speakers *disagree.* Such an account of the 'factual component' would simply amount to the claim that all truths (at least about 'standards') must be 'public', but why should one believe *this* unless one is a Majoritarian? (As we saw in Chapter 5, the claim that *all* truth is public is self-refuting.)

the truth of this statement are context dependent, interest relative, and vague. There is no reason to think that even 'in principle' there exists a *finite* expression in the language of physical theory which (in any physically possible world) is true of an *X* if and only if that *X* is thinking about Vienna. Not only might it be *false* that a finite equivalent in physicalist language exists for the ordinary language statement '*X* is thinking about Vienna'; even if such an equivalent *does* exist, the equivalence would be equivalence on the basis of an empirical theory or group of theories which are themselves not known (perhaps they are so complicated human beings will *never know* them), and which are certainly not part of the *meaning* of '*X* is thinking about Vienna'. In short, it is just false that '*X* is thinking about Vienna' *means* '*X* is in such-and-such a (physically or functionally specified) brain state.'

What holds for '*X* is thinking about Vienna' will hold for any ordinary language predicate whose conditions of application do not mesh well with those which govern physical concepts. '*X* is considerate' – even '*X* is brown', '*X* is an earthquake', and '*X* is a person' – are also not *translatable* into the language of 'physical theory'. What this means is that, if there *are* two components to the meaning of '*X* is considerate', then the only description we can give of the 'factual meaning' of the statement is that it is true if and only if *X* is *considerate*. And this trivializes the notion of a 'factual component'.

To say that the 'two components' theory collapses is not to deny that '*X* is considerate' normally has a certain emotive force. But it does not always have it. As we pointed out in Chapter 6, we can use the statement '*X* is considerate' for many purposes: to evaluate, to describe, to explain, to predict, and so on. Distinguishing the *uses* to which the statement can be put does not require us to deny the existence of such a *statement* as '*X* is considerate.'

Moore and the 'Naturalistic Fallacy'

Weber's claim that 'value judgments' cannot be rationally confirmed was the source of the present fact/value dichotomy; but the dichotomy was reinforced by G. E. Moore (contrary to his own intentions). Writing at a time when Bertrand Russell and

John Maynard Keynes, along with other future members of the Bloomsbury group, were still young students, Moore argued for the thesis that Good was a 'non-natural' property, i.e. one totally outside the physicalistic ontology of natural science. His defense of non-naturalism backfired; his students may have been convinced by Moore that there were such things as 'non-natural properties' (although Russell, at least, was to lose the faith) but later philosophers of a naturalistic kind tended to feel that Moore had provided a *reductio ad absurdum* of the idea that there are such things as value properties. In the 1930s Charles Stevenson and the Logical Positivists were to advance the 'emotive theory of ethics', that is the theory that '*X* is good' means 'I approve of *X*, do so as well!', or something of that kind. Value *properties* began to be rejected on epistemological grounds, but even more on ontological grounds; as John Mackie[2] has recently expressed it, it is compatible with natural science that there should be such things as *value attitudes* but it is not compatible with natural science that there should be such things as *value properties*. Value properties, Mackie claims, are 'ontologically queer' – i.e. they are funny mysterious properties in whose existence scientifically enlightened people should not continue to believe.

Moore's argument that Good cannot be a physicalistic property (a 'natural' property) was that if 'Good' is the same property as 'conducive to maximizing total utility' (or whatever natural property, physical or functional, you care to substitute), then

(1) 'this action is not good even though it is conducive to maximizing total utility'

is a *self-contradictory* statement (not just a *false* one).

But even a Utilitarian would not claim (1) is *self-contradictory*. And this shows, Moore claims, that although being Good and being conducive to maximizing total utility might be *correlated* properties, they could not be the same *identical* property.

Moore's argument turns on assumptions that I and many other philosophers of language would reject today, however. First of all, he implicitly denied that there could be such a thing as *synthetic identity of properties*. But, as I pointed out in Chap-

[2] *Ethics, Inventing Right and Wrong*, Penguin, 1977.

ter 4, this would rule out such accepted scientific discoveries as the discovery that the magnitude *temperature* is the same magnitude as the magnitude *mean molecular kinetic energy*. (One could use Moore's 'proof' to show that temperature must be a 'non-natural property', in fact. For one is not *contradicting oneself* when one says 'x has temperature T but x does not have mean molecular kinetic energy E', where E is the value of the kinetic energy that corresponds to temperature T, even if the statement is always false as a matter of empirical fact. So, Moore would have to conclude, Temperature is only *correlated* with Mean Molecular Kinetic Energy; the two properties cannot literally be *identical*.) In fact, Moore conflated *properties* and *concepts*. There *is* a notion of property in which the fact that two *concepts* are different (say 'temperature' and 'mean molecular kinetic energy') does not at all settle the question whether the corresponding *properties* are different. (And discovering how many fundamental physical properties there are is not discovering something about *concepts*, but something about the *world*.) The *concept* 'good' may not be synonymous with any physicalistic concept (after all, moral-descriptive language and physicalistic language are extremely different 'versions', in Goodman's sense), but it does not follow that *being good* is not the same property as *being P*, for some suitable physicalistic (or, better, *functionalistic*) *P*. In general, an ostensively learned term for a property (e.g. 'has high temperature') is not synonymous with a theoretical definition of that property; it takes empirical and theoretical research, not linguistic analysis, to find out what temperature is (and, some philosopher might suggest, what *goodness* is), not just reflection on meanings.

An idea which came into philosophy of language a few years after I introduced the 'synthetic identity of properties', and which enlarges and illuminates the point I have been making, is Saul Kripke's idea of 'metaphysically necessary' truths which have to be learned *empirically*, 'epistemically contingent necessary truths'.[3] Kripke's observation, applied to the temperature/kinetic energy case, is that, if someone describes a logically possible world in which people have sensations of hot

---

[3] Kripke's *Naming and Necessity*, Harvard, 1980 (lectures originally given in Princeton in 1970).

and cold, there are objects that feel hot and objects that feel cold, and in which these sensations of hot and cold are *explained by a different mechanism than mean molecular kinetic energy*, then we do *not* say that he has described a possible world in which *temperature is not mean molecular energy*. Rather we say that he has described a world in which *some mechanism other than temperature makes certain objects feel hot and cold*. Once we have accepted the 'synthetic identity statement' that temperature *is* mean molecular kinetic energy (in the *actual* world), nothing *counts* as a possible world in which temperature is *not* mean molecular kinetic energy.

A statement which is true in every possible world is traditionally called 'necessary'. A property which something has in every possible world is traditionally called 'essential'. In this traditional terminology, Kripke is saying that 'temperature is mean molecular kinetic energy' is a *necessary* truth *even though we can't know it a priori*. The statement is empirical but necessary. Or, to say the same thing in different words, being mean molecular kinetic energy is an essential property of temperature. We have discovered the *essence* of temperature by *empirical* investigation. These ideas of Kripke's have had widespread impact on philosophy of language, metaphysics, and philosophy of mathematics; applied to Moore's argument they are devastating. Moore argued from the fact that (1) *can only be false contingently*, that being *P* (for some suitable natural property *P*) could not be an essential property of goodness; this is just what the new theory of necessity blocks. All that one can validly infer from the fact that (1) is not self-contradictory is that 'good' is not synonymous with 'conducive to maximizing utility' (not synonymous with *P*, for any term *P* in the physicalistic version of the world). From this nonsynonymy of *words* nothing follows about non-identity of *properties*. Nothing follows about the essence of goodness.

Ruth Anna Putnam has pointed out that another common argument that goodness cannot be a natural property does not work.[4] This is the argument that '*X* is good' has 'emotive force', 'expresses a pro-attitude', and so forth.

---

[4] 'Remarks on Wittgenstein's Lecture on Ethics', in Haller *et al.* (eds.), *Language, Logic, and Philosophy, Proceedings of the 4th Intern. Wittgenstein Symposium, Vienna, 1980*.

What is wrong with the argument, Ruth Anna Putnam points out, is that many descriptive predicates naturally *acquire* an emotive force. In our culture, 'slobbers his food all over his shirt' has strong negative emotive force although the phrase is literally a *description*. Any word that stands for something people in a culture *value* (or disvalue) will tend to acquire emotive force.

The word 'good', in its moral sense, is applied to many things. Some of these – good states of mind, for example – may be naturally valued: it may be part of the content of that very state of mind that one values being in it. I don't mean to suggest the converse: that any state of mind that is naturally valued in this sense is good; that would be clearly false. Suppose 'good' were defined so that things which are naturally valued and are such that there is no good reason to *disvalue* them (as there is reason to disvalue certain drug-induced states which are naturally valued) count as 'good'.

Then one would expect the statement that something is good to have positive 'emotional force' *because of the nature of the property*. Even if one is *not* a Consequentialist (i.e. one who thinks *everything* with sufficiently good *consequences* is good), there is no doubt that the most common reason for calling an action good is that it has good consequences, among which might be that it ultimately promotes states or situations which are naturally valued; again, the very nature of the property explains why the description comes to have 'pro' emotive force.

Mackie defends his claim that goodness is ontologically 'queer' by introducing as a premiss the assumption that one cannot *know* that something is good *without* having a 'pro' attitude towards that something. This amounts to assuming *emotivism* in order to prove emotivism. The devils in hell are frequently depicted as using 'good' with a *negative* emotive force ('He has a deplorable tendency to moral goodness' one of them might say); contrary to Mackie, I do not find such uses to be linguistically improper or to involve any contradiction. And do we not hear people say, 'I know that's a bad thing to do but I don't care'? As Philippa Foot has pointed out, one can even rebuff appeals to morality by saying, 'I'm not out to be a good man.' What the possibility of these utterances shows is that while there is indeed a difference between the *describing use* of language and the *prescribing use* or the *commending use*, this difference in uses is not a simple function of *vocabulary*. 'Descriptive' words can be used to praise or blame ('He slobbers food all over his tie') and 'evaluative' words can be used to describe and explain. (Consider the following dialogue: 'John must have been an exceptionally good man to do such a thing.' 'No, he had never been a moral paragon, if anything the contrary; but he must have had a capacity for self-sacrifice we never suspected.' Here *moral* language is being used in an *explanatory* function.) To repeat Ruth Anna Putnam's point again, nothing about goodness not being a property follows from the fact that 'is good' is used to commend.

Professor Putnam points out that there is, nevertheless, something *right* about Mackie's argument. Some moral expressions undeniably do have a built-in orientation towards action. 'Should', 'ought', 'right', and 'must' are prime examples of such 'action guiding' words. The 'is/ought' problem is not the same as the 'fact/value' problem, as she points out. 'I am not out to do what I should' sounds much odder than 'I am not out to be a good man' (and 'I am not out to do what I must' sounds crazy).

Mackie points out that no physical property has a built-in connection to action (or to approval of an action), and concludes that 'being the right thing to do', etc., are 'ontologically queer'. But (besides depending on the assumption that the physicalist version of the world is the One True Theory), this argument proves too much. For some *epistemic* predicates (e.g. 'rationally acceptable', 'justified belief') are also action-guiding (taking 'action' in a wide sense, so that accepting a statement counts as an action). One can say, 'X is a good thing to do' and 'There is a good deal of evidence that Y' and not be committed to doing (or prescribing) X or to accepting Y; but if one says 'X is the right action to perform in this situation', or 'Believing that Y is completely justified', then one is oriented to doing (or prescribing) X and to accepting Y. 'Justified' (in the case of beliefs) has the characteristic of being action-guiding as much as 'right' in the moral sense does.

If we now mimic Mackie's argument and conclude that there is no such property as being *justified*, but only 'justification attitudes', then we land ourselves in total relativism. Before going so catastrophically far, we should pause to see *why* action-guiding predicates seem 'ontologically queer' to a committed physicalist.

In Chapter 2, I argued that *reference* itself should seem 'ontologically queer' to a committed physicalist. If only physicalistic properties and relations really exist, then reference, to exist, must be a physicalistic relation – but then the problem, as we saw, is an overabundance of 'candidates'. There are an infinite number of admissible reference relations (and all are physicalistic, or at least naturalistic, if we count *set theory* as part of the naturalistic version of the world). If one of these were *the* relation of reference, then *that* fact would itself be an *ultimate* metaphysical fact of a very strange kind.

What would make such a fact strange is that we have built a certain *neutrality,* a certain *mindlessness,* into our very notion of Nature. Nature is supposed to have no interests, intentions, or point of view. Given that this is right, then how *could* one admissible reference-relation be metaphysically singled-out?

It is this same mindlessness of Nature that makes the action-guiding predicates 'is right' and 'is a justified belief' seem 'queer'. If one physicalistic property *P* were *identical* with moral rightness or with epistemological justification, that *would* be 'queer' – queer for precisely the same reason that it would be 'queer' if *reference* were a physicalistic relation. It would be as if Nature itself had values, in the moral case, or referential intentions, in the semantical case.

For this reason, I think that Moore was right (even if his arguments are not acceptable) in holding that 'good', 'right' (and also 'justified belief', 'refers', and 'true') are not identical with physicalistic properties and relations. What *this* shows is not that goodness, rightness, epistemic justification, reference, and truth do not exist, but that monistic naturalism (or 'physicalism') is an inadequate philosophy.

The 'rational Nazi' again

What troubled us earlier was that we did not see how to argue that the hypothetical 'perfectly rational Nazi' had irrational ends. Perhaps the problem is this: that we identified too simply the question of the rationality of the *Nazi* (as someone who has a world view or views) with the rationality of the Nazi's *ends*. If there is no end 'in' the Nazi to which we can appeal, then it does seem odd to diagnose the situation by saying 'Karl has irrational goals.' Even if this is part of what we conclude in the end, surely the *first* thing we want to say is that Karl has *monstrous* goals, not that he has irrational ones.

But the question to look at, if we are going to discuss Karl's rationality at all, is the irrationality of his *beliefs and arguments,* not his goals.

Suppose, first, that Karl claims Nazi goals are morally *right* and *good* (as Nazis, in fact if not in philosophers' examples, generally did). Then, *in fact,* he will talk rubbish. He will assert all kinds of false 'factual' propositions, e.g. that the democracies are run by a 'Jewish conspiracy'; and he will advance moral propositions (e.g. that, if one is an 'Aryan', one has a *duty* to subjugate non-Aryan races to the 'master race') for which he has no good arguments. The notion of a 'good argument' I am appealing to is *internal* to ordinary moral discourse; but that is the appropriate notion, if the Nazi tries to justify himself *within* ordinary moral discourse.

Suppose, on the other hand, that the Nazi *repudiates* ordinary moral notions altogether (as our hypothetical Super-Benthamite did). I argued that a culture which repudiated ordinary moral notions, or substituted notions derived from a different ideology and moral outlook for them, would lose the ability to *describe* ordinary interpersonal relations, social events and political events adequately and perspicuously *by our present lights.* Of course, if the different ideology and moral outlook are *superior* to our present moral system then this substitution may be good and wise; but if the different ideology and moral outlook are *bad*, especially if they are warped and monstrous, then the result will be simply an inadequate, unperspicuous, repulsive representation of interpersonal and social facts. Of course, 'inadequate, unperspicuous, repulsive' reflect value judgments; but I have argued that the choice of a conceptual scheme *necessarily* reflects value judgments, and the choice of a conceptual scheme is what *cognitive* rationality is all about.

Even if the individual Nazi does not lose the ability to use our present moral descriptive vocabulary, even if he retains the old notions somewhere in his head (as some scholars, perhaps, still are familiar with and able to use the medieval notion of 'chivalry'), still these (our present moral descriptive notions such as 'considerate', 'compassionate', 'just', 'fair') will not be notions that he employs in living his life: they will not really figure in his construction of the world.

Again, I wish to emphasize that I am not saying that *what is bad* about being a Nazi is that it leads one to have warped and irrational *beliefs*. What is bad about being a Nazi is what it leads you to *do*. The Nazi is evil *and* he also has an irrational view of the world. These two facts about the Nazi are connected and interrelated; but that does not mean the Nazi is evil primarily *because* he has an irrational view of the world in the sense that the irrationality of his world view *constitutes* the evil. Nevertheless, there *is* a sense in which we may speak of *goals* being rational or irrational here, it seems to me: goals which are such that, if one accepts them and pursues them then one will either be led to offer crazy and false arguments for them (if one accepts the task of justifying them within our normal conceptual scheme), or else one will be led to adopt an alternative scheme for representing ordinary moral–descriptive facts (e.g. that someone is compassionate) which is irrational, have a right to be called 'irrational goals'. There is a connection, after all, between employing a rational conceptual scheme in describing and perceiving morally relevant facts and having certain general types of goals as opposed to others.

'But what if the Nazi gives no reason for being a Nazi except "that's how I feel like acting"?' This is a natural question, but here surely the natural answer is also the right one: in such a case the Nazi's conduct, besides being evil, would also be completely *arbitrary*. Notice that 'arbitrary' is one of the words I have been calling 'moral–descriptive', i.e. a word which can be used, without change of denotation, to evaluate (in this case to blame), to describe ('John quite arbitrarily decided to change jobs'), to explain (or to indicate that no explanation of a certain kind can be given), etc. Indeed, when I just said that Karl's decision to be a Nazi (in the case described) would be completely arbitrary, I was primarily *describing*, not evaluating. Many things I do are, quite literally, arbitrary – e.g. choosing one path across the campus rather than another; but this does not mean there is anything wrong about these actions. (The matters are simply too trivial.) Even if I do something important 'arbitrarily' – say, change jobs – if I don't have family responsibilities, etc., this may simply be my *right*. But if the action is one that *requires justification,* then performing it arbitrarily and with no justification will expose one to legitimate blame. Making a decision which adversely affects the lives of others (and perhaps one's own life) to a great extent with no justification, just as an arbitrary and willful (another of those moral descriptive words!) act, is a paradigmatic example of irrationality, and not just irrationality but perverseness.

We started our discussion in Chapter 7 by looking at Bentham's claim that 'prejudice aside' the game of pushpin (an ancient children's game similar to tiddlywinks) is just as good as 'the arts and sciences of music and of poetry'. In Bentham's view the only reason poetry *is* better than pushpin, ultimately, is the brute fact that poetry gives greater satisfaction than pushpin (or gives satisfaction to more people, or both). There are, basically, two things wrong with this view: one thing wrong is that 'satisfaction' (or 'self-interest') itself cannot be an aim of any being who does not have *other* aims. If I had no aim *other* than 'my welfare', then my 'welfare' would be a meaningless notion, a point which goes back to Bishop Butler. More important, some *satisfactions* are better and 'nobler' than others, and one can give reasons why. Poetry and music give solace, they enlarge our sensibilities, they provide important modes of self-expression to many people, including many of the most gifted people the human race has produced. Calling these reasons for valuing certain satisfactions above others 'prejudice' is actually closely connected with both the 'two components' theory *and* the idea that value properties are 'ontologically queer'. Bentham is operating with the model of 'neutral facts' and arbitrary 'prejudices'. Indeed, calling the preference for poetry a 'prejudice' is just Bentham's way of suggesting that the fact that poetry gives greater satisfaction than pushpin is the *only* consideration that is not 'arbitrary' in comparing the two; any preference for one *kind* of satisfaction over another (it is suggested) is arbitrary. But this is simply false, given the actual place in our conceptual scheme of the notion of an 'arbitrary' preference, and meaningless if 'arbitrary' is wrenched out of the scheme to which it belongs. (Similarly, the statement that preferring poetry to pushpin is a prejudice is *literally false*.) It is being suggested that it is somehow ontologically legitimate to admit that there are such things as *satisfactions,* but not ontologically legitimate to admit such things as enlarged sensibilities, enlarged repertoires of meaning and metaphor, modes of expression and self-realization, and so on. The idea that values are not part of the Furniture of the World and the idea that 'value judgments' are expressions of 'prejudice' are two sides of the same coin.

We have investigated the question whether 'value judgments' can be rationally supported. We have seen that various negative answers rest on dubious philosophical assumptions: that rationality itself is only good for 'prediction', or only good for getting 'consensus', or that there is only one Method for arriving at truth (where, sometimes, the only criteria for 'truth' are said to be prediction and consensus), or that value judgments have 'two meaning components', or that value properties are 'ontologically queer'. The position I have defended is that any choice of a conceptual scheme presupposes values, and the choice of a scheme for describing ordinary interpersonal relations and social facts, not to mention thinking about one's own life plan, involves, among other things, one's *moral* values. One cannot choose a scheme which simply 'copies' the facts, because *no* conceptual scheme is a mere 'copy' of the world. The notion of truth itself depends for its content on our standards of rational acceptability, and these in turn rest on and presuppose our values. Put schematically and too briefly, I am saying that theory of truth presupposes theory of rationality which in turn presupposes our theory of the good.

'Theory of the good', however, is not only programmatic, but is itself dependent upon assumptions about human nature, about society, about the universe (including theological and metaphysical assumptions). We have had to revise our theory of the good (such as it is) again and again as our knowledge has increased and our world-view has changed.

It has become clear that in the conception I am defending there is no such thing as a 'foundation'. And at this point people become worried: are we not close to the view that there is no difference between 'justified' and 'justified by our lights' (relativism) or even 'justified by *my* lights' (a species of solipsism)?

The position of the solipsist is indeed the one we will land in if we try to stand outside the conceptual system to which the concept of rationality belongs and simultaneously pretend to offer a more 'rational' notion of rationality! (Many thinkers have fallen into Nietzsche's error of telling us they had a 'better' morality than the entire tradition; in each case they only produced a monstrosity, for all they *could* do was *arbitrarily* wrench certain values out of their context while ignoring others.) We can only hope to produce a more rational *conception* of rationality or a better *conception* of morality if we operate from *within* our tradition (with its echoes of the Greek agora, of Newton, and so on, in the case of rationality, and with its echoes of scripture, of the philosophers, of the democratic revolutions, and so on, in the case of morality); but this is not at all to say that all is entirely reasonable and well with the conceptions we now have. We are not trapped in individual solipsistic hells, but invited to engage in a truly human dialogue; one which combines collectivity with individual responsibility.

Does this dialogue have an ideal terminus? Is there a *true* conception of rationality, a *true* morality, even if all *we* ever have are our *conceptions* of these? Here philosophers divide, like everyone else. Richard Rorty, in his Presidential Address[5] to the American Philosophical Association, opted strongly for the view that there is only the dialogue; no ideal end can be posited or should be needed. But how does the assertion that 'there is only the dialogue' differ from the self-refuting relativism we discussed in Chapter 5? The very fact that we speak of our different conceptions as different conceptions of *rationality* posits a *Grenzbegriff*, a limit-concept of the ideal truth.

    [5] 'Pragmatism, Relativism and Irrationalism', *Proceedings and Addresses of the American Philosophical Association,* August 1980. See also Rorty's *Philosophy and the Mirror of Nature,* Princeton University Press, 1979.

Appendix

Here is the Theorem referred to in Chapter 2.

Theorem Let L be a language with predicates $F_1, F_2, \ldots, F_k$ (not necessarily monadic). Let I be an interpretation, in the sense of an assignment of an intension to every predicate of L. Then if I is non-trivial in the sense that at least one predicate has an extension which is neither empty nor universal in at least one possible world, there exists a second interpretation J which disagrees with I, but which makes the same sentences true in every possible world as I does.

Proof Let $W_1, W_2, \ldots,$ be all the possible worlds, in some well-ordering, and let U_i be the set of possible individuals which exist in the world W_i. Let R_{ij} be the set which is the extension of the predicate F_i in the possible world W_j according to I (if F_{ij} is non-monadic, then R_{ij} will be a set of n_i-tuples, where n_i is the number of argument places of F_i). The structure $\langle U_j; R_{ij} \ (i = 1, 2, \ldots, k) \rangle$ is the 'intended model' of L in the world W_j relative to I (i.e. U_j is the universe of discourse of L in the world W_j, and (for $i = 1, 2, \ldots, k$) R_{ij} is the extension of the predicate F_i in W_j.

If at least one predicate, say, F_u, has an extension R_{uj} which is neither empty nor all of U_j, select a permutation P_j of U_j such that $P_j(R_{uj}) \neq R_{uj}$. Otherwise, let P_j be the identity. Since P_j is a permutation, the structure $\langle U_j; P_j(R_{ij}) \ (i = 1, 2, \ldots, k) \rangle$ is isomorphic to $\langle U_j; R_{ij} \ (i = 1, 2, \ldots, k) \rangle$ and so is a model for the same sentences of L (i.e. for the sentences of L which are true under I in W_j).

Let J be the interpretation of L which assigns to the predicate F_i $(i = 1, 2, \ldots, k)$ the following intension: the function $f_i(W)$

whose value at any possible world W_j is $P_j(R_{ij})$. In other words, the extension of F_i in each W_j under the interpretation J is defined to be $P_j(R_{ij})$. Since $\langle U_j; P_j(R_{ij})\ (i = 1,2, \ldots, k)\rangle$ is a model for the same set of sentences as $\langle U_j; R_{ij}\ (i = 1,2, \ldots, k)\rangle$ (by the isomorphism), the same sentences are true in each possible world under J as under I, and J differs from I in every world in which at least one predicate has a non-trivial extension. q.e.d.

Comment: If, in a given world W_j, there are two disjoint sets which are extensions of predicates of L in W_j under I – say, the set of cats and the set of dogs – then, if there are more dogs than cats (respectively, at least as many cats as dogs) we can take any set of dogs the same size as the set of cats (respectively, any set of cats the same size as the set of dogs) and choose a P_j which maps the selected set of dogs onto the set of cats (respectively, the selected set of cats onto the set of dogs) and vice versa; this will ensure that under J the extension of the first predicate – the one whose extension under I is the set of cats – is a set of dogs under J in W_j, or the extension of the second predicate – the one whose extension under I is the set of dogs – is a set of cats under J in W_j.

Second Comment: If there are objects – say, 'sensations' – which one wishes *not* to be permuted, because one regards predicates of those objects as 'absolute' in some sense, one simply stipulates that the permutations P_j are to be the identity on those objects. This will have the effect of making the restriction of any predicate of L to those privileged objects the same under I and under J in each world.

Third Comment: Since sentences receive logically equivalent truth conditions under I and under J, it follows that on the standard 'possible worlds semantics', *counterfactual conditionals* are also preserved.

Index